SCOTTISH METHODISM IN THE EARLY VICTORIAN PERIOD

SCOTTISH METHODISM
in the Early Victorian Period

The Scottish Correspondence of the Rev. Jabez Bunting
1800-57

Edited by A.J.Hayes and D.A.Gowland for the Edinburgh University Press

Edinburgh University Press
22 George Square, Edinburgh
ISBN 0 85224 412 6
Printed in Great Britain by
Redwood Burn Limited,
Trowbridge, Wilts.

Contents

Preface

In the year following the centenary of Jabez Bunting's birth, it is fitting to see the completion of the publication of his correspondence, commenced in 1972 by Professor W.R. Ward of the University of Durham. This work adds to the all-too-slender shelf of published work on Scottish Methodism. We are greatly indebted to the Edinburgh University Press for making available to a wider audience this 'overview' of the state of Methodism in Scotland for the critical years 1800-57.

We owe a great debt to Professor W.R. Ward for making available his initial transcripts of the Bunting correspondence; to Dr J.C. Bowmer and Mrs S. Himsworth for access to the Methodist Archives while they were still in City Road, London; to Dr J. Radcliffe and Mr D. Riley and the staff of the John Rylands University Library of Manchester for unfailing help and kindness in dealing with our queries once the Archives had been moved to Manchester; to the Librarian of the House of Commons; to the Librarian and Staff of the Edinburgh Public Library; to the Librarian of New College Library, University of Edinburgh for access to the Chalmers papers and to the Librarian of the University of St Andrews. Our thanks are also due to Mr W. Leary, the Connexional Archivist, for all his assistance and to the Rev. Dr O.W. Beckerlegge for making available some of his photographs. Letters No. 15 and 104 are published by kind permission of the Authorities of Drew University Library, Madison, U.S.A., and Letter No. 19 by permission of the University of St Andrews. Letters No. 8, 20, 23, 60 and 67 form part of the Correspondence of Thomas Chalmers, and are published by kind permission of the Librarian, New College Library, University of Edinburgh. We are grateful to the Royal Historical Society for permission to reproduce parts of Letters No. 8, 21 and 22, which have already appeared in *The Early Correspondence of Jabez Bunting 1820-1829*; and to Oxford University Press for permission to reproduce parts of Letters No. 43, 44, 50, 66, 69, 71, 76, 78, 79, 82, 96, 97 and 124, which have already appeared in *Early Victorian Methodism: The Correspondence of Jabez Bunting 1830-1858*. Plate 1 appears by permission of the National Monuments Record of Scotland, and plate 5 by permission of George Outram & Co. Ltd. Last (and most) we thank our wives for their forbearance and patience during the execution of this study.

A.J.H. *and* D.A.G.
Edinburgh & Dundee, June 1980

Table of Dates

1779	Birth of Jabez Bunting
1795	Plan of Pacification
1797	Foundation of Methodist New Connexion by Alexander Kilham; Wesleyan Conference adopts the Form of Discipline
1799	Jabez Bunting becomes Wesleyan Preacher
1800	Circuits in Scotland are Aberdeen, Brechin, Dundee, Edinburgh, Glasgow, Inverness (re-formed 1800)
1809	Banff Circuit separated from Inverness; Ayr Circuit re-formed from Glasgow; Perth Circuit separated from Dundee
1810	Arbroath Circuit separated from Dundee
1811	Formation of Primitive Methodist Connexion; Greenock Circuit re-formed from Glasgow
1812	Dunbar Circuit re-formed from Edinburgh
1814-20	Jabez Bunting Secretary of Conference
1814	Elgin Circuit formed
1815	Dunfermline Circuit formed
1817	Peterhead Circuit separated from Aberdeen
1818	Brechin Circuit united with Arbroath; Dunfermline Circuit united with Edinburgh
1820	Jabez Bunting President of Conference (first time); Paisley & Greenock Circuit united
1821-24	Jabez Bunting Connexional Editor
1822	Shetland Isles Circuit formed (later Lerwick)
1823	Yell Circuit formed
1824	Walls and Northmavin Circuits formed
1826	Dundee and Perth Circuits reunited
1827-28	Leeds Organ Case
1828	Jabez Bunting President of Conference (2nd time); Aberdeen and Peterhead Circuits reunited; Dunbar & Haddington Circuit reunited with Edinburgh
1829	Dundee and Perth Circuits separated; Dunbar & Haddington Circuit separated from Edinburgh
1833	Jabez Bunting settled permanently in London as Secretary for foreign missions; Greenock Circuit reunited with Glasgow
1835	Expulsion of Dr Warren from Wesleyan Methodist Connexion; establishment of Wesleyan Association; Jabez Bunting President of Theological Institution
1836	Jabez Bunting President of Conference (3rd time)
1842	Greenock Circuit re-formed from Glasgow
1844	Jabez Bunting President of Conference (4th time); Edinburgh and Aberdeen Districts united
1845	Airdrie Circuit separated from Glasgow
1849	Expulsion of Everett, Dunn and Griffith from Wesleyan Connexion; establishment of Wesleyan Reform Movement; Stirling and Doune Circuit separated from Airdrie
1850	Glasgow divided into Glasgow West (John Street) and Glasgow East (St Thomas's) Circuits
1851	Jabez Bunting retires from the full-time work of the ministry
1855	Dunrossness Circuit formed
1858	Death of Jabez Bunting

Introduction

1. The Scottish Correspondence of Jabez Bunting

a) Principles of Selection

The letters included in the present work complete the publication of the main part of the Bunting correspondence which was begun over a century ago by Jabez's second son Percy,[1] and resumed by Professor W.R. Ward, first in *The Early Correspondence of Jabez Bunting 1820-1829*, edited for the Royal Historical Society,[2] and more recently in *Early Victorian Methodism*.[3] When W.R. Ward commenced work, it was believed that the surviving portion of the Bunting correspondence ran to some 700 letters, about one-half of which merited publication. However, the holdings of the Methodist Archives and Research Centre[4] revealed the existence of more than 4,000 letters to and from Jabez Bunting and to these W.R. Ward added photocopies of six other collections of Bunting's papers which had been dispersed to the United States of America. These letters may be traced by the card catalogue at the Centre, now housed at the John Rylands University Library of Manchester. Since W.R. Ward completed transcription of the main Bunting collection, a further seventy-odd letters have been added by purchase. Their whereabouts since they were first separated from the main body of the correspondence remains something of a mystery, but they fill hitherto serious lacunae in the main body of the correspondence.

Bunting's biographer, his second son Percy, virtually ignored the Scottish situation, save for passing mention of two letters from Edmund Grindrod[5] to his father. In that portion of the biography completed by G. Stringer Rowe, however, the close friendship between Jabez and Thomas Chalmers is exposed to view, particularly in relationship to the 1843 Disruption in the Church of Scotland and the rise of the Free Church. In like manner the tremendous clash between Jabez and Samuel Warren, which convulsed the Methodist Connexion in the 1830s is considered in the broadest outlines only. This is particularly irritating, since local evidence[6] suggests increasingly that the Wesleyan Methodist Association secession had the most profound effects upon Scottish Methodism; more severe, perhaps, than the Reform disturbances some fourteen years later. However, Percy Bunting's deficiencies as a biographer have already been exposed by W.R. Ward in the *Early Correspondence,* so that it is unnecessary to re-iterate them here.

This failure on the part of Percy Bunting to document matters north of the Border, coupled with Ward's deliberate policy of exclusion of letters concerned with Scottish Methodism "which was always a law unto itself",[7] means that the bulk of the 127 letters included here have never been published, apart from a small number required in *Early Victorian Methodism* to illustrate the attitude of the Wesleyan Hierarchy to the 1843 Disruption and its aftermath. Those which have been excluded (17) have been done so using the same criteria as those used by W.R. Ward, namely (1) those of secondary importance or of purely local or personal interest (2) those concerned with missionary matters and (3) a very small number which duplicate others included in the collection. Nevertheless, editorial licence

1

has been used to include first a group of letters dealing with affairs in Dumfries, geographically in Scotland, but by virtue of its geographical isolation long included in the Carlisle District and secondly Samuel Dunn's account of the establishment of the Shetland Mission.[8] Since so much of Samuel Dunn's ministerial career is bound up with Scotland, this account forms a convenient starting-point.

As might be expected, few letters survive from the early period of Bunting's ministry. It is only following his election to the Secretaryship of the Conference in 1814 that the volume of correspondence suddenly increases, at a time when the state of Scottish Methodism was beginning to cause unease within the Connexion.

b) *The Character of the Scottish Correspondence*

The Scottish correspondence spans the whole of Jabez's active ministry and, as a result, the comments already made apply equally to this section of the material. The disparity between the numbers of in-letters and out-letters is again highlighted here. Up to the end of 1829, the proportion of in- to out-letters is 9 to 35, whereas after 1830 the proportions are 7 to 92. The life-style of the Travelling Preacher discouraged the majority of them from hoarding old letters and, indeed, many of them came from social levels where there was no such tradition. In contrast, Bunting kept many of the letters he received, particularly those addressed to him as President (together with his replies) which might be required for future reference.

As W.R. Ward has already noted in the case of the general correspondence, Bunting's Scottish letters undergo a change after 1829. Personal correspondence of the kind which provided such interesting sidelights from the early days of Bunting's ministry disappears almost completely, apart from a stream of letters to and from his protégé Maclean. This is partly as a result of the extent to which Bunting submerged his private personality in his official character and parallels his decline as a great preacher. In addition, the lack of personal correspondence is probably also partly due to deliberate action by Percy Bunting, who is believed to have removed everything written to or by himself and also whatever items he thought might be construed to discredit his father's career. Indeed, of the episode of the great Bunting-Warren conflict of 1834-35, little or nothing remains. The lack of Scottish correspondence from Warren is the more surprising since he was Superintendent of the Edinburgh Circuit from 1827-30, and was thus involved in the critical aftermath of the chapel speculations (e.g. Edinburgh, Leith, Haddington, etc). These papers may well have been destroyed soon after Jabez's death. Apart from this, the collection seems to have suffered no more than random losses since Percy first took it over for the purpose of writing the *Life*.

In many ways, the value of the collection as a thermometer with which to test the temperature of Scottish Methodism is enhanced by the preponderance of in-letters. Unfortunately their coverage of the country is extremely uneven, both in terms of time and space. As might be expected, there is a preponderance of letters from Edinburgh, with Glasgow coming a poor second, and the other major centres, e.g. Aberdeen, Perth, Dundee & Inverness producing a mere smattering or none at all. Indeed, in certain critical years (e.g. 1821, when the frightening financial implications of the chapel speculations of the previous ten years were finally coming home to roost), the surviving letters are largely concerned with such matters as the number of beds in the Dunfermline manse and the beginnings of the friendship with Thomas Chalmers. Likewise the sole letter from Scotland in 1835 deals with an internecine dispute between Edinburgh and Leith. The aftermath of the Warrenite secession, when Wesleyan Association chapels were set up in Aberdeen,[9] Edinburgh, Dundee and Glasgow, and where, in Edinburgh, a body of Trustees and many of the congregation seceded from the Nicolson Square chapel, go completely unnoticed. In the later years, the impressions of the state of Methodism north of the Border derive entirely from the inclination of the principal ministers to consult Bunting officially on their problems, and as such provide only a series of disconnected pictures, as of a jigsaw puzzle with many of the pieces missing. It is fortunate indeed, then, that Peter Duncan was stationed first in Edinburgh and then in Glasgow between 1842 and 1846, since he was a prolific letter-writer, who left a more or less complete record of the state of affairs in Scotland at a time when the intractable problems of the 1820s and 1830s were at last approaching solution. By the time of Peter Duncan's chairmanship, too, the character and territorial coverage of Scottish Methodism was changing. As a result of the pro-liferation of heavy industry in the Central Lowlands, Methodism was beginning to spread from its traditional strongholds in the main cities. This, in turn, meant that 'that Noble little fellow' Peter Duncan, now Chairman of the combined Edinburgh and Aberdeen Districts, was faced with the problem of dividing Circuits, not always in the best way either in terms of population or resources. This situation contrasts strongly with the North-East of Scotland, where circuit amalgamations, notably around Peterhead, had occurred in previous decades. Duncan's chairmanship marked the beginning of the proliferation of Circuits in Scotland, which was to continue for the next sixty years or so.

In the last ten years of Jabez Bunting's life, news from Scotland again becomes fragmentary. Whole years pass without a single letter from the 'northern realm'. There is, however, mention of the Evangelical Alliance - dear to Bunting's heart - and of the hostile reaction in Scotland to the expulsion of Everett, Dunn & Griffith by the 1849 Conference. By this time, however, Jabez had almost withdrawn from public life and, in any case, was too old and enfeebled to respond in the way in which he had done to the events of 1835. The correspondence closes with a group of letters from his protégé Maclean, both with suggestions for the future organisation and government of Scottish Methodism, including the revival of the idea of General Superintendents for Scotland (an idea first mooted by Wesley), a return to the practices of Wesley's days and with gossip on the religious state of Scotland. The last letter, sent only six months before Bunting's death, was written when Maclean was supernumerary at Dalkeith.

However, in spite of these shortcomings, the letters provide an invaluable social commentary by the Wesleyan Preachers themselves. The low state of Methodism in Scotland at the turn of the eighteenth century, the impact of the national retrenchments on Scotland, the proliferation of places of worship, the financial embarrassments and decline of the smaller and frequently also the larger chapels, the numerous separations, the occasional bright flickers, problems due to the with-drawal of preachers, the setting-up of the Shetland Mission, proposals to send supernumerary ministers to the smaller causes, advice on the selling of the Peterhead chapel to pay off the debt, proposals by a Chairman of District to release a Wesleyan minister to supply an Independent church, the finer points of doctrine, the Mussel-burgh 'foolishness', the gradual improvement in 1832-35, the non-observance of Methodist administration in the Aberdeen District, problems with the Edinburgh trustees, the aftermath of the Warrenite secession, unrest in Dumfries, the advent of the Shoebothamites in Dundee, followed by a final period of stability and a source of hope for the extension of Methodism are all revealed in the letters which follow.

c) *Editorial Practice*

The same editorial conventions have been followed as were previously used by W.R. Ward.[10] In the text of the letters, punctuation and the use of capitals have been modernised somewhat, and abbreviations have been extended. The frequently eccentric spelling of the early period has been left unchanged, since this gives some clue about the varied levels of literacy among the Wesleyan Travelling Preachers in the first quarter of the nineteenth century. A few passages have also been omitted on the same principles which have governed the omission of letters from the published collection. The subscriptions to the letters have also been omitted, being without significance. Such omissions are indicated by points (. . . .). Editorial emendations to the text appear in square brackets ([ ]), or in the case of emendations where the manuscript has suffered damage, in pointed brackets (《 》). Brief biographical details are provided for all the preachers and most of the laymen mentioned in the letters and there are notes on the principal *explicanda*. In a few cases, laymen or events cannot be identified and these are also noted. Such additions to the correspondence are contained in footnotes on the first occasion of mention and may be traced by means of the index. This procedure has been used to save an otherwise inordinate number of cross-references and it is hoped that it will prove convenient. In the period of the correspondence, as today, the Methodist Connexional Year began on 1 September; 1830-31 for example, implies one year's service from 1 September 1830 to 31 August 1831. However, the Wesleyan Conference met later than it now does, assembling for up to three weeks in late July and early August. For those readers who may not be familiar with the finer points of the Methodist system, amplified footnotes have been included where necessary, e.g. the establishment of the Chapel fund (p. 42).

2. Scottish Methodism during Jabez Bunting's Ministry

In 1791 when Wesley died, Scottish Methodism (the Edinburgh and Aberdeen Districts) boasted a combined total of 1179 members. A slow, steady increase began in 1801, until by 1819 the membership had reached 3,786.[11] Despite the fact that this was a period of connexional unrest, neither the Plan of Pacification of 1795, nor the Kilhamite secession appear to have disturbed the Scottish Societies. This is particularly surprising, since Alexander Kilham was Superintendent of the Aberdeen Circuit from 1792-94 and was already engaged in agitation. His attempts to convert the Aberdeen Methodists to his views failed completely, but the failure of the attempt in 1797 to admit lay representation to the District Meetings led to a number of members leaving the Aberdeen Society to form the first Congregational (or Independent) Church. Although there was considerable sympathy elsewhere in Scotland for the ideals and principles of the New Connexion, there is little evidence for the establishment of New Connexion Societies in Scotland, except in Glasgow and perhaps also in Edinburgh, and then only for a very short time.[12]

Much has already been said about Wesley's intentions for Scotland. Wesley Swift[13] inclined to the view that the ordinations of 1785-88, the wearing of gown and bands, the style and title of these ordinands as Reverend and Minister of the Methodist Church, together with the form of Communion being that used in the Church of Scotland, and the practice of holding Methodist services in church hours represented a last, despairing attempt by Wesley to retrieve the situation. Writing to Joshua Keighley, Wesley wrote

It seems that the people in the North of Scotland are of a different mind from those in the South. In the South, they flocked together in great numbers at first when the preachers began to officiate in church hours. But after a little while they began to fall off till they were at last the usual number. But in the North, you say, few would hear you at first, but afterwards the number increased. Before the time of the Conference we shall be able to judge which is more for the Glory of God & the increase of his Work in North Britain, the New or the Old Plan ...

Wesley Swift confessed that he was unable to identify the new plan, whether the ordinations or preaching in church hours

Wesley's plans and purposes for Scotland must remain obscure, though we may hazard a guess as to what lies beyond our range of vision. The key to the mystery, we may surmise, lies in the word expediency. In 1785, Wesley was an old man; his powers were not what they once had been. He was content to make his last despairing throw and to rejoice in its success ...

Thirty years later, however, W.R. Ward could write[14]

I have elsewhere given my reasons for believing that Wesley's intention in 1784-85 was to link Ireland, America and "other parts out of the kingdom of Great Britain" with the Methodism and church establishment in England, notionally by an itinerant episcopacy and substantially by a modernised prayerbook; each was to have its subordinate Conference, but was to be given, by the stationing of members of the Legal Hundred among them a toehold in the sovereign British Methodist Conference which also operated in an Anglican context ...

Unfortunately, the failure to implement fully these schemes led to confusion for those who wished to see a distinctly 'Scottish Methodism' develop and indecision by the Wesleyan Establishment as to the best course to adopt.

The year before Jabez Bunting's first Presidential Year (1820) Scottish Methodism reached its zenith and thereafter the numbers began slowly to decline, until in 1826 there was a sharp contraction. Throughout this period the pillars of the Wesleyan Establishment frequently spoke of abandoning the work in Scotland. In 1826, Adam Clarke considered that Methodism had no hold in Scotland except perhaps in Edinburgh and Glasgow. He felt that if all the other chapels were disposed of, it would be only a slight loss to pure Methodism but that the resultant saving in financial resources could be much better employed elsewhere.[15] As might be expected, Jabez Bunting pronounced bluntly

I think if Methodism in Scotland were put up to auction, it would be the best thing that could be done with it, except Glasgow, Edinburgh, Dundee, Perth and perhaps Ayr. We have spent more money in Scotland than we can account for to God, or to our people ...[16]

Even in the main centres of population where a secure hold had been established, the continuance of the Work demanded a heavy annual subsidy, but Methodism had by now reached out to the smaller towns and villages where the hold on the people was more tenuous. In the end, it was this part of Scottish Methodism that was 'put up to auction', with the result that many causes disappeared from the face of Scotland. Nowadays, it would be expected that new extensions of the Work would receive a subsidy, but in the early years of the nineteenth century budgeting on a Connexional basis was in its infancy, if it existed at all. The only source of subsidy at that time was the much maligned Contingent Fund ('that sick club box or parish fund to which all sick and needy subscribers may make application')[17] which was constantly in deficit as a result. In theory the individual Circuits were self-sufficient units, paying the Preacher's allowances (Quarterage) and other expenses, but if there were deficits, these were brought to the next District Meeting (Synod) and if they were not met at District level, then to Conference. The Conference charged them against the Contingent Fund, as long as any balance remained in that fund. Such payments had frequently been made during the Napoleonic Wars, but during the great financial crisis which marked the aftermath of the Napoleonic Wars, the 'long-stop' of the Contingent Fund induced payment on the 'never-never' pattern. Circuits frequently tempted additional Preachers to travel, thereby incurring deficiencies which someone else had to pay. In some years the total deficiency on the current account in the Scottish Circuits was as little as £200, whereas in other years it had increased five-fold. In addition to the 'ordinary' deficiencies at circuit level, there were also 'extraordinary' deficiencies, which were also chargeable to the Contingent Fund. These included Preachers' removal expenses and the rent of preaching-houses where the work was being extended. Occasionally, attempts were made to ease the worst of the situation, by means of a collection for an embarrassed cause being taken in neighbouring Societies or throughout the District, though in the Scottish context this usually meant the transfer of money from one near-empty pocket to another and therefore the net relief was slight.

It is easy, therefore, to sympathise with Jabez Bunting's view that Scottish Methodism should be put up to auction, but, indeed, the situation in Scotland was no different from that in Britain at large. Before 1815, financial difficulties had arisen from the fact that increasing numbers of Travelling Preachers had been called out without any calculations of the future financial liability for the preachers' families and children.[18] In like manner, large numbers of new preaching-houses were built with scant regard to their proper financing. The Minutes of this period are full of admonitions to Societies and Trustees to exercise restraint, but to no avail. Recognising the impending crises, therefore, Conference attempted to economise by the Preachers themselves becoming the guarantors of the Connexional debt (1816)[19] by means of reductions in the allowances (the 'retrenchments')[20] in 1817 and even on one occasion (1818) by half the Preachers' allowances being paid in the form of the unsold stock of the Book Room.[21] After the end of the Napoleonic Wars, however, matters became far worse, for the fall in prices multiplied the burden of debt and the restoration of the gold standard in 1822 meant that debts could no longer be paid off from inflation. The net effect was to make the bulk of the English Circuits insolvent and to destroy what little financial control had previously existed. If prosperous English Circuits could thus be reduced to penury, what hope remained for the financially shaky Scottish ones?

Not only were the current accounts of the Scottish Circuits in deficit at this time, but the majority also possessed extensive capital debts which eventually were to overwhelm many of them. Much has already been made of Valentine Ward's involvement in the Scottish chapel speculations, but indeed Ward was only acting in a similar way to the English Circuits in general, and it is safe to say that if some other Wesleyan Travelling Preacher had been Chairman of a Scottish District at this time, he would have been branded in the same way that Ward has been. In other respects, Ward was 'the most influential preacher that ever came to Scotland' and at first his colleagues 'wished him to continue his bishopric as his sway is so mild and his affection so sincere', but over the matter of chapel building and purchase, their reactions were very different. Nevertheless, in retrospect, it is clear that Wesley Swift's outright condemnation of Valentine Ward is a simplistic view of the situation. Where Ward fell down in his chapel schemes was first to finance them on short-term promissory notes and annuities and secondly that he did not account for these loans in any comprehensible way. Witness the 1820 Edinburgh District Minutes on the matter

Q. What is the opinion of this meeting respecting the Leith, Dunfermline, Greenock, Ayr and Perth chapels?

A. The debts and embarrassments of these chapels awaken painful apprehensions in our minds, but we find ourselves unable to dissipate the obscurity of the accounts and regret that we are not furnished with the means of stating anything more explicit: the Superintendents of the Circuits in which these chapels are situated not having been able to *obtain the information necessary from* Mr. Ward to whom they have made application for such information and, who alone was able to furnish it ...[22]

Indeed, by 1822, the Edinburgh District chapel debt alone had reached £34,000. In 1827, a special meeting of the President, Richard Watson, and Secretary of the Conference, Jabez Bunting, together with the preachers stationed in Scotland reported

The distressing embarrassments of several chapels in this District were taken into serious consideration and it was unanimously agreed to report the following particularly to the Conference.

(a) It is the opinion of this meeting that the chapels in Leith, Haddington, Tradeston, Greenock and Port Glasgow are so deeply involved in debt, as to afford not the least rational hope that they can ever be so effectually relieved as to be brought into a manageable state by any local exertions in which the Trustees and Societies in those places are capable.

(b) That the honour of our Connexion requires that some of the above cases be brought to a speedy issue, and we recommend that they be sold as soon as possible, though it should even be at a considerable loss, the deficiency to be provided for, partly by some arrangements with the creditors, partly by sacrifices on the part of the Trustees, and partly by grants from the General Chapel Fund. N.B. — In several cases opportunities for sale have been allowed to pass and we think ought to have been embraced.

(c) That on account of Mr. Valentine Ward's particular connexion with these chapels; his responsibility for monies borrowed upon them and the painful consequences which must result to the Trustees and to our Connexion at large, in the event of Mr W.'s demise -- we strongly recommend that he be stationed with instructions to dispose of the several chapels above named.

(d) That at an early period of the sitting of the Conference, a Committee be appointed to prepare special instructions for Mr W's. guidance and assistance in the disposal of the said chapels ...[23]

During this period, however, the financial embarrassment in Scotland became progressively more acute and at the 1829 Conference, Valentine Ward was authorised to travel around Great Britain during the following three years to appeal for subscriptions for the Scottish chapels.

Despite the imprudence of some of his schemes, much of what Ward did in Scotland was long overdue.[24] In Edinburgh, the Octagon chapel opened in 1765 by Christopher Hopper had become a 'dirty, dark, dangerous hole. which reflected dishonour on the whole Connexion'; despite the Superintendent's and Trustee's assertions to the contrary. This was demolished in 1815 as part of a road-improvement scheme incorporating the Regent Bridge. However, the new chapel in Nicolson Square cost £5,500 and left its Trustees with a defective title to the site, which required two actions in the Court of Session to resolve, and additional debts of £5,000 or so, which were finally paid off fifty years later.[25] In Leith, too, similar levels of debt plagued the Trustees for many years, while in Glasgow the Trust debt on three chapels had risen to £14,000 by the early 1830s.[26] In some towns, Valentine Ward's activities were dogged by ill-fortune. Thus, in Perth, Ward purchased Robert Haldane's Tabernacle (pronounced as 'likely to stand for 150 years'), which had cost nearly £4000 to build, for £1050. An opponent of Methodism in Perth contrived to have it condemned as unsafe, and in the end Ward had it pulled down and rebuilt with four shops below and a preacher's house above, thereby securing an income for the property at double the original capital cost. Other purchases or new buildings included Dunfermline, Greenock, Ayr and Strathkinness, all too large and expensive for their small (and usually impecunious) Societies to support. In Aberdeen he made a major blunder and the Society was left with a disused and unsaleable Octagon Chapel, a debt of £840 on the new chapel and a vacant site for which it had no immediate use. As a result, Aberdeen, which had been a self-supporting Circuit, fell into deficit, and as late as 1848 attempts were still being made to eliminate the debt. Conference's first reaction to the situation was to keep Ward in Scotland, but he finally offered for the mission field and died in Jamaica in 1834.

As early in his Scottish ministry as 1815, Ward had noted

As the matter of the chapels which I have been concerned in building in Scotland has caused much conversation and as the Providence of God has in my opinion been abundantly displayed throughout the whole business ...[27]

The debts, as we have already seen, not only caused much conversation, but awoke 'painful apprehensions' in the minds of his colleagues. By 1820 the situation was such that Conference directed the President (Jabez Bunting) to visit Scotland for a morale-boosting meeting with the preachers, and the following year George Marsden repeated the visit. When, in 1825, it was the opinion of the President (Robert Newton) that the state of the chapels in Scotland should undergo a full examination, Bunting was taken along as well, but on this occasion that arch-organiser failed to produce a solution. By 1829, the indebtedness in Scotland was hopelessly beyond the power of relief, progressively growing worse from year to year and now assuming an appalling prospect.[28] The effect upon the Societies was every bit as bad.[29] Whole Societies vanished without trace[30] and in places as far apart as Inverurie, Brechin, Duns, Lockerbie and Campbeltown, Methodism is no longer even a distant memory.

As a result of this situation, as W.R. Ward has already stated, the Wesleyan Connexional Establishment had three choices open to it. It could put Scottish Methodism up to auction and get out; it might strengthen the number and quality of the preachers and hope that the Work would become viable, or else it might convert Scottish Methodism into a low-cost enterprise more fitted to the needs (and pockets) of the country. That it adopted none of these courses and allowed the situation to muddle through, is ably explained by him in a recent paper.[31] The success of the Centenary Fund provided the Connexion with the means of freeing the most promising causes from their crippling debts, but by 1839 the whole mood of the connexion was towards centralisation; the net result being an institution for the training of preachers and the building of the Mission House.

This unhappy situation in the 1820s and 30s (and even later) meant that the more able preachers declined (as far as they were able) to go into Scotland and wrestle with these intractable problems; to that 'miserable makeshift establishment to which this Circuit (Calton, Glasgow) had recourse to provide itself with the labours of a second minister',[32] or to what John Maclean chose to call 'a penal establishment for disordered or suspected missionaries, who are here as free to follow their crudest ideas, as if they were in the wilds of Africa'.[33] To attempt to staff Scotland in this way, when as long ago as 1801 Bunting had been warned 'The Scotch are for the most part a well-informed people: they are very partial to a learned discourse from the Pulpit and think it little better than blasphemy for a person to preach who has not had an Academical Education'[34] was thus the greatest folly. In the circumstances it is not surprising that John Shipman[35] urged that the more northerly Circuits be staffed with 'veteran supernumeraries'. Bunting's reply to this novel suggestion was sweet reasonableness itself.

The end of the 1830s and early 1840s marked a turning of the tide and though there were occasional upsets, particularly in Dundee where the 'Shuffelbothamites' were still active,[36] and in Edinburgh where litigious Trustees were disturbing the Society,[37] the preachers increasingly sent in optimistic reports on the progress of the Work in Scotland.[38] Reduction of the capital debts via the Chapel Fund, larger numbers of members meeting in Society and larger numbers of adherents (and hence increased pew-rents) all give the impression of a return to better times.

The feeling that Scottish Methodism was in some way 'different' from the Methodism of the rest of the British Connexion manifested itself in different ways at different times. At the end of Wesley's lifetime, long before Jabez Bunting's heyday, there had been disputes over the hours of public worship (whether in church hours or not) and over the mode and frequency of celebrating Holy Communion.[39] Whereas in England the *Sunday Service of the Methodists* held sway, the Scottish Districts always adhered strictly to the 'order of administration of the Sacraments sanctioned by Mr. Wesley for use in Scotland, which is the same as that prescribed in the Church of Scotland'.[40] In addition, by Jabez Bunting's zenith, the Sacrament was usually celebrated in Scotland once a quarter, in conformity with Church of Scotland practice, whereas in England Communion was usually celebrated monthly.[41] It was much the same story with the gown and bands, which were allowed in Scotland,[42] but not in England. By the Bunting era (who supported the gown and bands for Scotland) the Glasgow Circuit was rent on this very point as between the native Scots (who wanted them) and the English and still more the Irish who would not have them at any price.[43] This 'different nature' of Scottish Methodism also manifested itself by periodic demands for a Scottish Conference, first heard in Wesley's lifetime,[44] resuscitated by Valentine Ward in the 1820s and again in the middle of the nineteenth century.[45] We have earlier noted W.R. Ward's assessment of Wesley's ultimate intentions, but it must remain a matter for speculation whether a subordinate or even a sovereign Scottish Conference would have proved any more successful in solving the problems of the first half of the nineteenth century.

3. Bunting and the Evolution of Wesleyan Methodism

In many respects the contrasts between Wesleyan Methodism at the beginning and at the end of Bunting's ministry are as great as the differences between the ecclesiastical order associated with Bunting and its twentieth-century successor. At the time of Bunting's entry into the ministry in 1799 Wesleyanism was still a loosely-controlled community of proliferating societies, equally vulnerable to a host of centrifugal forces and capable of constitutional developments in various directions. The connexion embraced a membership of 89,213 which represented an annual growth rate of 7.61 per cent, in itself not untypical of the period 1790-1820 as a whole when there were impressive annual gains particularly in the war years.[46] During the first half of the nineteenth century, however, the connexion became a highly organised unit with a much more expansive central administration designed to provide close supervision of the societies. By 1851, moreover, when Bunting retired from the active ministry, the membership had trebled to 280,054 while the annual growth rate for this year was of the disastrous order of −15.65 per cent. This last figure showed the immediate impact of the Wesleyan Reform Movement and was an extreme example of changing circumstances; the age of unbridled expansion had given way to a chequered period of less spectacular gains and more dramatic losses.

What was no less evident in the intervening period was the fact that Wesleyanism had shed the last vestiges of its identity as a societary movement and emerged as a fully institutionalised denomination. This process was marked by a number of developments and a range of conflicts, in all of which Bunting took up a decided position in shaping and interpreting the legacy bequeathed by Wesley. An increasing differentiation of roles and interests accentuated the problems of connexional management and resulted in numerous offshoots and divisions. Tensions between connexionalism and localism, between preachers and people, between the ministerial Conference and the lay-dominated local courts or between different social groups took many forms of uneasy coexistence and hostilities. On Wesley's death the term 'Methodist' could be more or less applied to a people within a single organisational framework, whereas by the time of Bunting's death the term had little meaning in

9

the absence of some designation indicating the particular brand of Methodism. Some of the new forms of Methodist organisation originated in spontaneous revivalism as was the case with the Primitive Methodists, the Bible Christians and the Independent Methodists. Other bodies emerged as a result of contests over the character of connexional government e.g. the Methodist New Connexion, the Protestant Methodists, the Wesleyan Methodist Association, and the Wesleyan Reform Movement. There were, too, the much smaller groups of the Methodist underworld, often more localised in appeal and usually the fleeting products of a particular period or issue e.g. Methodist Unitarians, Original Methodists, Magic Methodists, Teetotal Methodists, and Chartist Methodists.

The evolution of the Wesleyan connexion from a society or 'sect-type' organisation into a 'church' organisation found expression in a variety of ways. The change was as evident in the abandonment of the preaching room for the chapel as it was in the ruthlessness with which the upholders of religious order and discipline put down the practitioners of wildfire revivalism. It was no less apparent in the metamorphosis of the eighteenth-century itinerant preacher into the mid-nineteenth-century regular minister who, unlike his predecessor, had ordained status, college training and a chapel-based ministry. Furthermore, when Bunting's critics complained that he had turned an extraordinary mission into a vast regimented membership, they usually meant that he and the wealthy laity had settled for unevangelical respectability and for formalised types of worship that relegated lovefeasts, class meetings and revivalist activities to the status of fringe activities.

During the first half of his ministry Bunting laid the foundations of a form of systematic government that came under attack in the three major crises of the second half of his career: the Free Methodist secessions associated with the Leeds organ case of 1827-28, the Warrenite agitation of 1834-35 and the mid-century Wesleyan Reform controversy. Bunting's insistence on efficient and extensive administration was evident in his first minor commission to sort out some of the muddled connexional accounts. And it was no less apparent in his provision of a sound basis for the Methodist Missionary Society and his formulation of Sunday school policy. More importantly, this administration was based upon and influenced by a distinctive view of the ministry, often described as an integral part of 'High Methodism' in contrast to the main features of 'Low Methodism'.

It was in the wake of the Leeds organ case that the high Wesleyan conception of the Pastoral Office was expounded in considerable detail and in the belief that it was part of an undefined tradition implicit in Wesley's system. John Beecham, one of the younger preachers at the time of the Leeds crisis and later an important figure in defining official policy towards the Scots evangelicals,[47] faithfully reflected Bunting's position in one of the earliest essays on this theme. The substance of his argument was that Methodism recognised the legitimate and scriptural authority of the Pastoral Office as committed to the regular ministry. Beecham sought to demonstrate that the Pastoral Office, first filled by Christ and entrusted to the ministers in the church, involved the nurturing and governing of the people and that the only possible conclusion to be drawn from scripture was that ministers of the gospel alone acted as pastors. Beecham thus rejected the idea that the government of the church was vested in the whole church as was maintained by the exponents of 'Low Methodism' from the Kilhamites of the 1790s to the Wesleyan Reformers of the 1850s. He argued that the preachers in Conference constituted a collective pastorate that could not be shared with or surrendered to laymen. Separation from secular employment was one of the peculiar features of the pastor and, as such, local preachers and class leaders, whose respective preaching and counselling activities might have suggested otherwise, were barred from the office of pastor. In relation to Wesleyan polity this analysis meant that the important constitutional developments in the years immediately after Wesley's death had offered safeguards for the people but had not dispossessed the preachers of their power. Beecham was thus able to summarise his argument, 'We have seen that, in 1795 and 1797, the power of the pastor was not taken away from him, and given to others, or even shared with them; - that all the privileges then conceded by the Conference were only so many fences and guards thrown around the Pastor, to prevent him from using his power injuriously . . .'[48]

In their opposition to the nature and constitutional implications of this conception of the Pastoral Office, the Free Methodists insisted that they were reacting against a situation which was not of their own making. Their arguments were characterised by two general features. First, their understanding of Wesleyan polity was governed by what they regarded as a binding and comprehensive contract which had been made between preachers and people in the course of the major constitutional debates of 1795 and 1797. It was held that as a result of these deliberations Conference had transferred significant powers to the local courts and that a system had been established whereby the superintendent minister shared pastoral authority with laymen in the Leaders' Meeting. Secondly, it was claimed that during and after the Leeds organ case the preachers had taken the initiative in advancing a form of ministerial authority which was based on false premises and which destroyed the scriptural and constitutional rights of the people. The high Wesleyan conception of the Pastoral Office was neither a datum of scripture nor the underlying principle of the constitution. The preachers had in effect invented an artifice to enhance their own powers and status as well as to overwhelm allegedly undesirable elements.

The Free Methodist system of government asserted the influence of an essentially local, lay perspective or what may be classified as 'Low Methodism'. In these circumstances special emphasis was given to the need for minimal connexional ties and a weak central authority. A form of representative government was called into being which was analogous to constitutional developments in the secular world and which challenged one of Bunting's more famous dicta that Methodism was as opposed to democracy as it was to sin. Furthermore the full-time preacher under this system was denied the pastoral authority of the Wesleyan preacher and was no more than a 'hired servant' or 'speaking brother'.

It was against this model of church government that Bunting set his face and did not hesitate to deal with its advocates wherever and whenever they showed their hand. His connexional policies were designed to further the process of consolidation and integration. His critics, however, bitterly complained that they had the opposite effect and that Bunting was responsible for the division of Methodism and for the despoliation of Wesley's legacy. As the principal architect of a transformed administrative system, he commanded a personal authority and displayed political skills freely acknowledged by supporters and opponents alike. He was variously regarded as the indispensable ecclesiastical statesman, the Methodist Pope, the Conference 'buttoned up in a single pair of breeches', and 'the power-drunk minister of Christ'.[49] Although his pulpit talents first suggested high office, his keen regard for order and discipline proved his greatest asset. At the unusually early age of thirty-five he was appointed Secretary of Conference in 1814 and held the post until 1820 when he entered upon the first of four spells of office as President of Conference. After service as connexional editor in the period 1821-24 and further circuit duties he was permanently stationed in London as Secretary for foreign missions in 1833. A year later he became President of the newly-formed Theological Institution, the most controversial appointment of his career and one which precipitated the Warrenite agitation.

By the late 1830s and early 1840s, during the gathering crisis in the Church

11

of Scotland, Bunting's power and influence as connexional pilot, administrator and politician reached a peak and began to show incipient signs of decline. He had emerged from the Leeds organ case with enhanced authority, while the Warrenite episode, possibly the most exhausting contest of his career occupying him 'by night and day',[50] demonstrated his command of the Conference platform and his capacity to complete the first major revision of connexional rules since 1797. Bunting had become such an integral part of institutionalised Wesleyanism that one of the Conference sessions of 1837 was adjourned on the ground that no business could be transacted in his absence. He had within his grasp, moreover, an intelligence service and distribution network second only to that of the government; the nature and extent of these facilities are evident in the following correspondence, not least in the way in which Scots evangelicals like Chalmers and William Collins, the Glasgow publisher, requested Bunting to use his good offices to publicise their cause.[51]

The numerous and varied demands upon Bunting's time and energies are also well-illustrated by the correspondence. His punishing daily routine is evident in the bulk of the correspondence alone, especially in view of the fact that Scottish Methodism never accounted for more than fractionally over one per cent of the total British membership during his lifetime. Ministers and laymen relentlessly pursued him for advice on financial, theological, legal, constitutional and political matters. They requested his services as a preacher, sought his influence in obtaining appointments, and appealed to him as arbiter in a host of petty squabbles. He had of necessity to provide a guidance and counselling service, for the trials and tribulations of ministerial colleagues are apparent throughout the correspondence: the alcoholic problems of a superintendent's wife, the marital prospects of a young minister, or the mental disorders of one of his protégés. Keen to assert the professional status of the ministry, Bunting must have despaired occasionally when colleagues pleaded for living conditions comparable to their new-found status and grumbled about a miserably damp house in Glasgow or disputed responsibility for the purchase of a bed in Dunfermline.

As a family man and a public figure Bunting also had to contend with personal crises while continuing to deal with both routine administration and the promotion of a number of policies within and beyond the connexion. In 1836 Samuel Dunn, who was as quick to turn to Bunting for advice as he was to turn against him in the late 1840s, concluded a request for information by observing 'Some of these questions may appear trivial to you ...'[52] Bunting was probably inclined to agree at a time when the Warrenite controversy had scarcely subsided and the death of his wife twelve months earlier was still a deeply felt loss. But there was no relief from a multitude of commitments and troubles, and in 1840 when one minister appealed against an appointment to the Shetlands on the grounds of his wife's stomach troubles Bunting himself was virtually penniless and suffering a form of ill-health from which he was never to recover his full vigour.

By the mid-1840s the policy and character of Bunting's administration attracted formidable resistance. Fierce battles for the Presidential chair at this time demonstrated the growing strength of an 'official opposition' in Conference. Personality clashes and policy differences held together this anti-Bunting league amongst some of the ministers. Usually of liberal and dissenting views, such ministers opposed the platform on issues like Church-State relations, education, temperance and revivalism, though they shared the official view on the role of the ministry. They were strong enough to deny the chair to Buntingite candidates in the period 1845-47, but when the Buntingites finally rallied in 1848 and secured the election of Robert Newton, the most popular Wesleyan preacher of his generation, they mounted a campaign to smoke out their other critics, the underground opposition responsible for the *Flysheets*.

Published anonymously and in instalments between 1844 and 1848, the *Flysheets* savagely criticised Bunting's system of government under the heading of location, centralisation and secularisation. In effect the Bunting regime was held responsible for the construction of a London-based bureaucracy that was riddled with exclusiveness, favouritism and selfishness, that was contrary to the pristine qualities of Methodism and that was removed from and opposed to the provincial character of Methodism. The *Flysheets* might have remained simply the sharpest and most comprehensive of a series of criticisms but for the fact that they were used to reinforce support for the administration amongst the ministers. The declaration of loyal behaviour, which had long since become a hallmark of the Bunting regime in a crisis, was now employed yet again, as a result of which three ministers, James Everett, Samuel Dunn and William Griffith were expelled for their refusal to indicate whether they were associated with the *Flysheets*; Everett almost certainly had a hand in these publications, Dunn had for several years publicised his opposition to the Bunting oligarchy, and Griffith had pursued a stormy but hitherto inconsequential career as a radical politician. These expulsions heralded the last and most serious institutional break in Methodism with the appearance of the Wesleyan Reform Movement. The subsequent formation of the United Methodist Free Churches (1856), comprising the Wesleyan Methodist Association and the Wesleyan Reform Movement, was the first major Methodist Union.

Bunting was largely a spectator in these events, but when he was still at the helm in the 1840s he had increasingly struggled to control not only his open and conspiratorial ministerial opponents but also a mass membership exhibiting social-class divisions and cultural differences. The pressures and tensions most evident in the large urban societies of the North of England during the 1820s and 1830s were never far below the surface of Wesleyan life. The general influence of social-class status on relationships within such societies had resulted in a growing distinction between the wealth, authority and customs of a middle-class element and the aspirations, frustrations and practices of a predominantly artisan class. Bunting had forged an alliance between the ministry and the wealthy laity, which was based on overlapping interests in the maintenance of public order and disciplined societies; one of his main administrative achievements was to open up the large connexional business committees to the oft dubbed 'lay lords'. But this relationship was increasingly challenged by laymen whose social standing and financial resources were invariably less impressive, whose functions and outlook were essentially local, and whose distaste for central controls could be as strong as their opposition to any elevated view of the ministry.

It was from such quarters that there emerged a stream of protests against the political and social attitudes of Bunting and the hierarchy. The contrast between radical and liberal opinion amongst the rank-and-file and the conservative inclinations of the leadership was a standard feature of Free Methodist polemics. Bunting himself was never quite the doctrinaire Tory portrayed by some of his critics. Professor Kent rightly draws attention to the fact that Bunting gave a moderate welcome to the Reform Act of 1832 and that his tacit support for the deportation of the Dorchester labourers was support for a non-Tory administration.[53] Yet it was nevertheless the case that he was generally inclined to take a more favourable view of the Tories than of the Whigs. In the Liverpool parliamentary election of 1832, for example, he voted for Lord Sandon, the Tory candidate whose gradual emancipationist views on the slave question scarcely coincided with those of Wesleyans at large nor with Conference advice to pay a conscientious and paramount regard to this question. Furthermore Bunting was surrounded by some very pugnacious Tory supporters who possessed varying degrees of influence in the connexion.

His immediate family — especially his sons William and Percy — and some of his closest ministerial colleagues — notably George Osborn and Robert Newton — were no less than partisan Tories in their public activities.

During the period of the Disruption crisis both the passage of time and the pressure of events were beginning to expose limitations in Bunting's handling of public affairs. Immediately after a lengthy debate on the Disruption at the Conference of 1843 he expressed a wish to withdraw from some of the connexional committees, evidently believing that 'I cannot go on; I am conscious of failure'.[54] At the next Conference, when he was elected President for the fourth and last time, he so objected to resolutions carried against his advice that he dissolved the proceedings, though eventually he resumed the chair. In many respects, therefore, the growing conflict in the Kirk during the period 1834-43 coincided with an important transitional period in Bunting's ministry, during the course of which his physical powers visibly waned, his personal influence came under closer scrutiny and his policies on certain public matters were overtaken by events and subjected to fiercer questioning than in the past.

4. Wesleyan Methodism and the Disruption in the Church of Scotland

The following correspondence also offers insights into the impact of Scottish ecclesiastical developments upon Wesleyan opinion south of the border. The Disruption crisis in particular is of special importance in this context, and it provides, moreover, a fairly comprehensive commentary on a range of attitudes associated with the connexional management and most clearly demonstrated by Bunting as the acknowledged voice of official opinion. The protracted conflict in Scotland was accompanied by and related to a re-consideration of Wesleyan positions, most notably in the much-disputed territory of Church and State politics and the nature of ecclesiastical government.

Wesleyan support for the Scots evangelicals found full expression before and during the critical year of 1843. In March 1843 the London ministers headed by Bunting addressed a petition to parliament in which they expressed the view that in the absence of legislative action there would occur 'the lamentable secession of a large body of most valuable and excellent Ministers and Members of the Church of Scotland ...'[55] The Conference of 1843 endorsed this statement in a Pastoral Address that encouraged principled and pecuniary support for the Free Church. This response was predictable in view of the increasingly close relations between the Wesleyan leadership and the Scots evangelicals and most especially between Bunting and Chalmers. Bunting had corresponded with Chalmers since the early 1820s, in the first instance as an 'insignificant stranger' who had been 'refreshed in spirit' by the Scotsman's ministry and had been particularly impressed by his views on the management of religious causes in urban areas.[56] The personal rapport between the two men had its roots in a shared appreciation of evangelical principles, a common interest in the missionary cause and a similar assessment of the nature and value of established churches. While Bunting regarded Chalmers as one of the most illustrious men produced by Scotland, Free Church leaders were no less fulsome in their praise of Bunting and of the connexion at large.[57]

A major underlying theme of Wesleyan reactions to the Disruption crisis concerned the extent to which the evangelical party was performing in effect a Methodist role in Scotland. The connexional magazine believed that the evangelicals 'might have their *veto*, if they would give up their *Methodism*', and the mouthpiece of the Bunting administration, the weekly newspaper *The Watchman*, claimed that the evangelicals were under attack precisely because they 'have too much of what is called Methodism ...' while their opponents, the moderates, were suspicious of 'any tendency to Evangelism, Puritanism, Methodism or anything of the kind'.[58] At a time when other Protestant bodies in Scotland were either defective like the 'semi-Popish' Episcopalians or numerically small and uninfluential like the Dissenters, it was patently clear to the connexional management that the Free Church leadership shouldered the responsibility for an evangelical drive.

If this general attitude suggested an evangelical alliance in the making, a number of particular issues contributed to such an outcome. The controversy over Church-State relations was of crucial importance in this respect. The long-held view of the Wesleyan hierarchy reflected both the peculiar origins of Methodism and a general concern for the maintenance of the Church. It was axiomatic that the defence of the Protestant constitution involved at the very least a friendly disposition towards the Church. The Stephens case of 1834 had occasioned the most recent and comprehensive pronouncement on the subject. The young Wesleyan minister Joseph Rayner Stephens, who was soon to become the blood-curdling orator of the anti-poor law campaign, had been summoned before his ministerial colleagues to answer charges concerning his disestablishment opinions. It was judged that such opinions were 'inconsistent with those sentiments of respect and affection towards the Church of England which our Connexion has, from the beginning, openly professed and honourably maintained'. Shortly afterwards Bunting himself delivered a classic exposition of the official view in which he declared his marked preference for the Church rather than Dissent and insisted that a new constitution would be required if Conference joined the current campaign against the Church.[59]

Ten years later, however, the idea of a special relationship with the Church had received such a battering that Bunting was forced to conclude in a reference to the Disruption 'I once hoped that such a thing was possible as an Established Church without state interference. But I now see it to be impossible. I wish two thousand clergymen would leave the English church in the same way'.[60] The exhaustion of the fund of goodwill for the Church was due in part to the influence of the tractarian view of Methodism as a schismatic body with an invalid ministerial order. By the early 1840s there was a growing number of instances in which Puseyite clergymen displayed unrestrained hostility towards the Wesleyan cause. Yet while tractarianism presented the dangerous prospect of a Church dominated by hostile forces, the course of events in Scotland also prompted an agonising reappraisal of the principle of established churches and of the functions of authority in Church and State.

A central feature of the Wesleyan view of the Scottish situation involved support for a purified and spiritually free establishment in what was perceived as a conflict between religious liberty and state-thraldom. The editorial columns of *The Watchman* in the period 1838-44 revealed the difficulties surrounding attempts to uphold both the principle and specific expressions of established churches. It was frequently maintained that the establishment principle was being placed on weak ground and that only some of the misguided friends and the entire force of inveterate opponents of the establishment could benefit by a failure to back Chalmers and the evangelicals. Once initial hopes of a favourable response from the Peel Administration (1841-46) were dashed, the possible implications received much attention. In a major editorial in June 1842 *The Watchman* contrasted its earlier view that the abuses of establishments did not necessarily arise out of the principle with its current belief that 'the attempt now made on the spiritual independence of the Church of Scotland is neither more nor less than an endeavour to fix the abuse in the place of the original principle, and to subject the principle itself to continual abrasion, till not a single particle of it is left'.[61] Six months later and still defending the principle, *The Watchman* nevertheless warned that a secession from the Kirk would inflict a blow upon the principle of established churches which would shake them to their foundations. Soon after the secession was an accomplished fact, moreover, the change of tone and emphasis was complete; a weak, muted reference to the principle was overshadowed by the unequivocal statement that 'there is no Established Church in existence on behalf of which, as it now stands, we could conscientiously contend'.[62]

While such a statement did not portend an alliance with militant dissent through the recently-formed Anti-State Church Association, it did register a shift in opinion towards a far more neutral if not critical attitude to the Church than had previously been the case. A further and more important manifestation of this change was evident in the Conference debate of 1843, for the Pastoral Address asserted the right of every church to unfettered freedom 'in matters which are plainly, and in their very nature, spiritual and ecclesiastical, and especially in reference to the sacred functions belonging to the admission, appointment, ordination, suspension, or deposition of Ministers . . .'[63] This statement failed to carry unqualified assent, and Dr James Dixon, the ultra-Tory campaigning star of the evangelical Protestant platform, raised the strongest objections. Recognising that he took the unpopular view and that 'I almost tremble to differ in judgment from my friend Dr. Bunting . . .', Dixon nevertheless insisted that the 'very headstrong' Scotsmen had taken up positions 'in which we cannot agree'.[64] It was, indeed, the case that the statement went far beyond a declaration of solidarity and contained an important ecclesiastical principle, the implication of which was general opposition to all Protestant established churches. For his own part Bunting refused to yield in the face of Dixon's argument. He quibbled about the presentation of the statement but defended its substance. Similarly George Osborn, who had drafted the statement, resisted any amendment even though he had been a vigorous defender of the Church.

A further factor that influenced the Wesleyan assessment of events in Scotland was a deeply-ingrained anti-Catholic opinion. Keen identification with the Protestant platform emerged in the late 1830s, most conspicuously in the furious opposition to the government's education scheme of 1839. Strong reaffirmations of Reformation principles by the Scots evangelicals were warmly welcomed by Wesleyan leaders who observed an otherwise bleak landscape and concluded that 'Popery, everywhere struggling for ascendancy, is the object which, beyond all others, forces itself on our attention . . .'[65] The failings of the English establishment in this respect attracted a growing volume of critical comment. There were bitter complaints that while popery in Ireland was conciliated and tractarian influences were tolerated in the Church, the evangelicals in England and Scotland were 'alone to be thought unworthy of attention, and of concession . . .'[66] It was particularly pleasing to Wesleyan observers that the General Assembly of 1842 expressed its recognition of co-existent Christian churches and thereby distinguished itself from the Church whose policy drew scathing comment in the connexional magazine 'Vilified Rome is the only society, in this part of the world, that she will acknowledge to be a Christian church along with herself'.[67]

Protestant defences against the religious heresies of the day were viewed therefore as greatly dependent upon the combined operations of the Wesleyans and the Scots evangelicals. And while it was recognised that defeat of the evangelicals would strengthen the grip of the Kirk moderates and the Puseyite churchmen on either side of the border, it was also claimed that such an outcome would mean a decided victory for dissent and infidelity. This was a distressing prospect for Wesleyans who had so often distanced themselves from the Dissenters. It was no less alarming for the Scots evangelicals whose original intention had been to strengthen rather than subvert the Establishment and to defend the Kirk against Dissent.[68] Wesleyan fears were aroused because a failure to accommodate the

16

Scots evangelicals would strengthen the anti-state church argument and, worse still, improve the general status of Dissent in society at large. The complete subordination of ecclesiastical establishments to the civil power — commonly described as the secularisation of the church — would leave the Dissenters with 'the best of the argument' and with *influence and power*, as well as *truth*.[69] When the Conservative Member of Parliament, Alexander Campbell, unsuccessfully moved for a Select Committee to examine the dispute in the Kirk (March, 1842), the *Watchman* supported Campbell and argued that neither the Church nor the Conservatives could do without the evangelicals. Twelve months later *The Watchman* voiced the extreme opinion that the establishment principle would now be subjected to sterner questioning than at any time since the days of Constantine.[70] Meanwhile, the connexional magazine expressed its complete bewilderment at the sight of English politicians who, while professing to uphold the religious institutions of the country, seemed not only willing that the most powerful objections of Dissenters against religious establishments should be realised but also resolved to assist in realising them.[71] In the face of this condition and the light of Protestant divisions, rampant popery and widespread infidelity, it seemed that old theological controversies between the Calvinistic Kirk and Arminian Methodism were paling into insignificance; 'The Gospel itself' declared one Wesleyan commentator 'is now assailed; and, for its defence and establishment, all the energies of Calvinism and Arminians are required.'[72]

The Wesleyan response to developments in the Kirk was also influenced by the belief that legal decisions against the Scots evangelicals would open the door for all manner of interference with the non-established churches. The petition which was organised by Bunting in 1843 maintained that if parliament sanctioned court decisions concerning the spiritual functions and discipline of the Church of Scotland 'the religious rights and liberties even of those Christian Churches in this country which are *not established* may possibly be placed in jeopardy by the future extension, and application to *them*, under various plausible pretences, of the same principles...'[73] This important, if ill-founded, consideration reflected the long-standing concern of the connexional hierarchy to manage its own affairs without external interference. It was especially desirable in periodic dealings with dissident elements to avoid any encroachment on what was regarded as the proper jurisdiction of connexional courts. Bunting and his colleagues, moreover, were often nervous and assertive whenever chapel property rights became a matter of public attention in the civil courts, as was evident when Dr Samuel Warren had taken his case to law in 1835 and again when the Peel Administration pushed through the Dissenters' Chapels Act of 1844. This last piece of legislation, allowing Unitarians to remain in possession of chapels which they had held continuously for the last twenty-five years and for which no specific religious doctrines or mode of worship were prescribed in the original trust deed, was bitterly opposed by Bunting, mainly because in its unamended form the bill prejudiced efforts to recover property from Methodist seceders. During periods of internal unrest, in fact, the Bunting administration frequently appeared more concerned to keep control of property than to retain certain sections of the membership.

Opposition to the Dissenters' Chapels Act was also symptomatic of the growing disenchantment of the Wesleyan Tories with the Peel Administration. This attitude of mind perceptibly hardened as a result of the Disruption crisis, though it was also related to the general performance of the Administration ranging from the objectionable education clauses of Graham's Factory Bill (1843) to the most offensive of proposals to increase the grant to the Maynooth Catholic College (1845). At the height of the Maynooth conflict, William Bunting summed up the sense of shock and outrage felt by such individuals, 'I, who have taken some pains to lift the present Conservative party to power will, in my own place, as a Minister of religion, do my very best to help them out of power'.[74] Only a few Wesleyan Tories were now inclined to give Peel the benefit of the doubt; John Maclean belonged to this small minority and wrote to Bunting on hearing the news about the increased grant to Maynooth, 'I can't give up my confidence in Sir Robert Peel yet; but he would need (as our Scotch proverb says) "a *lang* spoon that sups wi' the Deil".'[75]

To a certain extent the Disruption crisis prepared the Wesleyan Tories for this hour in that the government's handling of the situation filled them with apprehension. Certainly the return to power of the Tories in 1841 had been welcomed by much of the Wesleyan establishment, especially in view of recent clashes with the Whig Administration over the education proposals of 1839 and the general association of whiggery with secularism. The high-water mark of Buntingism, as W.R. Ward argues, 'had come with the tory victory at the polls in 1841, which seemed to have completely vindicated the great man's foresight, and crowned a set of policies which might be supposed to have secured Methodism a considerable treasury of merit with Church and government'.[76] The conservative *Watchman*, which rarely concealed its distaste for the Whigs, persistently advised Peel to back the evangelicals against what it regarded as a high-Tory remnant in Scotland staunchly opposed to the Kirk. Hopeful and exasperated by turns, *The Watchman* lectured the Administration on the need to show that modern Conservatives were not simply old Tories under a new name, concerned only to oppose all popular rights and to advocate the church solely as an instrument of patronage. But as the crisis deepened it was increasingly recognised that the Administration had fallen far short of expectations, 'We did hope, therefore, that Sir Robert Peel would gladly have embraced the opportunity of vindicating Conservatism, by securing the Church in her just rights *as a church*, even, if necessary, by the alteration of the law. But we have been painfully disappointed'.[77]

More important, however, than these political consequences was the considerable emphasis upon the large amount of common ground shared by the Wesleyans and the Free Church in respect of ecclesiastical polity. At a Wesleyan Missionary Society anniversary meeting attended by the Moderator of the General Assembly, thunderous applause followed Bunting's reference to Robert Newton as 'The Very Rev. the Moderator (or President) of the Wesleyan Conference'.[78] Such a light-hearted reference was in fact indicative of the serious proposition that the Scots evangelicals were contending for the same principles of ecclesiastical polity already embodied in Wesleyanism. General similarities between Wesleyanism and Presbyterianism had been debated in Methodist circles since Wesley's day, but the subject became a matter of particular interest during the Disruption crisis. In 1839 Alfred Barrett, one of the most respected exponents of the high Wesleyan conception of the ministry, published an essay in which he argued that 'our general form of ecclesiastical polity is Presbyterian, combined with Episcopacy, *jure humano*. The Established Church of Scotland is not very dissimilar'.[79] John Beecham, whose mastery of Wesleyan polity was already established, also maintained that 'our polity is in substantial accordance with that of our evangelical brethren of the Church of Scotland . . .'[80] And in 1841 Edmund Grindrod made the same point in his handbook of Wesleyan laws and regulations, 'in our form of government we are a Scripture presbytery, resembling, to a great degree, the Established Church of Scotland . . .'[81] Grindrod maintained that the courts in both bodies were similar in number, order, status, composition and functions. What differentiated the two systems in his view was the superior degree of authority entrusted to the ministry in Wesleyanism.

This distinction, however, was of vital importance when set against the full

18

meaning of the authoritarian conception of the ministry on the Wesleyan side. Certainly neither Grindrod nor Barrett, for example, overlooked the contrasts, yet during the Disruption crisis some observers considered that the differences were muted or misunderstood. Wesleyan spokesmen paid much attention to the issue of the admission and ordination of ministers in the Kirk, whereas the real question in Scotland concerned the local appointment of ordained men. It was all very well to adopt Beecham's line of argument that the Quarterly Meeting in Wesleyanism had the right to approve of any candidate for the ministry and 'that we have even a *fuller* system of non-intrusion, in our own body, than that for which the Free Church contends'.[82] But it was in fact the case that the appointment of ministers was entirely in the hands of the ministerial Conference, and this arrangement could not be modified in view of the implications of the high Wesleyan conception of the Pastoral Office.

A further aspect of the unease felt by dissentients like Dixon was the impact of close identification with the Free Church upon the laity. By displaying a dangerously partisan interest in the affairs of another church, Conference was playing with fire if its public policies served only to encourage the laity to discuss the points raised by the controversy in the Kirk. Dixon himself was most concerned about the likely effects if the Free Church 'turn into a democracy' and if Wesleyan laymen took it into their heads to retain the services of a minister without regard to the rights and interests of the connexion.[83] Similar grave anxieties were shared by other ministers, one of whom held that it was unwise in a Pastoral Address 'to set our people thinking and talking about debateable and complex questions of Church politics'.[84] Such a view of the laity was not untypical and it arose out of an apprehensiveness heightened by periodic explosions of unrest. Thus, for example, had it not expired in 1839 the *Christian Advocate*, regarded by the Bunting administration as a gadfly throughout the 1830s, would have continued its generally disparaging references to Chalmers and the establishment principle, thereby fermenting lay opinion. The general argument concerning the inappropriateness of a public declaration on a dispute in another church could not have been lost on Bunting who was forever complaining about the volley of external criticism whenever disputes beset the connexion. Yet on this matter as on the question of the establishment principle there was much substance to the impressions of one commentator who described William Bunting's contribution to the Conference debate of 1843 in a railway metaphor. 'His position did not substantially differ from his father's, and it carried its line over the same Chat Moss without sinking any concrete for the support of his train of argument.'[85]

In these circumstances the warm embrace of the Free Church cause by the Wesleyan leadership bore the suggestion of a need to overcome the peculiarly isolated position of Wesleyanism in the interstices between Church and Dissent. In the face of internal disturbances and public criticism, advantages could be derived from emphasising, albeit in an exaggerated manner, the amount of common ground shared with the Scots evangelicals rather than stressing the *sui generis* character of the connexional system. During the Disruption period, especially, the connexional leadership often felt bereft of allies and showed an uncertain sense of identity as it was attacked by Puseyite and evangelical elements in the Church and by Dissenters at large; 'our position as Wesleyans' commented *The Watchman* in 1843 'is encompassed with as much difficulty as the opposition of many who *ought* to be our friends can gather around it. But are we to give way to despondency on that account? In no wise'.[86] At least support for the Scots evangelicals provided a ray of hope, though in the longer term it was not repaid in equal measure.

Immediately after the Disruption the Scots were effusive in their expressions of gratitude to the Wesleyan leadership. In 1845 the Marquis of Breadalbane, one

19

of the few artistocrats to join the Free Church, spoke of the high obligation owed to the Wesleyans; Fox Maule, a Whig Member of Parliament, was unable to forget the interest taken by the Wesleyans in the Free Church cause; and Thomas Guthrie promised that 'if the Wesleyan Methodist cause has ever its "back to the wall", they have only to send across the border, and they will find in Scotland, perhaps hands not so full of gold, but hearts as full of love, and tongues as loud . . .'[87] Neither financial assistance nor strong local support, however, was evident on the outbreak of the Wesleyan Reform troubles in 1849, even though the Scottish public was immediately treated to a pamphlet by William Horton, Chairman of the Scottish District. *The Watchman* commended this pamphlet to the English public and claimed that it 'will be still better appreciated in the Presbyterian North'.[88] The Scottish press, however, completely disagreed with this suggestion and sympathised with Wesleyan Reformers; neither the *Dundee Advertiser* nor the *Aberdeen Herald*, for example, could understand why English Methodists had tolerated a system of clerical despotism for such a long time.[89]

The Free Church leaders were put on the spot and at best offered lukewarm and generally private support. Horton explained to Bunting that they entertained more favourable views of the official line than they were prepared to express, mainly because of 'the stupid prejudices which generally prevail in Scotland with regard to us'.[90] The initial reaction of the *Free Church Magazine* in September 1849 was hostile to Conference; its wounding advice to the Wesleyan leadership was to remodel the connexional sytem of government so as to bring it into harmony with the Free Church view of the scriptural plan. Meanwhile the *Wesleyan Times*, the major organ of the *Wesleyan Reform Movement*, reinforced this argument and quickly dismissed any suggestion of similarity between the Wesleyan and Free Church polities.[91]

No less depressing for the Wesleyan leaders was the effect of their policies upon the fate of Methodism in Scotland. At the time of the Disruption Bunting received regular reports that the pro-Free-Church stand was creating a favourable state of public opinion for Scottish Methodism.[92] But if the Free Church was God's elected instrument for evangelising Scotland, as one such report suggested in 1845, then the role of Methodism required definition. John Maclean, for example, believed that Scottish Methodism could serve to abate the severity of Calvinism, to moderate hostility to the residuary church, and to act as a breakwater to the ferocity of anti-episcopal wrath. This last function was based on 'our known friendship for the Church of England (which I trust in God we shall never sacrifice). . .'[93] This position, however, no longer corresponded to the widespread sense of reluctance to take up the cudgels on behalf of the Church. In any case Maclean had earlier expressed the fear that Conference might overlook the state of Scottish Methodism in its support for the Free Church, 'Let us give as much money to the Free Church as we can spare from our people — but don't let us hand *them* over too'. In a Conference debate on the subject in 1844 Dr Joseph Beaumont, who was familiar with Scottish Methodism, was no less assertive in objecting to the lavish sympathy for the Free Church when the Scottish circuits were struggling to keep alive.[94]

The lengthy correspondence between Maclean and Bunting, which concludes the following selection of letters, bears witness to what the connexional hierarchy no doubt regarded as another unwanted by-product of the Disruption, namely the proposed adoption of certain Free Church principles by the Wesleyans in Scotland. By the time of this correspondence Bunting had stood down from the active work, while periodic treatment at the Royal Asylum was about to force Maclean into a supernumeraryship. But it was not a disordered mind that put the case for a special arrangement whereby 'a regulated power of vetoing a minister . . .

might . . . be safely and very advantageously committed to our congregations.'[9][5] Bunting's reply has not survived, yet little imagination is required to gauge the probable reaction of a man who had consistently upheld the high Wesleyan conception of the Pastoral Office, who had repeatedly resisted any lay encroachment upon the power and responsibility of the ministry, and who had vigorously dismissed any suggestion that Methodism should inbibe the spirit of the times whether in the specific form of a Veto Act or in the more general demand for a democratic system of church government.

Against the background of the various strains and conflicts accompanying the evolution of Wesleyan Methodism, Bunting retained confidence in the value and correctness of his policy to the end of his life. In what proved to be his farewell message to the Conference of 1857 he testified to this effect 'I regard my policy, that is, the course which I have seen it my duty to pursue to have been right. It was the best for Methodism. *I am a true Methodist.* . .'[9][6] What emerges quite clearly is his key role in the connexional affairs of this period. In the context of the tangled history of Scottish Methodism, the letters which follow themselves provide the most eloquent testimony to Bunting's efforts (and frequent failures) to bring some order out of the prevailing chaos. The pressing demands imposed upon him by ministers and laymen from Lerwick to Dumfries demonstrate that if he had not existed he would have been a necessary invention.

Notes to Introduction

'Op.cit' in the notes after letters corresponds to a reference in this list.

1. T.P.Bunting *The Life of Jabez Bunting D.D.* (London: T.Woolmer 1858-1887). Cited below as *Life.*

2. W.R.Ward(ed.) *The Early Correspondence of Jabez Bunting 1820-1829* (London: Royal Historical Society Camden 4th Series 1972). Cited below as *Early Correspondence.*

3. W.R.Ward(ed.) *Early Victorian Methodism. The Correspondence of Jabez Bunting 1830-1858.* (Oxford: Oxford University Press 1976). Cited below as *Early Victorian Methodism.*

4. Methodist Archives and Research Centre; the John Rylands University Library of Manchester, Deansgate. Abbreviated below to M.C.A.

5. Edmund Grindrod to J.B. 1827. *Life* ii, p.226-227.

6. A.J.Hayes 'A Warrenite Secession in Edinburgh', *Journal of the Scottish Branch of the Wesley Historical Society* 10, 3-18 (1977a); *ibid.* 11, 3-6 (1978a). See also Letter No. 51 regarding Aberdeen.

7. *Early Victorian Methodism,* x.

8. H.R.Bowes *Methodism in Shetland and Orkney 1822-1825* (privately printed 1976); also *Journal of the Scottish Branch of the Wesley Historical Society* 5, 6-17 (1975); *ibid,* 6, 9-20 (1975).

9. See Letter No.51. James Rosser to J.B. Aberdeen 30 March 1837.

10. See *Early Correspondence* and *Early Victorian Methodism.*

11. Wesley F.Swift *Methodism in Scotland* (London: Epworth Press 1947).

12. O.W.Beckerlegge 'The Methodist New Connexion in Scotland', *Proceedings of the Wesley Historical Society* XXIX(7), 160-161 (1954); Hayes (1977a) op.cit.

13. *Wesley F.Swift* op.cit.p.56-63.

14. W.R.Ward 'Scottish Methodism in the Age of Jabez Bunting', *Scottish Church History Society Records* XX(1), 47-63 (1979). See also W.R.Ward *The Legacy of John Wesley* In *Statesmen, Scholars and Merchants* (A.Whiteman, J.S.Branley & P.G.M.Dickson,Eds.) (Oxford: Oxford University Press 1973).

15. Wesley F.Swift op.cit. p.70.

16. Wesley F.Swift op.cit. p.70.

17. J.Crowther *Thoughts upon the finances or temporal affairs of the Methodist Connexion...* p.5 and 16, (Leeds, 1817).

18. *Minutes of the Methodist Conference,* 1805. (Cited below as *Minutes.*) 'Let greater caution be used as to multiplying chapels so as not to load Societies with heavy debts...'. See also *Minutes* 1815, 1819, 1822.

'If a new chapel is built, is an additional preacher required, and can he be supported from the funds of the chapel or the Circuit? (*Minutes* 1813).

19.   See *Minutes* 1816.

20.   See *Minutes* 1817. (See also W. Pierce *The Ecclesiastical Principles & Polity of the Wesleyan Methodists* (London:Wesleyan Conference Office 1873). See also Letter No. 7. Duncan McAllum to J.B. Dunbar 1 July 1819.

21.   See G.Smith *History of Wesleyan Methodism* (London: Longman 1864), iii, p.5.

22.   See *Edinburgh District Minutes* 1820 (M.C.A.) 'Q. What is the opinion of the meeting respecting the adoption of the 'Bill Trade' in the case of the Scotch Chapels?
A. That it greatly regrets to find that such a trade exists at all among us, and much more that it should have been carried to the allarming [sic] extent to which it has — as it is a direct violation of our own rule on that subject and that in consequence of the very awfully involved state of the accounts of our chapels, the meeting thinks it necessary that a clerk be appointed to draw up a statement to be presented to Conference from documents to be furnished by Mr Ward...'

23.   See *Edinburgh District Minutes* 1827 (M.C.A.).

24.   See Letter No. 13. Valentine Ward to J.B. Glasgow 6 June 1821 (M.C.A.).

25.   See A.J.Hayes *Edinburgh Methodism 1761-1975. The Mother Churches* p.120 (Edinburgh: privately printed, 1976a). Fragments of Valentine Ward's diary were copies into Tyerman MSS iii, f. 528-534 by Tyerman, which give financial information missed by Wesley F.Swift op.cit. See also A.J.Hayes 'Valentine Ward: A reassessment', *Journal of the Scottish Branch of the Wesley Historical Society* 8, 2-19 (1976b).

26.   Wesley F.Swift *Methodism in Scotland* (London: Epworth Press 1947).

27.   V.Ward *Free and Candid Strictures on Methodism* (Aberdeen: 1818).

28.   Nor did the speculations entirely cease when Ward finally left Scotland. See A.J.Hayes 'The extinct Methodist Societies of South-East Scotland. 3. Musselburgh', *Proceedings of the Wesley Historical Society* XLI(3), 77-85 (1977b). See also Letter No.7. Duncan McAllum to J.B. Dunbar 1 July 1819: 'As to Leith, Dunformilen [sic] & Perth, only Mr.Ward can explain how they stand. I believe but so so.' As to Dunfermline, see 'The extinct Methodist Societies of South East Scotland. 1. Dunfermline', *Proceedings of the Wesley Historical Society* XLI(1), 12-21 (1977c).

29.   See Letter No.36. James Anderson to J.B. Hamilton 25 September 1830.

30.   See Wesley F.Swift op.cit. Also O.W. Beckerlegge 'In search of Forgotten Methodism', *Proceedings of the Wesley Historical Society* XXXII(5), 109-114 (1960); A.J.Hayes (1977d), 'The extinct Methodist societies of South-East Scotland. 2. Haddington'. *Proceedings of the Wesley Historical Society* XLI(2) 43-52. *Ibid.* 1978b 4. Dalkeith XLI(4) 104-117.

31.   See W.R.Ward (1979).

32.   See Letter No.112. Thomas R.Jones to J.B. Glasgow 6 July 1848.

33.   See Letter No.126. John Maclean to J.B. 1 April 1857.

34.   See Letter No.3. Thomas Preston to J.B. Edinburgh 6 March 1801.

35.   See Letter No.29. John Shipman to J.B. Liverpool 21 July 1826; also Letter No.27. J.B. to John Shipman Manchester 11 May 1826.

36.   A.N.Cass 'Development in Dundee Methodism 1830-1870', *Journal of the Scottish Branch of the Wesley Historical Society* 2, 4-17 (1973).

37.   See Hayes (1977a, 1978a).

38.   See Letter No.81. P.Duncan to J.B. Edinburgh 27 March 1843; Letter No.83 P.Duncan to J.B. 30 September 1843.

39.   John Pawson to Charles Atmore Edinburgh 8 October 1785; 20 October 1787; 27 October 1787 (M.C.A.).

40.   Wesley F.Swift op.cit.

41.   See Letter No.29. John Shipman to J.B. Liverpool 21 July 1826.

42.   John Wesley to Joseph Taylor, London 6 November 1877 (M.C.A.). 'I desire you would not wear the *surplice* nor administer the Lord's Supper any more'.

43.   B.Gregory *Sidelights on the conflicts of Methodism* p.333. (London: Cassell, 1899) Also David Wilson *Methodism in Scotland* p.18-20. (Aberdeen, 1850).

44.   See also Letter No.90. P.Duncan to J.B. Glasgow 18 November 1844; P.Duncan Letter No.111. P.Duncan to J.B. postmarked Glasgow 8 September 1846; Letter No.113. Thomas R.Jones to J.B. Glasgow Calton 11 July 1848.

45.   Tyerman MSS iii f.173 (M.C.A.). See Letter No.126. John Maclean to J.B. 1 April 1857.

46.	R.Currie, A.Gilbert, and L.Horsley *Churches and Churchgoers: Patterns of Church Growth in the British Isles since 1700* p.40 (Oxford, 1977).
47.	See Letter No.71. J.B. to John Beecham Manchester 13 January 1842 (M.C.A.).
48.	J.Beecham *An essay on the constitution of Wesleyan Methodism* p.108 (Second edition: London, 1850).
49.	Modern scholars have been as divided as Bunting's contemporaries in their assessment of his role and significance in nineteenth-century Methodism. For a sympathetic study see J.Kent *Jabez Bunting, The Last Wesleyan* (London 1955). A strongly unfavourable view is expressed by R.Currie *Methodism Divided* (London, 1968). A detailed study of the high Wesleyan conception of the Pastoral Office is provided by J.C.Bowmer *Pastor and People: A Study of Church and Ministry in Wesleyan Methodism from the death of John Wesley (1791) to the death of Jabez Bunting (1858)* (London, 1975). For the most extensive use of Bunting's correspondence see the works by W.R.Ward cited above.
50.	See Ward (1976) op.cit. p.xxii.
51.	See Letter No. 17. Valentine Ward to J.B., no place or date (M.C.A.). Letter No.67 J.B. to Thomas Chalmers, London 23 January 1841 (New College, Edinburgh).
52.	Letter No. 47. Samuel Dunn to J.B. Edinburgh 21 October 1836 (M.C.A.).
53.	R.Davies, A.R.George and G.Rupp (eds.) *A History of the Methodist Church in Great Britain* vol. 2, Chapter VI J.Kent 'The Wesleyan Methodists to 1849' (London, 1978). For further discussion of Wesleyan political opinion during this period see W.R.Ward *Religion and Society in England 1799-1850* passim (London, 1972) and D.A.Gowland *Methodist Secessions* p.119-39 (Manchester, 1979).
54.	B.Gregory op.cit. p.352.
55.	*The Watchman*, 8 March 1843.
56.	J.Bunting to T.Chalmers, 1821 (MSS. New College, Edinburgh).
57.	See *Wesleyan Methodist Magazine*, June 1842 and June 1845. See also T.P.Bunting op.cit. p.319-20.
58.	*Wesleyan Methodist Magazine*, July 1841 and January 1843. *The Watchman*, 30 March 1842 and 24 May 1843.
59.	See Smith (1864) op.cit. iii, Appendix G. B.Gregory op.cit. p.162.
60.	B.Gregory op.cit. p.349.
61.	*The Watchman*, 1 June 1842.
62.	*Ibid.* 31 January 1844.
63.	*Wesleyan Methodist Magazine*, December 1843.
64.	B.Gregory op.cit. p.347-50.
65.	*The Watchman*, 2 January 1839.
66.	*Ibid.* 21 September 1842.
67.	*Wesleyan Methodist Magazine*, September 1842.
68.	G.I.T.Machin *Politics and the Churches in Great Britain 1832 to 1868* p.112-13 (Oxford, 1977).
69.	*The Watchman*, 9 March 1842.
70.	*Ibid.* 15 March 1843.
71.	*Wesleyan Methodist Magazine*, January 1843.
72.	*Ibid.* November 1845.
73.	*Ibid.* April 1843.
74.	A.S.Thelwall (ed.) *Proceedings of the Anti-Maynooth Conference of 1845* p.164 (London, 1845).
75.	See Letter No. 97. John Maclean to J.B. Edinburgh 6 February 1845 (M.C.A.).
76.	W.R.Ward *Religion and Society in England 1790-1850* pp.251-2 (London, 1972).
77.	*The Watchman*, 30 March 1842.
78.	*Wesleyan Methodist Magazine*, June 1841.
79.	A.Barrett *An Essay on the Pastoral Office* pp.132-3 (London, 1839).
80.	*The Watchman*, 28 June 1843.
81.	E.Grindrod *A compendium of the laws and regulations of Wesleyan Methodism. With notes and an appendix* p.ix (Third edition: London, 1848).
82.	*The Watchman*, 28 June 1843.
83.	B.Gregory op.cit. p.349-50.
84.	B.Gregory op.cit. p.348.
85.	B.Gregory op.cit. p.350.
86.	*The Watchman*, 25 January 1843. See also Letter No.67. J.B. to Thomas Chalmers London 23 January 1843.

87.   *Wesleyan Methodist Magazine*, June 1845.
See also Letter No.86. Peter Duncan to J.B. Edinburgh 21 March 1844, Note 1.

88.   *The Watchman*, 19 September 1849.

89.   *Wesleyan Times*, 3 September 1849 and 15 October 1849.

90.   See Letter No.119. William Horton to J.B. Edinburgh 27 October 1849 (M.C.A.)

91.   See *Wesleyan Times*, 12 August 1850.

92.   See Letter No.81. Peter Duncan to J.B. Edinburgh 27 March 1843 (M.C.A.).
See also Letter No.96. John Maclean to J.B. Edinburgh 30 January 1845 (M.C.A.).

93.   Letter No.96. John Maclean to J.B. Edinburgh 30 January 1845.

94.   See J.Beaumont *The Life of the Rev Joseph Beaumont, M.D.* p.134 (London, 1856).
B. Gregory op.cit. p.363.

95.   See Letter No.124. John Maclean to J.B. Edinburgh 18 August 1855 (M.C.A.).

96.   Quoted in J.Kent op.cit. p.62.

Plate 1. Nicolson Square, Edinburgh, erected 1815. Engraving by J. Storer, 1820.
Reproduced by permission of the National Monuments Record of Scotland.

Plate 2. The Calton or Green Street Chapel, Glasgow, erected 1844.
Photograph Dr O.W. Beckerlegge.

*Plate 3. Anderson Cross Church, Glasgow, erected 1819.
Photograph Dr O.W. Beckerlegge.*

Plate 4. Tradeston Chapel, Bridge Street, Glasgow, erected 1813.
Photograph Dr O.W. Beckerlegge.

Plate 5. Wesleyan Methodist Association Chapel, Paisley. Reproduced by permission of George Outram & Co. Ltd, Glasgow.

The Letters

1. *From Thomas Preston*[1]   Dunbar, March 11, 1800

For some months I have been in expectation of a letter from you and many times
have wonder'd much [why] you did not write me; but having this morning received
a letter from Mr. Farrar,[2] I understand you are expecting a few lines from me. I will
therefore now remove the hindrance.

You may perhaps wish to know how I like [it] in Scotland? Upon the whole
I like it very well, I have enjoyed a far better state of health than I did in Manchester,
for which mercy I desire to be thankfull.

I am very fond of Scotland, also for the many opportunitys I have for making
improvement in usefull knowledge. Our Circuit is different from most in England.
We have but three place[s] where we preach on a Sunday, Edinburgh, Dalkeith
and Dunbar. The preachers in Edinburgh and Dalkeith change every fortnight. At
Dunbar (which is 27 miles east of Edinburgh) we stay for three months, except the
Superintendent who stays only about one month.

Dunbar is my province at present, and will be till about the 15th of May.
Here I have to preach five times a week, (and once a fortnight to walk eleven miles
to preach at Haddington) and meet two small classes and attend three prayer
meetings. I take a walk out by the sea-side before breakfast and then sit down to
read till three or four o'clock in the afternoon ...

The people of Scotland for the most part are a knowing sencible [sic] people;
but there is not that depth of piety, which knowledge require[s] to keep it in its
proper place. Nevertheless, there are a few piouse persons, as any I have ever known.
This is the only thing I have against Scotland, or else according to my present views,
I would live and die among them. But there [is] no necessity that a preacher should
drink into their spirit, and the more he is spiritual in his conviction, the more he is
respected by them.

Our success in the work of the Lord is small, but we have good reason to
believe that we do not labour altogether in vain. Messrs Kershaw[3] and White[4] are
very agreeable sencible men, we labour together in unity and love ...[5]

1. Thomas Preston (1775-1834), Probationer, Edinburgh Circuit 1799-1800.
2. John Farrar (d. 1837 aet. 71), Preacher, Oldham Circuit 1798-99.
3. John Kershaw (1766-1855), Superintendent, Edinburgh Circuit, 1799-1801.
4. George White (d. 1801), Preacher, Edinburgh Circuit, 1798-1800.
5. This is a very early letter, written to Bunting at his first station in the Oldham
   Circuit. See Hayes (1977d).

2. *From Thomas Preston*   Dunbar, October 24, 1800

I am sorry that you have taken up so great a part of your letter in apologising for
not writing sooner, as one line might have answered the same end. It gives me great
pleasure to hear that you have been so much assisted and supported under the
exersises of mind you have had to pass thro' the last year ... I perfectly agree with
you with respect to the Life of an Itinerant Methodist preacher being a sphere of

action, in which if a man be faithfull, he may be far more useful and holy than in any other calling whatsoever. Indeed holiness and usefullness ought to be the great concern of our life; and in this respect we are I believe furnish'd with such helps as no other body of people ...

No man, I have ever met with has been so usefull to me in every respect, as Mr. Kershaw. My last year was in many respects the best year of my life. My opportunities for the cultivation of my mind and of pursuing those studies which are likely to be very usefull to me ...

3. *From Thomas Preston* Edinburgh, March 6, 1801

Yours of Jan 10th, which I had expected some weeks, came safe to hand, and would have been answered before this had I not been prevented by a little indisposition of body which rendered me unable to think, or write with any propriety. . .

You ask what is the state of Methodism & Religion in Scotland? Both are very low. Very little of the power of Godliness is known amongst them. The Scotch are for the most part a well informed people; they are very partial to a learn[ed] discourse from the Pulpit, & think it little better than blasphemy for a person to preach who has not had an Academical Education. I have more than once been asked at what College I study'd. We never hear any Amens. This is altogether unfashionable. We have a few very pious persons amongst us, & thro' mercy we are increasing a little. We have added a few to the Society since Conference, & have reason to hope several have got good.

The great bar which prevents Methodism from prospering in this Country is the Doctrines of Calvin [being] nearly universally received, so that as soon as a general salvation is offer'd we are looked upon as deceiver[s] of the People and many to this day believe the Methodists to be the false prophets mentioned in Scripture. At present Salvation is seldom heard in the churches, the Gospel being preach'd rather as a system of Doctrines than as truths which are to be experienced.

After all I think a young man may make more improvement in knowledge than in any part of the Connection I know. But there are not so many helps to practical religion, as in Yorkshire & Lancashire. We have nothing particular in a religious way that I know of at present.

I hope to hear from you soon . . . Remember me in love to all my Manchester friends. Do you hear anything of Mr Farrar? . . .

4. [Printed Broadsheet]. *Copy of a Letter from the Rev. Richard Heape*[1] *of Crieff*[2] *in Scotland, to the Rev. John Armitage*[3] *of Stockton-upon-Tees.*

As the following letter contains intelligence which will be gratifying to many, and especially to those who have long felt deeply concerned for the interests of religion in the North, it has been deemed advisable to give it publicity, as an encouragement to such as pray for the peace and prosperity of Zion.

Crieff, February 19, 1816

I make free to write to you again because I have more pleasing intelligence to communicate. For sometime after I wrote last, I felt grieved that I had sent you such a black account of Scotland: I thought though it was true, it would do no good, and pain your mind by the appearance of so much labour and expence being lost. After our great sifting at *Perth,*[4] seventeen, or eighteen were added, in one fortnight, who appeared to be on the threshold of the Kingdom. The last time I was there (about seven weeks since), we had a Love-feast, in which a Gentleman got up and told us, that he was so powerfully affected, and deeply awakened, on the 21st of May last, while I was lecturing on Luke xiv. 16-23 that if I had spoken a few minutes longer

26

he should have been obliged to "bawl out": and altho' he did smother his feelings as much as he could, yet most in the Chapel observed him, which so much ashamed his wife, that she would not come near a meeting for sometime afterwards, and prevented him as often as possible ...

Two of our Missionaries from Ireland, who have lately visited Edinburgh and Glasgow have been made very useful. *Mr. Ward*[5] writes from Edinburgh (January 14th) saying, there was such a glorious work going on there as he had never seen before, but gives no particulars. A Local Preacher in Glasgow, from whom I have lately had a Letter, informs me, that *Mr. Noble,*[6] on his way to Ireland had been a few days in that place. After preaching on Sunday evening, he told them, he had just come from Edinburgh, where twenty souls had found divine peace in one meeting. This account shook the dry bones and after wrestling sometime in prayer, he dismissed the congregation. But when the people were nearly all out, he observed two families weeping in their seats. He then begun to sing, and the people returned into the Chapel, where they continued till about ten o'clock. On Monday evening Mr. Noble preached again; and after exhorting his hearers to obey the voice of God, just as he was looking for a Hymn, a Woman stood up, in the presence of about a thousand people, and desired permission to tell what God had done for her since the night before. She said, she had often *heard* of conversion, but never *felt* it till Sunday evening; and that the peace and joy she experienced was indescribable. Then the fire kindled and began to blaze! ... On Monday, Tuesday and Wednesday evenings were most glorious meetings. They continued from seven, till about twelve o'clock. Indeed the people would not go away; for whenever the Ministers concluded, some of the Brethren gave out a Hymn and prayed again ...

Yesterday morning, whilst lecturing on John xiii. 18-30 I felt affected and blessed, as were many besides; but in the afternoon the power of God was most eminently present ... Although the like of this was never known in Crieff before, I have not heard one jest made upon it, nor the least abuse of it ... It came so unexpectedly, that I was utterly confounded for a short time, and neither knew what to say, nor what I did say: all indeed seemed astonished and overpowered. O, that God would ride on! Such has been the unanimous, and earnest prayer of this little Society for some time; but my belief is so strong, that I fear the work will not continue ...[7]

[Endorsed] J. Armitage to Jabez Bunting Stockton, April 2, 1816

1. Richard Heape (1789-1874), Preacher, Perth Circuit, 1814-16.
2. There was a short-lived Society in Crieff c. 1815-17.
3. John Armitage (left ministry 1839), Superintendent, Stockton Circuit, 1815-16.
4. This refers to a revival at Perth in 1814-15, but unfortunately no further details survive.
5. Valentine Ward (1781-1834), Superintendent, Edinburgh Circuit, 1815-17; Chairman of the Edinburgh District, 1815-16.
6. Arthur Noble (d. 1862 aet. 78), Missionary, Londonderry and Antrim Mission, 1815-19. Remained in Ireland for the rest of his life.
7. The date of this letter antedates the opening of Nicolson Square Chapel, Edinburgh, by some months, so that these events must have occurred within the Masons Hall, Niddry Street. See Hayes (1976a).

5. *From D. McAllum*[1]   Dunbar, April 2, 1818

As the President and you[2] are expected to visit Edin[bu]r[gh] & Glasgow on your way to Ireland & make the collections to help their distressed chapels, I have appointed our District Meeting to be held the second week in May not to interfere with your visit.

I write to you now for your opinion & advice. How far is your law to be conceived of and acted upon respecting retrenchments as to allowing or not allowing for servants?[3] Suppose you appoint young men to circuits where they receive all their demands upon the spot as to Br. Dredge[4] in Edin[bu] r[gh] & Br. Bell[5] in Glasgow, but others are sent without their consent to places where all their allowance comes from Conference — suppose Messrs. Crabtree,[6] Hamer,[7] Millar[8] & Bridgman,[9] they get nothing from either source. Now how shall I act to be impartial & maintain equality or satisfy the disappointed Brethren? Have the goodness to write me soon & give me your opi[ni]on & advice whether the law is intended only to affect those circuits which are unable to meet their expenses & the unfortunate brethren in them but none others.

I fear you must carry retrenchments much farther yet before your finances equal your expenditure — perhaps quarterages reduced to £4 or even to £3 3/- and also children to £1 11/6 if not £1. 1. 0 pr. Qur. I know retrenchments are very unpalatable yet I foresaw the necessity thereof years ago and proposed it in our District Meeting at Shields; but it was not relished or seconded. I for[e]saw & lamented many years ago, step after step taken that led to our present embarrassments. The Disease is now self-evident, but a radical easy cure is difficult.

Please inform me when you expect to pass through Dunbar. If you could spend *one* night with me it would gratify me much ...

Our new chapels in this country are sadly burdened with debt that the interest scarcely can be raised. The debt upon Haddington through my son's[10] exertions is reduced since Conference about £140, but is still too heavy for the Society to bear ...

1. Identified from letter as Duncan McAllum (d.1834 aet.78), Superintendent, Dunbar Circuit 1817-19.
2. Bunting was now Secretary of the Conference, The President was John Gaulter (d.1839 aet.74).
3. Owing to the financially embarrassed state of the Connexion, it was agreed at the 1817 Conference that no Preacher should receive from the Contingent Fund the allowance for a Servant unless he had travelled at least ten years or unless he had one or more children. When a Preacher not having travelled ten years has only one child, he shall be allowed only £4 per year towards the expense of a Servant, but if he have more than one child he may claim the full allowance of £8. No Circuit shall receive from the Contingent Fund any money towards *Ordinary Deficiencies*, in which the regular allowance to the Preacher has been more than 14/- per week, unless
   (1) The Yearly Collection has exceeded the claims for deficiencies.
   (2) There are more than four children in the Preacher's family chargeable on the Circuit.
   (3) The Preacher shall have travelled more than twenty years.
   (4) There was a special exemption by Conference on the recommendation of the District Meeting.
   Any claims for house rent were to be closely examined by the Chairman and other members of the District Meeting, in order to reduce expenditure under this heading. These retrenchments were confirmed at the 1818 Conference, where the general debt of the Connexion was divided between all the Circuits in proportion to their membership and this sum was expected to be raised locally. (*Minutes*, 1817-18). See also *Life* ii, pp.96-97; Miles Martindale MSS to J.B.
4. John Dredge (d.1820), Preacher, Edinburgh Circuit, 1816-20.
5. Alexander Bell (1788-1851), Preacher, Glasgow Circuit, 1816-20.
6. Abraham Crabtree (1785-1851), Superintendent, Dunfermline Circuit, 1817-18.

7. Thomas Hamer (1792-1846), Superintendent, Ayr Circuit, 1817-19.
8. James Millar (d.1832 aet.60), Superintendent, Greenock Circuit, 1817-18.
9. Thomas Bridgman (d.1832), Superintendent, Perth Circuit, 1817-19.
10. Daniel McAllum, M.D. (1794-1827), son of Duncan McAllum.

6. *From Robert Melson*[1]   Pickering, April 12,1819

I wish to inform you that Mr J.W. Barritt[2] who is in the North of Scotland is my wife's brother and as they are the children of a Methodist Preacher they have been at a distance from each other almost all their lives, and are very desirous to be accommodated by becoming members of one family if the favour can be grantted [sic]. And as a kind Providence seems to open the way to this he being a single man, and we having the single man boarded with us, and as our Stewards and Leaders desired me to do what I could in order to this, I have to beg of you Sir the favor of your influence in Connexion with Mr H. Moore[3] is our representative and engaged to do what he can for us in this business.

In respect to the distance, that can be no great object as he is a single man and we are in the North of Yorkshire and only 18 miles from Scarborough and 21 from Whitby so that he could come nearly all the way by sea.

Now, Sir, I persuade myself that you will have the goodness to interest yourself in our behalf as you will conclude that it must increase the domestic comfort of my wife and family, and will also meet the *earnest desire* of our Brother together with our Stewards and Leaders, and cannot possibly infringe upon the rights of any. But, Sir, I also encourage myself from what I have observed in your conduct in reference to accommodating your absent brethren in former Conferences.

I know Sir that it will afford you pleasure to hear that I have had a very pleasant and agreeable year among our friends in this Circuit and have a colleague worth the world. And if I cannot have my Brother in Law the next year, I should beg his re-appointment (as he was unanimously invited) to spend a third year in this Circuit but he is desirous to remove. May the Lord be with and direct you in all things.[4]

1. Robert Melson, Superintendent, Pickering Circuit 1818-21. Disappeared from ministry between 1847 and 1853. Melson had previously served in a number of Scottish circuits: Inverness 1808-10; Brechin 1810-11; Arbroath 1811-12.
2. John Wesley Barritt Jnr (d.1861 aet.70), Preacher, Banff Circuit,1818-19. He was *not* appointed to the Pickering Circuit at the 1819 Conference.
3. Henry Moore (1751-1844), Superintendent, York Circuit, 1818-20; Chairman of York District, 1818-20.
4. In 1847, Melson wrote a long and passionate letter to Conference (M.C.A. MSS August 2 1847) calling for reform, a complete change in the Mission House staff (including Bunting), an end to institutionalisation and a return to primitive simplicity in Methodism. On April 26 1850, Melson wrote again to Bunting ascribing the chaos in Methodism to Bunting's constitutional legislation. Melson probably disappeared from the ministry as a result of this episode. See *Early Victorian Methodism* p.183 and 396.

... Nothing remarkable in this District. Some good doing. Our deficiencies one fourth less than last years. But still great. Most of the chapels lately built are sadly burdened with debt. I believe Edinburgh Chapel is sinking deeper in to debt about £70 or £80 every year. Ayr & Greenock worse in proportion to the population & members in Society. Glasgow with difficulty may pay their interest altho' they have all the ordinary collections given to help.[2] As to Leith, Dunformilen [sic] & Perth, only Mr. Ward can explain how they stand. I believe but so so. Haddington is £480 in debt & unless some help come from some quarter, the Society in the place will never be able to redeem it. I believe you are one of the members of the Committee of Distribution. If you can help Haddington more or less, it will be gratefully received. It is mentioned in the District Minutes.[3] £5 went to the fund.

Our friends here (I believe in general) earnestly wish *I and my son*[4] to continue a third year. I hope there will be no objections; it is a circuit that scarcely any will covet & the smallness of the chapels & the moderate distance for changing suit me as well as any I can at present see. Third year appointments have lately become common when desired.

What I write chiefly at this time is to ask your advice, at least to have your opinion − I write to you in confidence, not having mentioned the affair to any individual, directly or indirectly. I think in the Conference of 1784, Mr. Wm. Thompson[5] introduced a law that every young preacher must travel four years upon trial before he be received into full Connection and that he must not marry till his four years be finished. This law never afflicted me, for I was married before it was made, having travelled nine years single. However this law, altho' a wise measure in itself has been over & over dispensed with. Also some married men rec[eive] d without families & even some with families. I need not mention names, as you know some of them. Now my request is that you will give me your opinion candidly, whether you think considering the present state of our Connection, Conference would give a dispensation to my son to marry this year, having travelled only two years. The reason assigned for the law when passed, so far as I can recollect were, First that the young men before they had the cares of a family might apply themselves the more intensely & successfully to study so laying in a good store of useful knowledge. As to this first reason I may venture to affirm owing to his previous advantages, strength of intellect & intense application he can bear a scrutiny being endued with an acceptable & useful talent. A second reason and a chief one is to prevent expenses. This reason is weighty & ought not to be lost sight of; but if the dispensation be granted I may venture to promise that no additional expenses will be incurred, I understand [in] the New Connexion of Kilhamites[6] the only punishment they inflict upon a young man marrying before his time is to make him bear his own extra expenses. The young woman I believe is truly converted to God, of an excellent & useful character, & a Methodist in sentiment & principle, has been a communicant a few times & would willingly meet in class as soon as convenient ...

1. The date on this letter is incorrect, as Daniel McAllum died in 1827. The correct date is clearly 1819, when both McAllum's were stationed in the Dunbar and Haddington Circuit.
2. This situation also applied to Edinburgh. See Hayes (1976a,b).
3. M.C.A. Edinburgh District *Minutes*.
4. Daniel McAllum, M.D.
5. William Thompson (d.1799 aet.63), President of the Conference, 1791.
6. Alexander Kilham founded the Methodist New Connexion in 1797. See *Early Correspondence* p.181.

8. *From Edmund Grindrod*[1] Newcastle, March 11, 1820[2]

... In a letter from Mr Marsden[3] some tim⟨e⟩ ago, he mentions that you and he thought the Conference would approve of my going to Edinburgh or Glasgow, next year, provided I would consent. The former place, I should think, will not be at liberty. I have no objection to go to either, nor *except the distance* to Aberd⟨een⟩ from which place I have had three letters of request. I have declined North Shields chiefly because I would like a place where I should have more leisure for study. But I am quite easy about my future station. The friends here have requested Mr V. Ward,[4] and he has given his unreserved consent. I should think either Glasgow or Aberdeen will be my destiny. There has been, it is said, a separation[5] at Glasgow. I hear it has been a year of dissention there.

I hope we shall see you in the chair at the next Conference. Many of the junior brethren, I am persuaded, intend to give you their votes: and, I hope, if spared so long Mr Geo. Marsden will follow you: but that is looking into futurity. It would be well if those who take the lead in our affairs would understand each other, and not be so divided as they were last year ...

1. Edmund Grindrod (1786-1842), Superintendent, Newcastle Circuit, 1817-20; Preacher, London East Circuit, 1820-23; Superintendent Glasgow Circuit 1823-25; Superintendent, Edinburgh Circuit, 1825-26.
2. Part of this letter is already published in *Early Correspondence* p.28. The holograph of this letter is at Southern Methodist University, Dallas, Texas.
3. George Marsden (1773-1858), succeeded Bunting as President, 1821-22.
4. Valentine Ward, Superintendent, Aberdeen Circuit 1817-20; Superintendent, Glasgow Circuit, 1820-22.
5. The Methodist New Connexion chapel was opened in Glasgow between 1817 and 1818. This may well be a belated reference to this secession. See Beckerlegge 'Early Glasgow Chapels', *Proceedings of the Wesley Historical Society* 30(1), 7-12 (1955).

9. *From Valentine Ward*[1] Aberdeen, August 18, 1820

Thro[ugh] the mercy of our gracious God I arrived safe here last evening, and found my family pretty well. I trust you are well after the fatigues of Conf[erenc] e. and that we shall have a good year in every part of the connexion.

Mr Neil[2] who has been helping me nearly two years as a hired local preacher, is willing either to continue to be employed in a similar way or to go back to his business, but he w[oul] d prefer the former, it being understood that his being so employed shall not hinder his being called out regularly in the course of the year if needed. I believe there would be plenty of employment, and such provision as w[oul] d satisfy him either in the Glasgow Circuit, or that of Paisley and Greenock. Would you approve of my mentioning it at the Financial District Meeting,[3] and employing him as above in one of those Circuits if the preachers and people wish it so? Mr Neil wishes to know how many names stand before his on the List of Reserve. As Mr Bursdall[4] knows the Glasgow and Greenock Circuits, especially the former, you can, if you please, consult him before you send an answer ...

I wish you would speak to Mr Watson[5] on the subject of taking some notice of those Scotch publications which have lately so shamefully vilified the Methodists and especially Mr Wesley. Perhaps he had better reply to them in an Appendix to his review of Southey's life of Wesley. I am sure that such statements going thro[ugh] this country uncontradicted, do us great harm, and I should like much to be freed from the temptation of scribbling on the subject. The works to which I allude are, Sir H. Moncrieff's life of Dr J. Erskine. The Review of that work by

the seceders in their work called the Christian Repository for August &c 1819
and the Edin[bu]r[gh] Christian Instructor [for] Feb[ruar]y and June 1819 ...

Disapprove of *Hired* Local Preacher. This is a peculiar case; 1st because Neil has
been in that way 2 years already, & is not likely to be soon called out regularly;
& 2ndly. because Glasgow is a field for more labourers. I therefore do not *object*
if Q[uarterly] Meet[in]g & Financ[ia]l Dist[rict] Meet[in]g agree to his employ-
[men]t at *Glasgow*, but not Greenock. My positive sanction they will not press?
Neil one of *ten* on my select list; but I have *discretion*.

1. Valentine Ward, Superintendent, Aberdeen Circuit, 1817-20; Chairman, Aberdeen
   District, 1817-20; Superintendent, Glasgow Circuit, 1820-22. This letter was
   written after Ward had returned from the 1820 Conference, immediately prior
   to his removal to Glasgow.
2. Francis Neal (1795-1859), called out at the 1820 Conference; received into
   Full Connexion at the 1825 Conference, Preacher Glasgow Circuit, 1825-27.
3. The Financial District Meeting had its origins in 1817, when the Conference
   resolved: 'Every Superintendent is required earnestly to invite & urge the attendance and assistance of the Circuit Stewards at the District Meeting, according
   to our rule, during the time when the financial affairs of the district to which
   they belong are under consideration. And, in order to facilitate this object,
   let it be understood and announced, that the financial business of the district
   shall, in future, always commence at 10 o'clock in the forenoon of the second
   day of every district meeting' (*Minutes* 1817). By 1820, however, a regular
   Financial District Meeting was ordered by Conference;
   'It is agreed that a Financial District Meeting shall be held in each district in the
   month of September, consisting of such preachers as can conveniently attend
   (the superintendent at least of each circuit) & also of the circuit stewards throughout the district, whose presence as the official financial representatives of their
   several circuits shall be most earnestly requested. The place of meeting shall be
   so fixed as to precede the Michaelmas Quarterly Meetings' (*Minutes* 1820).
4. John Burdsall (d.1861 aet.85), Superintendent, Glasgow Circuit, 1818-20. He
   had just left Glasgow for his new Station when this letter was written.
5. Richard Watson (1781-1833), Secretary of the General Chapel Fund, 1822-26
   and one of the principal Methodist Theologians of his day.

10.   *From James Beckwith*[1]   Bridlington, January 27, 1821
I take the liberty to solicite [sic] your advice on the following subject, as I find
myself at a loss how to act. At the Conference 1818, I was stationed for Dunfermline
in Scotland;[2] I was the only preacher in the circuit, but changed occasionally with
the preachers on the Edinburgh Circuit of which Mr Jno. Lancaster[3] was Superintendent. As the House in Dunfermline had only one bed in it, and as Mrs Beckwith
had to be confined, another bed was of necessity wanted, and the Circuit not being
able to purchase one, I consulted the Chairman[4] and Mr Lancaster, who both
advised, to borrow one at so much per week. Accordingly when I was over in Edinburgh, Mr L and I engaged one, which was kept until the following Conference. As
Mr L and I both left Scotland, we had no opportunity of bringing the bill forward
at the next District Meeting; but as a bed was wanted in the Leith house, we expected that the Stewards of the Edinburgh Circuit, would purchase the bed which
had been returned from Dunfermline; and on this consideration the friend of whom
it had been borrowed, engaged to charge nothing for the time we had had the use

of it. Under the impression that the bed would be bought we left the country for
our different circuits. It seems however that it was not bought, and the charge for
the time I had the use of it amounts to £5 0. 2d. This has never been paid, the person is now dead, and I received the other day a letter from an Attorney, stating that
he had applied to the Dunfermline people for the money, who, directed him to
apply to me for it. As I did not wish to trouble you, I wrote to Mr Ward who is now
the Chairman of the District, but he seems completely to have misunderstood me;
and supposes, that there were two beds in the Dunfermline house when I went to it,
which is a gross mistake; for there was neither a second bed, nor the *smallest particle*
of anything belonging to a second bed, until the one I alluded to was borrowed ...
I feel persuaded you will be able to give me every necessary direction. This, my dear
Sir, is what I earnestly request; and as there ought to be no delay lest ⟨the a⟩ttorney
should write me another⟨letter⟩ you will do me a favour by writing immediately;
and rest assured, your advice shall be minutely attended to.

[Endorsed]   Ans[were] d. February 6, 1821

As he individually hired the bed, he is legally responsible. Advise him immediately
to settle the matter with the owner & to apply for remuner[atio] n to the Dunfermline Society who are in equity bound to pay it. If they refuse appeal to the Edinburgh
District Meeting.

1. James Beckwith (d.1852 aet.58), Preacher, Edinburgh Circuit 1817-18; Preacher
   Dunfermline Circuit, 1818-19; Preacher, Bridlington Circuit 1819-21.
2. Dunfermline was a short-lived Circuit and Society which lasted from 1817 to
   c.1827. See A.J. Hayes (1977c).
3. John Lancaster (d.1829 aet.47), Superintendent, Edinburgh Circuit, 1817-19.
4. The Chairman of the Edinburgh District was John Burdsall. See also Letter No. 13.

11.   *From Valentine Ward*   Glasgow, April 9, 1821

... I take it for granted that no change has taken place either in your mind or
arrangements to prevent us having the pleasure and advantage of your company in
June, and we are making our plans accordingly.
       We are faint yet pursuing — but our Bro[the] r Cadell[1] can tell you more
particularly of our case.
       Have you an excellent•young man who w[oul] d think it a priviledge [sic] to
come here and help us till after Conference. My reasons for asking are 1. I am going
into Shropshire for a few weeks for the improvement of my health. 2. Bro[the] r
Mollard[2] is not very strong. 3. We are on the eve of opening another place of worship.[3] 4. The time is approaching for preaching out of doors and 5. I expect to go
to Conf[eren] c[e] .
       We have an excellent young man who has passed our Quarterly Meeting today
who is willing to go to any part of the world. Are you likely to need him immediately after Conf[ere] c[e] . If so and you cannot send us one, may we employ him
as a hired Local Preacher till Conf[eren] c[e] is over.
       What method sh[oul] d be taken in bringing a preacher in another District to
trial for things done in the District which he has left. I think we want a [regulation]
on the subject. Excuse great haste & blunders ...

[Endorsed]   Ans[were] d May 14 [1821)

We do want a rule on the point he mentions. At present I think any charge must
be bro[ugh] t first in the District in wh[ic] h a preacher *now* labours. If they found

that it cannot be fairly & full investigated there or at a distance, they may appoint from among themselves a Minor District Meet[in]g in the usual way to hear evidence on the spot, & decide accordingly.

1. William Cadell (? d.1845), last survivor of the Calton (Green St.) Trustees still resident in Glasgow. He was also associated with Tradeston and was one of the Trustees of the Bloomsbury Chapel. See Glasgow Circuit Records, City of Glasgow Record Office.
2. Thomas Mollard (1788-1827), Preacher, Glasgow Circuit, 1820-21.
3. This could well be the Anderston Chapel in Warroch St., Glasgow, but is most probably the Calton Chapel (later Green St.) See Beckerlegge (1955) op. cit.

12. *From Richard Tabraham*[1]   Buckie in the Banff Circuit, June, 1821
[Inscribed] To the Revd. J. Bunting, President of the Methodist Conference and the preachers assembled at Edinburgh.[2]

... Not finding it convenient to attend your meeting at Edinburgh, and hoping that you would not think me rude I have taken the liberty to express my thoughts on the general subject of your meeting.

As this is my first year in this part of our Connection and as I have not had much opportunity to extend my inquiries I can say nothing about "Methodism in Scotland in general". However in refference [sic] to these parts I would observe that the people in general are in lamentable ignorance, prophaneness [sic] or self-righteousness rendering every possible effort to promote their spiritual good absolutely necessary — that there is a wide uncultivated field for benevolent effort in consequence of the comparatively little ministerial or other religious aid afforded them — that tho[ugh] many have a disposition to hear, yet in consequence of their peculiar views, habits and employment much self denial, perseverance and watchfulness are necessary to succeed in establishing congregations and especially in forming and preserving societies — that tho[ugh] many can read and will read almost anything that is put into their hands yet thro[ugh] their general poverty and other causes most of them have very few books, are extremely ignorant of Methodism and possess but very limited means of instruction — that in consequence of their mistaken idea of the kind of education that is a necessary qualification of the work of the ministry, it is extremely difficult to secure any aid from local preachers — that the collection after eve[r]y sermon is an advantage, yet as the population is small and scattered the congregations are small and consequently the collection must be small also and as there are but few friends who find it convenient to accommodate the preacher with board and lodgings his support is rather expensive.

On the whole there appear many difficulties in the way of the spread of Methodism in these parts and that to remove them or triumph over them will be a work of some time and labour but to well directed perseverance, success is certain.

Perhaps the general probable means to secure success are the appointment of men possessing missionary qualifications — deep devotedness to the work — the evident possible circulation of some of the cheapest and best of our books — and the general reappointment of preachers two and in some cases three years. Through rich mercy we have seen a little prosperity in our circuit — a disposition to hear plain words — to join in Church Communion — to unite in plans to promote the general good — to live to God — and plead for the outpouring of the divine Spirit — tho[ugh] our number is so very small we have had a few turn from the "Holy Commandment delivered unto them" — and one called into eternity — yet their places have been filled by others who bid fair for the Heavenly Kingdom

34

and we have a very small increase ... I confess from general appearances I did not even hope for the fruit that has been seen. May more appear to encourage us in the work of the Lord ...

1. Richard Tabraham (1792-1878), Preacher, Banff Circuit, 1820-22.
2. These comments were sent to Bunting during his Presidential visit to Scotland. See also M.C.A. MSS. Edinburgh District *Minutes* 1821. This visit was a preface to annual visits paid by the President at the instruction of Conference from 1824, in view of the critical financial situation which had developed. See Hayes (1976a) op. cit. Indeed, this visit in 1821 was at the express request of the Conference of 1820. 'The President is requested to visit Scotland on his way to Ireland: and as many of the preachers, stationed in Scotland, as can make it convenient, shall be directed to meet him in Edinburgh, at the time which he may appoint'. (*Minutes* 1820).

13. *From Valentine Ward*   Glasgow, June 6, 1821

... Our friends rejoice greatly at the prospect of seeing and hearing you, and we are praying that the Lord may prosper your way unto us, and bless us when we meet together.

Mr Bell[1] lives next door to the chapel in Nicolson Square. If none of our fri[en]ds are looking out for you at the Coach Office, you will have no difficulty in finding the place ...

I have formed the following plan which I hope will be agreeable to you.
Sund[a]y the 17th Edin[burg]h Forenoon and Evening & Leith Afternoon.
Monday 18 Leith
Tuesday 19 Edin[burg]h
Wed[nesda]y meet [?]
Thursday 21 Glasgow Jno. St.
Friday 22 [?]
Sat[urda]y 23[r]d Paisley
Sun[da]y 24 hear Dr Chalmers[2] and preach once in Jno. St. and once in Tradeston.

Owing to Dr Chalmers's great liberality and condescension I shall be able to introduce you to breakfast with him at his own House.

My reason for making the remark and asking the question contained in my former letter was several persons in this place having made complaints ag[ains]t Mr Burdsall's conduct as Sup̧erintendent of this circuit the last year. The amount is as follows. First, making arrangements for the single preacher to live at Paisley, and after the App[ointmen]t of Mr Beaumont,[3] promising the Leaders meeting in Glasgow that he Mr B[eaumon]t sh[oul]d go and reside there, and afterwards allowing the Leaders and Quarterly meetings to be agitated by the discussion of the subject of Mr Beaumont's place of residence. This they consider the grand cause of the Division. Secondly. Allowing the indulgence and expression of bad temper and improper language in both parties during these discussions. Thirdly. Encouraging the erection of two chapels in the suburbs of Glasgow,[4] to the injury of the other chapels without consulting any Leaders, Quarterly or District Meeting, or the Chapel Building Committee,[5] and which buildings are now a burden to the Trustees and no relief can be obtained according to Rule. Fourth. Receiving a considerable sum of money from this circuit towards bringing himself and family here and he ⟨took⟩ again from it when he was going away though he was leaving a circuit debt of near £300 accumulated during his superintendency.

The fifth and last is personal, and is that Mr Burdsall tried and condemned me, and *recorded* the condemnation in the District Minute Book without me knowing anything about the matter.

35

I will thank you to let Mr B[urdsall] to see this part of the letter, and I believe I may safely leave it to yourself what course sh[oul]d be taken. My own opinion is that justice cannot be done to Mr B[urdsall]'s character and the cause of Methodism without an investigation on the spot either while you are here or immediately after conference. The former w[oul]d be best if Mr B[ursdall] could meet you in Glasgow. In that case you co[ul]d collect evidence and lay it before Conference ...

[Endorsed]   Shewed to Burdsall June 9 1821

1. Alexander Bell, Superintendent, Edinburgh Circuit, 1819-21.
2. Thomas Chalmers (1780-1847), theologian, Leader of the Disruption in the Church of Scotland, 1843. It seems probable that the friendship between Jabez Bunting and Chalmers stems from this meeting. See *Life* ii. p.190-193.
3. Joseph Beaumont, M.D. (1794-1855), Preacher, Glasgow Circuit, 1818-19. A prominent spokesman in Methodism for liberal political views, he was accused in his official obituary of infidelity to connexional discipline (*Minutes* 1856). See also Letter No. 9 Note 4.
4. These could well be Anderston and Green Street (or the Calton) Chapels. See Beckerlegge (1955).
5. The Chapel Building Committee was first established by Wesley in 1790 and consisted of six travelling preachers. The rules under which they operated were very simple:
   (1) All preaching houses are to be settled on the Methodist Plan.
   (2) All preaching houses are to be built, in future, on the same plan as the London or Bath Chapel.
   (3) Everything relative to the building or repairing of preaching houses is to be referred to them.
   (4) No house shall be undertaken without the consent of the majority of them: and not a stone laid till the house is settled after the Methodist plan, verbatim. N.B. No lawyer is to alter one line, nor need any be employed.
   (5) No building is to be undertaken till an estimate of the expense is made & two-thirds of the money raised or subscribed.
   (6) Every preaching house equal to or less than the Bath house, is to be built on the plan of the new chapel in London, both within & without (*Minutes* 1790).
   Various measures were adopted between 1790 and 1817, to prevent the imprudent erection of new chapels. However, by 1817, it was agreed that further measures were necessary to curb the proliferation of new chapel buildings: 'As the repeated cautions and entreaties of the Conference have in various instances been disregarded, we now deem it necessary to the honour and security of the Connexion to appoint 5 brethren annually as a chapel committee. To this committee every proposal for the erection or purchase of any new or additional chapel, with clear and full explanations of the necessity alleged, of the expense contemplated, & of the subscriptions & other local income, likely to be raised, shall be submitted by the superintendent of the circuit, before he shall give any sanction to such erection or purchase or allow any steps to be taken in the actual execution of the proposal: and no chapel shall be built or purchased without the consent of a majority of this committee' (*Minutes* 1817). The following year, these regulations were further strengthened: 'No case shall be sanctioned by the committee, unless it shall come before them as having received the previous approbation of the Quarterly Meeting of the circuit, and shall be recommended either by the annual district meeting, or, at least, by three superintendents in

the neighbourhood who shall certify their approbation in writing' (*Minutes* 1818). Further amending regulations were added from time to time. See Pierce, W. *Ecclesiastical Principles & Polity of the Wesleyan Methodists* (London) (1873).

14. *From James Anderson*[1]   Dunbar, Sept[embe]r 15, 1821

I have received a letter from Mr Beaumont,[2] who was stationed at Haddington last year; but from which the Preacher has been withdrawn this year,[3] and concerning which he observes — "E're this you will have discovered the dilemma in which poor Haddington is left. The history of the matter is shortly this — when I found no Preacher appointed to Hadd[ingto]n, I wrote to the Conference, thro[ugh] the President, stating and proving, that it would be no pecuniary relief to take the man away from Hadd[ingto]n, if the Chapel were continued — that the Chapel could not be supplyed by local preachers — that Hadd[ingto]n had had but a short trial — that the Chapel I believed could not be sold but at a great loss — that the trustees could not sustain that loss &c. &c. I waited patiently till the end of the Conference, which being come, noone was appointed, & I learned from Dr McAllum[4] that my letter was not communicated to the Conference, and that the Chapel was not authorised to be sold. I have written to Mr Ward on the subject, stating my regret that my letter was not communicated to the Conference, and the probable consequence of the measure adopted. I wished him to write to you on the subject. In his answer he says he has not done so; & thinks that "Hadd[ingto]n may have a good supply from the regular service of Mr Anderson and what the Edinburgh circuit and local Preachers can do for it". In my reply, I told him "that as to the Edinburgh local Preachers supplying it, that it was out of the question altogether, the expence that would be incurred by such a measure, could not be born".

From the above, it appears that Mr Beaumont's mind is very sore about the business, & I do not wonder at it, as the Preacher was withdrawn from Hadd[ingto]n by the recommendation of Dr McAllum & himself at the District meeting; what they then said on the subject, I have no doubt you will recollect.[5] At that time, it was *supposed* that the Chapel might be sold, at little or no loss to the Burgher Congregation, who wished to have a better chapel than their own; but having lately repaired it, all expectation from that quarter is fled and gone. Hearing of the alarming circumstances of the case I went over to Hadd[ingto]n last Monday, & found the few pious souls there overwhelmed with not only *grief*, but *fear* and *dread*, so much so, that some of them told me that when they went about their business, they did not know what they were doing. I inquired minutely into the whole of the business, & found a commodious Chapel, strongly built with stone, that will contain about 500; compleately pewed below, & galleried round, with a debt of about £480 upon it. The weekly income from the *ba bee*[6] collection & class money, from 12 to 15 shillings; on some occasions when the Preacher is popular, from £1 to £1 6/-. The morning congregation, about 100, the afternoon, about 150, & in the evening generally well filled — the Society 16 in number. £200 is on the Chapel by way of mortgage, due to an indifferent person in Hadd[ingto]n; £230 to a friend that lives under me in Dunbar, upon a *note in hand*; £50 more upon a note in hand, from an old faithful servant of an old Methodist in Dunbar, now deceased; & which by care and industry, she had saved for a support in old age. If no Preacher is sent to Hadd[ingto]n, the interest upon the first £200 cannot be paid, in which case the bond will be executed, & the Chapel sold, & the opinion is that it will not bring more than £200, although, as a Chapel, it is well worth from £600 to £650; and what will become of the poor old people with their £230, and the old servant with her £50!! The case is truly distressing, & especially as there is in my opinion, no necessity for it. The withdrawing of the Preacher from

Hadd[ingto]n was a *rash, thoughtless, unnecessary* measure; and on the part of
the Conference, it may be said — "in ignorance they did it"; for I am sure that had
we been informed of all the circumstances in the case, we never could have done
it. To the best of my recollection, the reasons that Messrs McAllum & Beaumont
assigned at the District meeting for withdrawing the Preacher, were, that the
Congregation was not steady, and the society did not increase; but all who know
the Scotch Character, know, that it requires time to establish a society & Congregation in Scotland. Hadd[ingto]n chapel has been built only five years, &
there are but few places in Scotland that has [sic] done so well, in so short a
time, & which requires so little assistance from Conference!! If Preachers must
be withdrawn from places on the account of our temporal embarrassment, why not
begin with those which require large sums every year, not only in Scotia, but in
England. In Scotland, there is Peterhead with its £62 deficiency[7], & two preachers.
Dundee £38 and one Preacher. Montrose £107 and two preachers. Banff £55 and
two Preachers. Elgin £62 and one Preacher. Inverness £49 & one Preacher. Greenock
& Paisley £54 & two Preachers. Ayr & Kilmarnock £82 & two Preachers (1 now
gone). Perth £62 & one Preacher. In England there is Windsor with its £50 def-
ficiencies [sic] & one Preacher. Leigh £43 & one Preacher. Chelmsford £51 & one
Preacher. Manningtree, £44 & two Preachers. St Neots £83 & two Preachers &c.
The list might easily be multiplied, but it is not necessary; and what is the enormous
sum required by Dunbar, with even Hadd[ingto]n united? £37 12/-, sixteen of
which goes to Hadd[ingto]n, which, with £6. 15 from the Chapel Fund, makes
the whole expence of Hadd[ingto]n to the Conference £22. 15: and for the sake
of this small sum we have exposed ourselves in all probability, to a payment of
£280, to prevent certain ruin to six trustees, who, if there [sic] beds were sold
from under them, could not raise a third part of the sum required. Had I known
these things before, I, for one, would not have remained silent in Conference when
the Preacher was withdrawn from Hadd[ingto]n. I am surprised beyond measure
how the District meeting could be induced to recommend such a measure. It
appears that those who first moved it, are now heartily ashamed of it, & grieved
for it; & so they ought for a more imprudent, inconsistent aye, & cruel measure,
I never knew since first I knew Methodism. But now what can be done? Hadd[ingto]n
can recieve [sic] but little help from me: I might go once in about six weeks,
but to go oftener, would be highly injurious to Dunbar. At present we are doing well,
with the prospect of doing better. I have certainly no appointment for Hadd[ingto]n,
only to Dunbar, & its dependencies. So I understood it: so the Conference understood it, & hence the change was appointed between Dunbar & Berwick every
quarter: nevertheless I am willing to do what I can for Hadd[ingto]n yet so as not
to injure Dunbar. The Local Preachers coming from Edinburgh 17 miles by coach,
with paying for their loss of time, & board while there, would be more than the
weekly income; & in this case the seats would not let, & the interest could not be
paid. Whether the travelling preachers could be spared from Edinburgh is doubtful;
they would have 17 miles to come and I 11 to go. I am fearful that a young man
could not be called out for the purpose of supplying Hadd[ingto]n; at least he
could not receive his quarterage from the grant made to the District, as such a circumstance was not taken into the account, when that grant was made. An acceptable
local Preacher who would be willing to devote all his time to Hadd[ingto]n for the
year, & take what the place would produce for his support, & with whom I could
change, would do; but I know of none such hereabouts. Could any assistance be
received from Missionaries previous to their going on foreign service? The communication from London by Steam Packet is now frequent & cheap & they would have
a good opportunity of improvement by reading & study while in Scotland. Is Mr
Wilson[8] of Aberdeen likely to be employed in foreign service? He would do very

well. Something must be done & that speedily, to prevent the most disastrous consequences. I think I have made out a case which deserves attention & relief.

I am exceedingly pleased with the remarks in the Magazine[9] for Sept[embe]r respecting Scotland: they are just & correct; for I believe the good that is done in Scotia by the Methodist Preachers, will not be fully known till "the last trump shall sound & the dead shall be raised"; for I have no doubt, but that thousands & tens of thousands are gone to glory who were brought to God by their preaching; but who were never in our society, not even stated, but only occasional hearers. My good friend Mr Ward seems very easy on the business, but when he talks of a *regular supply* from Mr Anderson, & the Edinburgh Circuit, & local Preachers, he certainly talks without book; but the Hadd[ingto]n chapel is not one of those with which he is connected, & *this* may in some measure account for it. I have written to the President upon the subject, nearly a *duplicate* of this letter, that if he should have occasion to consult with you, as ex-President, you might be in possession of all the circumstances without his having the trouble of stating them to you: and this I have informed him of. Next Sunday week I intend to spend at Hadd[ingto]n. The expence concerned with Dr McAllum and I changing would have paid one half of a Preacher's quarterage at Haddington — altogether it is an unwise business. Haddington contains about the same population with Dunbar — from 4 to 5000. Methodism in Dunbar was much lower at one time than at Hadd[ingto]n; but it is now "not the least among the Princes of Judah". We hope? that next year it will appear upon the minutes as being the least expence to Conference of any place in Scotland with the exception of Glasgow: both Edinburgh & Aberdeen will now have larger demands by far; only this will in a great measure depend upon my giving Dunbar a regular supply; for were I to leave this to go to Hadd[ingto]n, the congregation would be scattered, & the income, of course, materially lessen'd.

A thought has just struck me — what would you think of employing B[r] o-[the]r Flint;[10] by referring to my notes which I took at Conference, I see that he is suspended for one year; but that "... if the President find it necessary to employ him in the course of the year, he is at liberty to do so". The circumstance, I believe, is not known in these parts, & I should prom⟨ise⟩ it should not get in the wind thro[ugh] me. I have mentioned this also to the President. This, I should think may do, if we cannot do better; providing he has got no family, as there is but one room, with a bed closet, for the Preacher there, being a single man; with 1 child, he might do; but perhaps he is a single man all the while, so much the better. Should I succeed in obtaining a supply for Hadd[ingto]n I can change with the preacher there which will superceed [sic] the necessity of changing with the Berwick Preacher; and which will save from 8 to 10 pounds to both places, the distance being 30 miles, and Hadd[ingto]n only 11. This I can walk ...

1. James Anderson (d.1840 aet.73), Superintendent, Dunbar and Haddington Circuit, 1820-23.
2. Joseph Beaumont, M.D., Preacher, Edinburgh Circuit, 1821-24.
3. In the event, the preacher was not restored until the Conference of 1825, when John Maclean was sent. See Hayes (1977d) op.cit.
4. Daniel McAllum, M.D., Preacher, Edinburgh Circuit, 1820-22.
5. Edinburgh District Minutes, M.C.A. The District Minutes of 1821 recommend that the Haddington preacher be withdrawn unless a pledge (of financial support) was given.
6. This refers to the keeping of a plate at the door of the chapel during public worship. A bawbee was originally ½d Scots. See also Hayes (1976a).
7. All deficiencies in the quarterage of preachers, preachers wives, children and all demands concerning rent, furniture, lighting and heating, which the local circuit

could not immediately pay, were brought to the notice of the District Committee and ultimately settled at the Conference (*Minutes* 1794). These deficiencies were paid out of the Contingent Fund, which was financed out of a yearly collection originally taken up at Christmas (*Minutes* 1763). The Contingent Fund — one of the oldest funds in Wesleyan Methodism was originally set up to defray the Connexional Debt (mainly on chapels) and to send preachers into new areas for the extension of the work. See Pierce op.cit. p.535ff.

8. William Wilson 1st (1779-1848), spent 10 years as a Missionary in the Bahamas.
9. The *Methodist Magazine* for September 1821 (Vol.44 pp.689-690) reported on a meeting held in Edinburgh on Tuesday June 19, 1821 at which the prosperity of Methodism in Scotland was considered. 'It clearly appeared that the value and success of the labours of the Methodist Preachers in Scotland could not be estimated simply by the numbers of members in Societies, since there is a much wider indirect influence'.
10. William Flint (left the ministry, 1832), Preacher, Truro Circuit, 1820; suspended for one year at the Conference of 1821; returned as Preacher, Arbroath, Montrose & Brechin Circuit, 1822-24; Superintendent, Peterhead Circuit, 1824-25. See also Letter No. 15. All the evidence suggests that Haddington arose as a result of local interest and was little influenced by the presence of Valentine Ward in the Edinburgh District. See also Hayes (1976a, d)

15. *To George Marsden*[1] *(Leeds)*   London, September 25, 1821[2]

I had this morning an opportunity of laying your letter and that of Mr Anderson before several of the brethren. We all concur in opinion with you, that something should be done, if possible, to give Haddington another year's trial. You will, if all be well, have an opportunity next year of investigating the circumstances at the District-Meeting,[3] when some final conclusion may be recommended to Conference. One thing is clear, that, after our *very large increase* of the Grants to the Scotch Districts at our last Conference, we cannot further augment our allowances to that country. But perhaps some other place can be given up with less difficulty, & one not so hopeful, as Haddington is now said to be. We think it would be well if Brother Flint could now go to Haddington. It would be a mercy at once to *him*, & to the small *Society* there. He might go by *sea* from Cornwall to Glasgow, & so on to Edinburgh & Haddington. The £70 or £80 to be allowed him from the Book Room, with what it appears he might raise in collections, would *tolerably* well support him & his family for the year, pay his Travelling Expences, & afford him, perhaps, the means of taking lodgings rather more suited than the present to his family ...

1. George Marsden, President of the Conference 1821.
2. The holograph of this letter is at Drew University Library, Madison, N.J., U.S.A.
3. This strongly suggests that the President attended the Spring District Meetings of the two Scottish Districts from 1821 onwards to obtain first-hand information on the current situation. See Hayes (1976a).
   It is clear that James Anderson's letter had struck a soft spot, but in the event William Flint was not sent to Haddington, which remained without a resident preacher until 1825. See also Letter No. 14.

16. *From Valentine Ward*   Glasgow, October 17, 1821

... Your answer came in time and answered the end. We soon finished our business and spent a few hours in reading the results of the conversations respecting the best means for promoting the revival and extension of the work of God, as printed in the Minutes of the last two Conferences, and in further remarks applicable to the peculiarities of our present scene of labours. We had a good Miss[ionar]y Meeting in the Evening of which you have a brief account on the other side of this letter. Perhaps you may think it proper to insert it in the Miss[ionar]y Notices.

Messrs Chalmers and Collins[1] have given me the following list on the Scotch Periodical Works ... I could send them out at the beginning of each month to you in a parcel ...

Please let me know of your mind in reference to these publications.

The Brethren when here last week were very anxious that I should correspond with Mr Watson respecting his visit to Scotland, and get him to say as soon as possible what part of the year is most likely to suit his convenience. Perhaps you will converse with him on the Subject.

Will you also tell Mr Taylor[2] to send at least twice the usual number of Miss[ionar]y Notices & Papers — and w[oul]d it not be well to send one in each parcel directed to Dr Chalmers and one to Mr Sword.[3] The Brethren and friends were glad to be remembered by you.

I am writing by this post to request Mr Butterworth[4] to use his influence with Dr Clarke[5] to get him if possible to visit us, and Preach us a few Anniversary Sermons. If you sh[oul]d happen to meet Mr B[utterworth] you will I know use your good offices for us.

P.S. I have often thought of asking how it happened that the Leeds Conf[erenc]e plan[6] of releiving [sic] the chapels was so readily abandoned. Perhaps it cannot be revived.

Missionary Meeting

On the Evening of Wed[nesda]y the 10th of Oct[obe]r, a Public meeting was held in the Methodist Chapel, John St. Glasgow for the purpose of exciting an increased interest in the minds of our members and others in this City in behalf of our Missions. James Sword Esq. of Annfield Presided on the occassion [sic] ; the Chapel was well filled with people who appeared to feel a rekindling of the flame of Missionary Zeal, while they were addressed by several Ministers, (Revd. Messrs Mainwaring,[7] Beaumont, Dr McAllum, Anderson, Vevers,[8] Agar,[9] and Ward) and by Messrs Cormi[10] and Bains[11] from Burslem.

1. William Collins (1789-1853), publisher, philanthropist. Associated with the Free Church from the Disruption. Member of the Kirk Session of the Tron Kirk in Glasgow when Thomas Chalmers was inducted as Minister in 1815, & moved to St. Johns with Chalmers. Opened the first Sabbath School on the Chalmers Plan. Advocated the abolition of slavery & therefore became an associate of Wilberforce, Macaulay, etc. Founder of William Collins & Sons, the publishing firm.
2. Joseph Taylor (1779-1845), Secretary of the Methodist Missionary Society, 1818-24; President of the Conference, 1834.
3. James Sword of Annfield (1749-1832) second son by second marriage of James Sword of Lanark (d.1767), a local landowner and philanthropist. He loaned £4000 in 1817 towards the construction of Chapels in Glasgow and was also associated with the building of the Tradestown Chapel. His son, Robert Sword, is mentioned in 1854 in connection with Trust affairs at St Thomas's, Glasgow. See also Glasgow Circuit Records, City of Glasgow Record Office. In *Life* ii, p.190-191 James Sword is described as a 'member of the Church of Scotland but friendly to the Methodists, and a great supporter of Mr Ward in his enterprises for the promotion of our cause in Scotland ...'
4. Joseph Butterworth, M.P. (1770-1826), founder of the famous law publishing firm; pressed Conference to form the Committee of Privileges in 1803, and was

one of its first members. He was Independent M.P. for Coventry 1812-18 and for Dover 1820-26. See *Life* i, p.230.

5. Adam Clarke (1762-1832), Preacher, Salford (Manchester) Circuit, 1820-23, Chairman of the Manchester District 1820-23; President of the Conference, 1801, 1822. See also Letter No. 24.

6. The Leeds (1818) Conference plan (*Minutes* 1818) referred to the setting-up of a General Chapel Fund, supplied (a) by Private Subscriptions (b) by a Public Collection in February (c) by Legacies and the establishment of a Chapel Building Committee to oversee new buildings and to veto injudicious projects. This scheme was, in fact, never abandoned, but was strengthened at a number of subsequent Conferences (e.g. 1821).

7. George Mainwaring (1788-1825), Superintendent, Edinburgh Circuit, 1821-22.

8. William Vevers (d.1850 aet.58), Preacher, Glasgow Circuit, 1821-23.

9. Joseph Agar (1788-1830), Preacher, Glasgow Circuit, 1821-23; son of Joseph Agar who later became Sheriff of York. Became a Wesleyan Preacher 1810 and died 1830. See *Early Correspondence* p.179.

10. John Cormie (d.1854 aet.72) originally came from the North of Scotland. He was the first local preacher employed north of Aberdeen. Subsequently settled in Burslem and died in London.

11. The identity of Mr Bains remains unknown.

17. *From Valentine Ward*   No place or date

In a few days I expect to send you a parcel to the care of Mr Blanshard[1] containing Scotts Periodical Publication, and shall perhaps write you again. In the mean time I beg leave to second the proposal of Mr Collins. It seems that the worthy D[octo]r thinks more of his Civic Economy[2] than of all his other works together, and is most anxious for its extensive circulation, and ⟨esp⟩ecially that we should approve of it.

I can see no reasonable ground of objection to the plan proposed in this Letter by Mr Collins, but perhaps Mr Blanshard may ⟨not?⟩ enter into it unless you stimulate him ...

I have lately heard good news from several Stations in Scotland.

[It seems highly probable that the following letter from William Collins to Jabez Bunting was first sent to Valentine Ward for onward transmission. Clearly, Ward was acquainted with the contents of the letter.]

From William Collins   Glasgow, November 3, 1821

Knowing the numerous and important avocations in which you are engaged I feel extremely reluctant to engross any of your time, but the deep concern you take in every thing designed to promote the interests of Christianity, and particularly in those specualations of our mutual friend Dr Chalmers which are so well calculated to give a wise and official direction to Christian Philanthropy, will I know render any apology for this intrusion unnecessary.

When I had the pleasure of seeing you in London I mentioned to you Dr Chalmers very great anxiety to have the plans developed in his Civic Economy extensively known and adopted; and it was with much regret he learned after my return, that in Liverpool, Manchester, Leicester, York and other places I visited the existence of the Work was scarcely known. I have therefore been devising every means for bringing the Work and his plans into general notice; and in conversation with your friend Mr Ward I learned that the Ministers in your connection were in the habit of disposing of such Publications as were calculated to promote the interests of Christianity and that a monthly parcel of Magazines and other Publications was sent to each of them for that purpose. It immediately occurred to me that if the measure met your approbation, we would place as many copies of the Civic Economy as you might judge proper, at the disposal of Mr Blanshard, to enclose a copy in the next monthly Parcel to each of your Ministers, and request them to use their prudent endeavours to dispose of the Work. In this way I conceive it might be widely circulated and the Knowledge of Dr Chalmers Plans most extensively diffused; ⟨ ? ⟩ many of those who might purchase the work ⟨ ? ⟩ lend themselves as ready agents to ⟨as⟩ sist in carrying the designs which it reveals into operation, in connection with your Ministers at their various stations.

Should you approve of this measure I would esteem it a particular favour if you would have the goodness to write a circular, which could be printed by Mr Blanshard *at our expence*, and a copy of it sent with the Volume to each Minister, commending the Work to their attention, stating it as the wish of the Conference that they should make themselves intimately acquainted with the system, and as opportunity might offer to give it publicity in their respective stations ...

I shall take it very kind if you will favour me with your sentiments on this subje⟨ct⟩, and if your convenience would permit you to write to early as to enable us to place the work in the hands of Mr Blanshard in time to be enclosed in the parcels for December we would immediately dispatch them to his care. I need not say how ⟨Dr Chal⟩mers would be gratified by such an act ⟨of kindness ?⟩ on your part. I have mentioned to him ⟨this suggestion ?⟩ and he is not only exceedingly pleased with the idea, but has high anticipations for the success of such a mode, in extensively circulating a work on which his heart is so much set, and which you will agree with me in thinking is calculated to tell most effectually on the moral destinies of Great Britain.

I shall be glad to know if the Local system of Sabbath Schools[3] has been introduced in London, and whether it has been entered on by any of your own Body in England. I am sure a short experience will commend it to their regards, and all who embark in it would soon feel the comfort and efficiency of the system ...

1. Thomas Blanshard (d.1824 aet.49), Connexional Book Steward, 1808-23.
2. Thomas Chalmers *The Christian and Civic Economy of Large Towns* 3 vols, Chalmers & Collins (1821-26).
3. See Letter No. 28.

18. *To Thomas Chalmers (Edinburgh)*   Tradestown Chapel House (Glasgow)
1821[1]

Your goodness, I hope will excuse the liberty which I take in obtruding this note upon you, for the purpose of soliciting, that, if the Pamphlet[2] you were so kind as to propose sending to me be within your reach, it may be forwarded by the Bearer. If this cannot be done with perfect convenience, Mr Ward will have the pleasure in conveying it to me at any future opportunity.

Allow me, while I have my pen in exercise, to offer to you my most cordial acknowledgements for your hospitable attentions to me yesterday, in consequence of which, the most pleasing recollections will ever be associated with my short visit to Glasgow. I hope I may also be permitted to say, how much I was gratified, and I trust instructed also, and refreshed in spirit, & by my attendance at your Church[3] this morning, by the incomparable discourse which I had the happening of hearing from your lips. I most earnestly pray that the best blessings of our common Lord and Saviour may rest on yourself, your family, & your ministrations ... Pardon this freedom of an insignificant stranger. It is prompted by the warm emotions of Christian respect & gratitude ...

1. The original of this letter is in New College, Edinburgh. CHA 4.17.27
2. The Pamphlet is most probably *The Application of Christianity to the Commercial and Ordinary Affairs of Life* published by Chalmers & Collins in Glasgow, 1820.
3. Thomas Chalmers was minister of St Johns Church, Glasgow. See also Letter No. 13.

19. *To Thomas Chalmers*
Wesleyan Mission House London
February 27, 1822[1]

I am directed, by the Committee of the Wesleyan Methodist Missionary Society, to express to you their most respectful and earnest request, that you will confer upon the Society the high honour of preaching one of the three Sermons at its approaching Anniversary in London. The time fixed for our Public Meeting is Monday, April 29th., to which we are necessarily confined, because all the subsequent days in the two following weeks are engaged, by other leading Institutions, for the like purpose. Our Annual Sermons, therefore, must be on the preceding Thursday and Friday; viz. the 25th and 26th of April.

I am further directed to state, that, although other Sermons in behalf of our Mission will be preached, as usual, in all our Places of Worship, on Sunday, April 28th., the Committee cannot presume to solicit, however much they would value, your assistance on that day, in addition to the Week-day Sermon to be delivered before the Society. But they are of opinion, that you would most essentially serve the cause of Public Morals in their Metropolis and its vicinity, if, while you remain in London you would oblige by preaching a Sermon (also on a week-day, - say, Tuesday, April 23rd.,) to recommend the continuance and extension of some efforts that have been lately made, by a number of pious and benevolent persons, to put into operation the great principle of *Locality*, which you have so excellently developed in your "Civic Economy".

We venture to hope that, by combining to *two objects*, to which I have adverted, viz. the advocacy of our *Missionary* Institution, and the encouragement of *Localization*, a motive will be presented sufficiently powerful to induce you to favour us with a visit at the time specified.

With respect to the first, — the Report of the Wesleyan Missions for 1821, just published, which I shall have the honour of forwarding to you immediately by another conveyance, will, I trust be sufficient to interest your christian benevolence in their behalf. Our establishments among the Negroe[sic] Slaves in the West Indies, those in Western and Southern Africa, in South India, Ceylon, New South Wales, and New Zealand, and, especially our Schools for Negro & for Cingalese Children (in which not less than 4200 of the former, and 4900 of the latter, are receiving a *christian* education,) will appear, we hope, to deserve your public countenance, and to furnish good grounds of appeal to the liberality of religious & philanthropic persons of all Denominations. Never would you confer a greater favour on our Society, by pleading its cause, than at the present time, when, (owing to the great increase of our Foreign Work), the expense of numerous additional out-fits, occasioned by Deaths of Missionaries, &c.,) our Treasurers are in advance, according to the Accounts appended to the Report, to the amount of upwards of £7500. Our case is one of real necessity: and we anxiously hope that you may be induced to afford us, in this exigency, that important assistance, which, we are sure, would result from your acceptance of our invitation.

With respect to the second object, I am happy to state, that your plan of *Locality* has made a powerful impression on many persons here; and that there is a strong disposition to apply it to some of the most wretched Districts of our

44

metropolis. A beginning, on a small scale, has been made in a parish contiguous to St Giles's, and, I believe, in Spitalfields also; and already, enough has been seen to induce the belief, that your principle is the only one which will effectually reach the mass of our ignorant and vicious population. Mr Butterworth, who has, with his wonted benevolence, zealously occupied himself in these preliminary efforts, will probably express to you his opinion on this subject. I will only beg permission to state my conviction, that a Sermon from you on the duty of thus carrying the light and influence of our religion to our poor and careless neighbours, would, at this particular crisis, be attended with incalculable benefit to the great cause; and might probably, by the divine blessing, give a most effectual stimulus, and practical direction, not only in London, but in all parts of England, to the good feeling excited by your "Civic Economy". Deeply interested as I am in the success of your recommendations, I earnestly hope that you may consider this opening for extensive usefulness as a call of duty.

Allow me to intreat the favour of an early answer, directed to me, at 77, Hatton Garden. Should you accede to our wishes, it will give us the highest pleasure to make every possible arrangement for your convenience and comfort, while in Town, I think it will be quite practicable to guard against the intolerable pressure of some of those annoyances, of which, I recollect, you complained, when you were formerly in London.

If you feel any insurmountable objection to preaching for our Missions, *generally*, you would greatly oblige and serve us by pleading *specifically* for our *Negro-Missions* in the West Indies, or for our *Mission-Schools* in Ceylon and the West Indies. I am not aware of any such difficulty as this suggestion supposes; but if it should exist, this plan would, I trust, satisfactorily remove it.

I have to apologise for this long intrusion on your time. Your goodness will excuse it, as resulting from my anxiety about the success of our application. The invaluable service which your compliance would render us would, I humbly hope, be acceptable to our common Lord and useful, in no small degree, to the cause of Christianity at large; — while, by the friends for whom I act, it would never cease to be most gratefully appreciated.

I will only add the expression of my best thanks for the kind and condescending attentions with which you honoured me when I was in Glasgow last Summer ...

1. The holograph of this letter is in St Andrews University Library. MS.30385/87.

20.   *To Thomas Chalmers*   London, September 10, 1822[1]

Mr. Butterworth, now on a visit to the Isle of Wight, for the recovery of his health after the fatigues of the late Long Session of Parliament, has just informed me, that you are likely to be in London on the two last Sabbaths of the present month. He unites with me, and with my Brethren in the Methodist Ministry now stationed in and near the Metropolis, in most earnestly soliciting that you will confer on our Body the favour of preaching *at least once* in one of our large and central Chapels, during your stay in Town. I think that if you knew how highly and how gratefully such a favour would be appreciated, your benevolence would induce you to grant the prayer of our unfortunate petition. Nor would our own People only be indebted to you; but Christians of other Denominations might be very extensively accommodated, as several of our Chapels are of suitable dimensions, & very conveniently situated ...

A few lines in reply directed to me at No. 14, City Road, London, will exceedingly oblige us all. You will add to the favour if you can find leisure just to intimate to me, at what times & places you are likely to preach. I anticipate much delight & profit from attendance at your Ministry; I wish to make beforehand such arrangements as will enable me to avail myself of *every* possible opportunity ...

1. The holograph of this letter is in New College, Edinburgh. CHA 4.19.23. This letter was redirected from Glasgow Care of Dr. Stock, Clifton near Bristol. Some five months later, Butterworth also wrote to Chalmers:

Bedford Square, London, 4.2.1823

... At a meeting of the General Committee of the Wesleyan Missionary Society held yesterday, it was most cordially resolved to request you to oblige the Society by preaching one of their Missionary Sermons at their next annual meeting at the end of April & I was desired to convey their most unanimous and earnest request ...

21.   *From Adam Clarke*[1]   Dublin, June 27, 1823[2]
...   When the⟨ese⟩ letters [from Bunting enclosing minutes of the two special Missionary Committee meetings on Ireland] came, I had almost given ⟨up⟩ *all hopes of Ireland* — I have travelled ⟨th⟩ro the nation from the remotest North ⟨to⟩ the South, preaching to the uttermost of my strength: travelling both in Scotland & Ireland, at the rate, on an average, of 40 miles per diem, ho[l] ding meetings & preaching in various places ...
        I held a miss[ionar] y meeting in Edinbro. & preach'd from the chapels — both there & at Leith & preach'd for the Missions at Glasgow ...

1. Adam Clarke, President of the Conference, 1822 (third time); President of the Irish Conference, 1823.
2. The bulk of this letter was published in *Early Correspondence*, p.89.

22.   *From Edmund Grindrod*[1]   Green Street, Calton, Glasgow
                                                                January 12, 1824[2]
...For some weeks past the Lord has been reviving us in this City. Several profess to have found peace with God in the last fortnight. In the prayer meetings at John Street[3] awakened sinners have been crying aloud for mercy. I trust these are but drops before the shower. Please to give my love to all the preachers ... We have had many afflictions since we came here. Two of the children have been at death's door, but are now out of danger ...

1. Edmund Grindrod, Superintendent, Glasgow Circuit, 1823-25.
2. The bulk of this letter was published in *Early Correspondence* p.92.
3. John Street Chapel, Glasgow.

23.   *To Thomas Chalmers*   London, January 16, 1824[1]
We are directed by the Committee of the Wesleyan Methodist Missionary Society most respectfully and earnestly to solicit the favour of your preaching one of their Three Anniversary Sermons in London; the regular day for which services will happen this year, to be Friday, April 30th, being the Friday next preceding the first Monday in May.
        The Committee received with gratitude the intimation conveyed in your letter to Mr Butterworth, in answer to their application to you for similar aid in 1823, that it was possible that your new engagements at St Andrew's[2] might afford you more leisure for assisting, at some parts of the year, the cause of General Benevolence, than that which you could so appropriate during the continuance of your pastoral charge in Glasgow. Most happy & thankful will be our Committee, and the Society at large, if it should be possible for you to do them the high honour of pleading the cause of their Missions at the ensuing Anniversary ...

46

Every facility as to Travelling, and accommodations while in Town, so as to make your visit as little annoying as possible to you, would be gratefully provided ...

1. The holograph of this letter is in New College, Edinburgh CHA.4.31.26.
2. Chalmers left Glasgow precipitately in 1823 to become Professor of Moral Philosophy at the University of St Andrews. See also Letter No. 20.

24.   *From Adam Clarke*[1]   July 24, 1824

[This letter was written as marginal notes on a letter first addressed to Joseph Butterworth M.P. from Samuel Dunn, with a long account of his activities in Shetland. Adam Clarke redirected this letter to Jabez Bunting at Leeds, where Conference was being held.]

You will find this a very important Letter — take time to read & consider it. Pray, for God's sake, get two able men for Shetland. Mr Dunn[2] should be chairman, have the general management of all our work in the Islands, as no one else can manage the building concerns & much will depend on the men we send to him. The dog in manger wretches will now throw in their Decree men to unhinge a people whom they did not before strive to save. Let us counteract [yrn ?] by sending such men as they shall not be able to gainsay.
      Will you have time to drop me a line ? Mr Manson[3] will see that his five bills have been met. Strive to make out my marginal scraps, or write as you can.
      Dunn & Lewis[4] keep their places — we cannot do better. But we should have a man for the *Orkneys*. If the Conference think I can help them by labouring for the Shetland Mission, I am willing to try longer. But it is not pleasant to be always without any kind of appointment. I may be well [?] asked, what work are you doing and, by what authority?
      For Scotland we can do but little, but we may do much for the Shetlands Orkney & Western Isles.[5] Is there no zealous, able young man who can speak Erse? *Mull* the property of my maternal ancestors has a population of 5000 souls and not a place of worship on the whole Island ...
[Enclosed]
From Samuel Dunn to Joseph Butterworth   Lerwick, Shetland. July 14, 1824
Your very kind letters of the 15th May and the 6th Ult. should have been answered long before this opportunity offered but no vessel has sailed from this for several weeks, with the exception of one which accidentally called in here while I was in the country & by which Mr Lewis wrote you. It did my soul good to hear that you had again been able to proclaim from the pulpit great glad tidings of great joy, though you recover but slowly ... I feel pained to think of the trouble you take on behalf of poor Shetland, and should beg you to desist, had I not been conscious that you are doing a "great work" and a work which no man in the connexion would be able, nor many of them perhaps, willing to perform. Were you to decline, I fear the great work which has been set a going, and which is now in such a blessed state of progression would soon retrograde. As for myself therefore, like our *noble benefactors*, I cannot think of working with *any other person*[6] than yourself in this business. So that unless the brethren at the Conference will leave Shetland in your hands the coming year, I hope they will remove me, or at least not expect me to labour as I have done for the past two years, for how can I unless I have a suitable person to send me wholesome advice and pecuniary assistance. I need not add that it is the wish of all brethren that these Islands be left still in your hands ... The neat Chandelier sent us by W. Williams Esq M.P.[7]

and the very handsome and substantial Bible presented by his excellent lady came
to hand safe and sound. They were seen in the Chapel last Sabbath for the first
time when I told the hearers to whom we were indebted for such valuable presents.
I also rec[eive]d the *night sack* sent by my very kind friend Mrs Williams. It is a most
useful article. I know not how to express the gratitude I feel for such kindness ...

Conference not having given me the £100 last year explains the mystery
which so puzzled me. If you can get it into the buildings it will be a fine thing.
Now is the time to do something for Shetland. If no heavy debts are left, I believe
the cause will do well here as long as the world lasts, but if the station be once
embarrassed in money matters, it will not perhaps be so easy some years hence
to get disentangled.

Since receiving your last I have fixed on having the Dwelling House in Lerwick
a storey higher than I first intended, as the situation is so very eligible and so well
sheltered from the winds. It will now have three floors besides an under ground
cellar, the whole length and breadth of the House, consisting of a parlour & a
kitchen & four or five very good bedrooms. So that it will cost more than we first
expected. I need not say that such a House is always likely here to make its money
by letting, as we intend always to occupy it ourselves. We can have a well in the
cellar, which will be most valuable as water is remarkably scarce during the summer
months. The walls are now about three fourths up, & will be finished I hope in
another fortnight. I think I never saw better stones than those we are using, & as
we have had hardly any rain since we commenced, the walls are most substantial.
Further particulars of the House, I must leave for a future letter. I will now extract
a little from my Journal.

May 28. 1824. Left Lerwick this morning and walked to Scalloway, then took
    boat and rowed with one man 7 miles to Sand where I preached at 8 o'clock
    this even[in]g. We see but little fruit here.

    29. Preached early this morn[in]g to a larger congregation. Walked on to Grutting
    & preached at 12. & met the class, even[in]g. I exhorted a good number in
    Bayhall, to *Bless the Lord who daily leadeth us with benefits*. met the class.
    they are doing well. before long I think we shall have *here* the best Society
    in Shetland.

    30. At 10 this morn[in]g I invited a large company who sat on the stones, to
    the fountain opened for sin & uncleanness. met the class, *one hundred and
    ten* present. I spoke to about forty, gave the Tickets and thirty three notes
    of admittance on trial. Then went out and preached to the great congregation,
    & again at 5 in the even[in]g. after which I administered the ordinance of
    the Lord's Supper in our large dining room. Sixty two knelt down & partook.
    It was a time of refreshing from the presence of the Lord. May this day be
    long remembered!

    31. Preached this morn[in]g at 8 from 15 John 14 then took boat for the
    island of Vaila, where I met with a cordial reception from John Scott Esq.[8]
    who generously *gave* me a piece of ground in the parish of Sandness for the
    purpose of building a Wesleyan Methodist Chapel on it. May my God remember
    him for good, for this good deed which he has done! I returned & exhorted
    as many as a large cottage could conveniently contain, to *Behold the Lamb
    of God*. I then stated that after the congregation was dismissed, I would
    talk to all plainly and personally who desired it. a great number remained,
    I spoke to all who had not met in class before. They appeared to feel. May
    it be lasting!

June 1 I arrived in Burostow this morn[in]g in time to go by one of the large boats
    to the island of Papa, where we safely landed after three hours sail. I preached
    out of doors at 2 and in a very full house at 6. then took boat for Sandness,

where I was glad to find all the friends well.

2. After exhorting them this morn[in]g to *continue in prayer*, I went & marked off the ground for the Chapel. after which with my worthy Friend Mr Couper,[9] I sailed in a boat 14 miles to the parish of Northmavin, which I had not visited before. Preached at 8 p.m.

3. After speaking early this morn[in]g I walked four miles to Tanwick, where I was kindly received by John Cheyne Esq.[10] and obtained a most excellent horse to ride to Stenness, one of the largest fishing stations. As the weather was unfavourable, the men were all inshore, so I spoke from the *drag net which gathers every kind* to about 250 of them, who all sat on the beach in their fishing habiliments & paid the greatest attention, at 8 I went down to the place again, & spoke to a still greater number. A more interesting sight, I think, I never beheld. It forcibly reminded me of the multitudes who attended the preaching of my Master on the sea coast of Zebulon and Nephthalim.

4. I went again early this morning to Stenness, & spoke on the beach with much freedom as several women were present the congregation was even larger than yesterday and I trust good was done. I only regretted that for want of a convenient place, I was prevented from proposing to meet any of the seriously disposed in Class. Preached in Hilswick at night.

5. I expected the Boat several hours earlier this morn[in]g otherwise I should have preached. Arrived safely in Sandness about 4, preached at 7, met the Class & closed the week in peace.

6. Preached this morn[in]g in the open air to a very large number from *Philip's success in Samaria & never felt* the sun so oppressive before in Shetland. Met the class *ninety* present, to whom I continued speaking until 2, when I went forth to the multitude, most of whom had been sitting on the grass since the conclusion of the first service, & spoke on the *wickedness, repentance & restoration of Manasseh.* at 5 took my stand again behind Mr Couper's house, & directed the attention of the people to the *holy life & peaceful death* of the *venerable Simeon.* I then gave the Tickets & about 25 notes of admittance, & appointed three Leaders, the first in Shetland, which took me until 11 o'clock. As certain individuals, *who should look nearer at home*, for want of something else to say, have often asserted that we are too lax in our discipline, we have acted with the greatest caution from the beginning & did as long as we could without leaders, but as *this & some other societies* (glory be to God) are now got so unwieldy as to render it impossible for the Preachers regularly to meet them, we are obliged to appoint those of our members, who are best qualified for the important office. I have not neglected to give Mr Wood's excellent advice to those who have been this day appointed.

7. At 9 o'clock this morn[in]g after singing and prayer, Mr Couper laid the foundation stone of the Chapel about to be erected in the parish of Sandness, on which a short history of Methodism was given, & a sermon preached from 122 Psalm 6 to a very attentive & much larger congregation than I expected as many of the fishermen were gone to sea. I then engaged with labourers for the work, visited some sick people, spoke at night in Mr C's parlour & met the class.

8. Preached this morn[in]g in Sandness, afternoon in Bayhall met the class, three new ones. Walked on to Grutting, spoke at 8 gave the tickets to the members, & seven notes of admittance.

9. Walked 4 miles to Reawick without either boot or shoe, preached at 12, took boat across the bay and walked in to Lerwick. Ten years have this day elapsed since I first met in Class. How time flies! How many things have occurred to humble me, & many to make me thankful.

10. Set the masons to commence building the Preacher's Dwelling House in Lerwick, evening preached from 126 Psa. 6. Brothers Raby[11] & Thompson[12] present.

11. Br Raby left here for the Conference, probably not to return here again. May he have a prosperous journey! I expected to have the pleasure of visiting England with him, but the way was not open. I therefore am content. May we meet in a better world!

I cannot conclude without giving you an account of a still more recent visit to the West.

June 25. Walked over the hills to Scalloway through a very thick fog. took boat to Sand. sound walked on to Grutting, where I arrive too late to preach.

26. Rose early this morn[in]g from my bottle of straw, in the old barn, walked alone to Sandness. Preached at night & met the class.

27. Preached three times in the open air to very large congregations from Malachi 3.16, 17, 34 Psa. 8-9 Acts 9.36-42. gave the tickets to the four classes. several notes of admittance, baptised a child, & on the whole had a most blessed day. To God be all the praises!

28. Preached in Sandness in the morn[in]g in the island of Papa at 2 formed a class for the first time, 10 remained who had not met before. returned & preached in Sandness in the even[in]g.

29. At 8 spoke in Sandness, at 1 in Dale, met the Class, proceeded on to Burostow, took boat for the island of Vaila, met with a cordial reception from the proprietor Jno. Scott Esq who signed the Disposition for the ground of Sandness Chapel, & then generously offered to *give* as much as we need for building a Chapel in Walls which I gratefully rec[eive]d. Such acts shall not be forgotten. at night preached in Bayhall, met the class & returned to Burostow.

30. Awoke very early this morn[in]g with a sore throat & quite in a fever. I got to my feet bathed & lay until 3 in the afternoon, when finding myself much better, I went to Bayhall, but could proceed no further. I however was able to preach, meet the class, give tickets, & 7 notes of admittance.

July 1. Marked off the ground for the Chapel left Walls about 12. Walked to Sand, took boat, & rowed with one man about 3 hours against a strong wind to Scalloway. Preached, baptised a child, then walked in to Lerwick.

You see from what I have written that the name of *Scott* will long be associated with the Shetland Mission. Mr Scott of Vaila, who is one of the principal lairds in Shetland, is a very worthy gentleman. I think his kindness to us should be acknowledged in the Magazine. He has given the ground to the Connexion forever only with this proviso, that the Chapels be continued as *places of worship*. The Dispositions are made out in my name as the other. The drawing of them has cost nothing, a young man, who has lately joined the Society, qualified for the work, has done it gratis.

The walls of Sandness Chapel are about two thirds up. I hope to get on with Walls. In Dunrossness we want one very much, more than 100 members there, & no place to meet them but a cottage, but I cannot find time to go see about ground & materials. I bought a cheap lot of wood lately at a public sale. Mr Lewis is gone to North Mavin, he will make some enquiries about ground for a Chapel there. My feelings about staying I stated in my last letter. I want nothing but a *fair understanding*. It was our unanimous opinion at the District Meeting that into however many circuits Shetland may be divided, one man must keep all the general acc[oun]ts order for books, draw for monies & that there can be but one Quarterly Meet[in]g at least for a while. If we get *two good men*, which I hope the Conference will send us, we shall do well. The Congregational Union of Scotland has sent over two men, one to itinerate for 2 or 3 months, the other to remain over the winter. The Dissenters are

50

very busy in endeavouring to make proselytes, but they do not succeed well, though they sometimes descend very low. Opposition from different quarters increases. The vilest reports are daily circulated, & what is remarkable they are all levelled at *me*. The other brethren escape, they have even placarded me as a liar in the public streets & on the kirk door. Very few Dutch ships have been in here this summer, whether the weather or what else has been the cause of it I know not; but the general report is that I wrote to the Dutch Cammt?[13] But blessed be God, in all these matters, I can say *no man convinceth me of sin*. These vile reports no doubt keep many from coming to hear us, yet I rejoice that those who do come in general feel the word to come with power. Six have joined in Lerwick within the last 2 or 3 weeks, and I have just heard that about 15 more joined the Class in Papa *after I left* last week. To God be all the praise: We are not likely to be able to preach on every inhabited rock very soon with our [pr]esent forces. I am very sorry that I cannot send you before Conference a map of the islands of inhabitants[?] but you shall get these matters as soon as possible, nor a detailed state of the word. There are now very nearly *Four hundred* meeting regularly in class, and these all *on the mainland*, with the exception of those whom I last week met in Papa isle to the West. I am afraid it would not be prudent for me to go to Yell just now as I have so many things on my hands, but I will visit it if possible. *I feel for it.* Will anything be done for the *Orkneys*? If Conference thought proper I think I could visit them for a month or two in the spring, should not *a Preacher be now appointed* & depart at the next Conference. Could you send me any glass, as it is exceedingly dear here? We shall want 170 panes $14^3/_8$ by $10^3/_8$ 30 panes $11^6/_8$ by $8^6/_8$ 100 panes 10½ by 8 for the House & three Chapels. If you think you can send it, let it be cut into panes before being sent off, we shall want it very soon, however I shall do nothing until I hear from you ...[14]

[Marginal comments]

I heard from Mr Raby the day after his arrival in Leith but not since. It is Mr Lewis's fault that the house here is so public, therefore he ought not to have complained. I have told him of it more than once. I hope your remarks will be of use. I shall not *insist* on any kneeling to receive the Lord's supper, but I do not think we shall have much need, all the members fall in with it. I have paid the brethren £1 each, as I see Mr Kershaw[15] has credited me with the £4 so kindly sent us by Mr Scott. I gave Mr Raby £2 to pay his travelling expenses. His next circuit of course will pay for his luggage. We now always change the Tracts in the Chapel. Next Sabbath day I intend to try to form a Sunday School, it is much wanted, there are difficulties in the way but I think to surmount them. You shall know how I succeed in my next letter.

Mr Mason sent me a Bill value £260.3 . I shall when I [?] draw on him for the balance. It is safer & more convenient for me to draw than for him to send me bills. You may, I believe, place the greatest confidence in me as to prudence & economy. Prodigality is a charge I have never had brought against me. I think I am not of sufficient sanguine temperament to be extravagant. You may be assured that not a penny shall be wasted while I am in Shetland.[16]

1. Adam Clarke (d.1832) supervised the setting-up of the Shetland Mission. After the list of Preacher's Stations in the Conference Minutes for 1824, and until Dr. Clarke's death in 1832 was printed the following note: Dr. Clarke is requested to correspond regularly with the preachers in the Shetland Isles, and to give them such advice and directions as he may deem necessary. Dr. Clarke is also authorised to receive donations for the chapels, and for the support of the preachers in those islands; which donations shall be regularly paid, on account to the treasurer of the Contingent Fund.

2. Samuel Dunn (1799-1882), founder of Methodism in Shetland 1822-26; Superintendent, Lerwick Circuit, 1822-25; expelled from the Wesleyan Conference 1849.
3. John Mason (d.1864 aet.82); Secretary, Methodist Missionary Society, 1824-27.
4. John Lewis (1788-1826), Preacher, Yell Circuit, 1823-24. Chairman of the Shetland Isles District, 1824-25.
5. Dr Adam Clarke had written to the Superintendent of the North Isles (Shetland) Circuit in the summer of 1824: 'Strive to get a preacher for the Orkneys. I have written to Mr Bunting on the Subject'. The Conference of 1824 instructed Samuel Dunn, then stationed at Lerwick to 'visit the Orkney Islands, in the next spring'. Dunn's visit lasted some months; he preached at Kirkwall, Sandwick and many other places in Orkney, but unfortunately this work was not followed up. The next preacher to visit Orkney was John Knowles, junr., LL.D., Ph.D., (1804-88) in June 1834. In 1835, the Shetland preachers went again at the instruction of the Conference, preached at Kirkwall and Stronsay, and formed a Society at the latter place. The Conference of 1835 stationed two preachers in the newly-formed Orkney Isles Circuit. Subsequently, the Orkney and Wick Circuit disappeared from the Minutes after 1840, and there is reason to think that the chapel at Stronsay was taken over by the Free Church of Scotland after the Disruption of 1843. (Wesley Swift (1947) op.cit.) As far as Mull and the Western Isles were concerned, John MacLean was sent on a visit in 1827, but reported that the time was not opportune for an extension of the work.
6. A reference to Robert Scott of Pensford, near Bristol, of whom Adam Clarke wrote to Richard Tabraham: "*Entre nous*, he is much prejudiced against the Conference, at least the powerful leading men in it ... As Mr S sees it, not one of the Preachers has ever helped in this work, he believes they have prejudice against Shetland, and that they care not for the people's souls. He has again and again told me that 'if either I give up the Shetland Stewardship, or God should remove me from it, he would from that day give up contributions towards it, as he would *not trust one of them*'. I have laboured to give a better impression, but in vain". (Letter of 13 October 1830, M.C.A.).
7. William Williams, M.P. (1774-1839) of Belmont, Surrey, M.P. for Weymouth and Melcombe Regis, 1818-26. Supported the cause and maintained the principles of civil and religious liberty. Possibly he was a friend of Joseph Butterworth, M.P. (q.v.) at this time.
8. John Scott (1804-50) of Melby, in the Parishes of Walls & Sandness, eldest son of John Scott the Younger (1782-1813) of Melby. One of the principal landowners in Shetland. See Grant, Sir F.J. (1893) *The County Families of the Zetland Islands*, Lerwick.
9. John Cheyne (d.1840) of Tangwick, in the Parish of Northmavin. Another of the principal landowners in Shetland. See Grant op.cit.
10. The identity of Mr Couper is at present unknown, apart from the fact that he was not a Shetlander.
11. John Raby (1790-1858), Superintendent, Yell Circuit, 1823-24.
12. Samuel Thompson (1797-1839), Preacher, Yell Circuit, 1823-24.
13. Bowes renders this 'Consul'.
14. The order for glass was carried out for £17 3/- and dispatched from London by the King George to Leith on August 4, 1824 (*Christian Missions*, p222).
15. John Kershaw (1766-1855), Preacher, London North Circuit, 1823-27; Connexional Book Steward, 1824-27.
16. This letter was addressed to Joseph Butterworth, M.P. and marked in the corner 'A.C.' Adam Clarke wrote in the margins and redirected it to the Rev Jabez Bunting, Methodists Chapel, Leeds, where Conference was sitting. The letter

throws a vivid light on the early development of Shetland Methodism, two years after Samuel Dunn and John Raby were sent at the Conference of 1822. This arose as a direct result of Dr Daniel McAllum's visit to Shetland in 1822, to meet John Nicolson & to report on the possibility of a Mission to Shetland. From 1822 to 1832 Adam Clarke masterminded the Shetland Mission, arranged for financial assistance and channelled extra preachers to the Islands. See also Bowes, H.R. (1976) *Samuel Dunn's Shetland & Orkney Journal* (privately printed).

25. *From Adam Clarke*[1]   No pl. August 9, 1824

I have just seen a copy of the stations,[2] & one thing distresses me, relative to the Shetland Isles. *Lewis*[3] is an excellent man, & does faithfully the work of an evangelist, & in these respects *Dunn*[4] is every way equal to him, but there are other respects, & these apparently, essential to our work in the Shetlands, in which Lewis can do but little — he has not the powers, address and influence of Dunn. Dunn alone can be the man who can stand between the *Conference* & the *Shetlands*. Everything relative to our Shetland affairs, as to secular matters, must be done by *him*. In all our *building* concerns he must be the chief Director. He alone *can* & must *plan*, engage *workmen*, superintend the *buildings, receive* & *pay* all the monies. As he alone can do these matters is it right not only not to appear to *authenticate him* at all, but to place him under one who is *junior* in the *Islands?*

The Conference must do what they think good: & I have no doubt, that they will do all for the best but in my opinion "John Lewis, Chairman of the District" and "The Preachers in the District will change under the Direction of the chairman",[3] is not likely to answer the best end for those Islands. *I know Mr Dunn's mind* — & thus to unqualify him from every important act except that of labouring *as he may be sent, by one*, who, however excellent, has not his knowledge nor experience in those things, which are so highly at stake, will induce him, if he have timely information, to request his recall. Pray let some alteration be made in these things. It distresses me to write thus because of the very high opinion I have of Mr L. but he is not qualified to take upon himself the secular part of our work there. I will propose nothing — I leave it with you & write what I have written, *sub rosa*. I have laboured night & day for this mission and I was willing to labour on — may God prosper him who next takes the management of that which I am satisfied, is *the most promising & most important mission in the Methodist Connexion* ...

1. Adam Clarke, Preacher London West Circuit, 1823-25.
2. One of the particular features of Methodism is its itinerant and imposed ministry; ministers being appointed to Circuits, not to individual churches, by the Conference, on the recommendation of the Stationing Committee. The first Committee appointed to draw up a Plan for stationing the travelling preachers was formed in 1791, the year of Wesley's death. The committee was composed of one member elected by each of the newly-formed District Committees and met at the Conference venue three days in the week prior to the Conference to draw up the plan. The title of the Plan is frequently abbreviated to "the Stations". See also Pierce op.cit.p.477ff.
3. John Lewis, Superintendent, Walls Circuit, 1824-26; Chairman of the Shetland District 1824-25.
4. Samuel Dunn, Superintendent, Lerwick Circuit, 1822-25. This letter indicates the great esteem in which Samuel Dunn, the first Methodist Missionary to Shetland, was held by Clarke, & of his misgivings at the action of the Stationing Committee in appearing to demote Dunn. See also Bowes op.cit.

26. *From Edmund Grindrod*[1]   Edinburgh, December 1, 1825

Mr. Thomas Stanley[2] informs me, in a letter which I received from him a few days ago, that it is Mr President's[3] opinion, that the state of the Chapels in Scotland[4] should undergo a full examination when he visits us, and that, on this account, he wishes you to accompany him. I am exactly of his mind; and I now write most earnestly to request you to comply with the wishes of the President, and be his companion in his Northern tour. I expect he will write to you shortly to express his request, and to agree upon the most convenient time for your visit. Any part of the month of April or May, will suit us better than June or July. When I have heard from you I will arrange the plan of your labour during your stay and send it to you. I have thought that the following plan would answer:

Friday. Paisley, Entwistle.
  Dundee — Bunting
Sunday, first — Glasgow — Entwistle
  Edinburgh — Bunting
Monday — Glasgow Missionary Meeting
Tuesday — Do. Transact a part of the regular business of the District Meeting from 6 in the morning, until twelve, from 12 until 4 examine the state of the Chapels: at 7 pm the President to preach his Visitation Sermon.
Wednesday — at 6 in the morning resume the examination of the state of the Chapels; and employ the remainder of the sitting until 9, in a conversation upon the general state of Methodism in Scotland.
Wednesday (cont[d].) From 10 until 3 finish the regular business of the District Meeting, and from 3 to 4 receive the President and Secretary's advices. Mr Bunting to preach the same evening at 7pm., after which you and the President will be requested to attend a meeting of the Leaders, to give them your judgement upon the question still in debate among them, relative to the re-union of their three Meetings.
Thursday & Friday. At leisure to see the country. Perhaps you will be inclined to visit Ben-Lomond, and the Loch of the same name, about 40 miles distant from Glasgow.
Sunday. Glasgow. Bunting.
  Edinburgh — Entwistle.
Monday. Edinburgh Missionary Meeting.
Tuesday. Leith Missionary Meeting. In the morning attend the Meeting of General Assembly, if your visit be in the 3[d.] or 4th week in May.
Wednesday. Take a view of this interesting City.
Thursday. Bid adieu to Caledonia.

---

1. Edmund Grindrod, Superintendent, Edinburgh Circuit, 1825-27; Chairman of the Edinburgh District, 1825-27.
2. Thomas Stanley (d.1832 aet.59), Superintendent, Dudley Circuit, 1827-30.
3. Joseph Entwistle, President of the Conference (2nd time), 1825.
4. Between 1813 and 1829, Valentine Ward had acquired at least 14 new Chapels, the cost of which proved totally beyond the power of the congregations to sustain. In all this Ward behaved as the English Connexion, & like them he had the misfortune to acquire a mass of debt immediately prior to the severest deflation of recent times. The crippling increase in the debt occasioned by the restoration of sound money (Britain resuming the gold standard in 1822) produced a crisis situation in Scotland, where as early as 1822, the District Chapel Debt stood at £34,000; £11,000 of which was in Glasgow. It was to this situation that the Conference directed the President to visit Scotland, to give

the preachers moral support and advice, & hopefully some guidance on the way
out of the impasse. As a result, many Societies folded up and others carried a
burden of debt for the following 40-50 years. See also Wesley Swift (1947),
Hayes (1976a, b). Jabez Bunting was Secretary of the Conference 1824-27.

27.   *To John Shipman*[1] (Aberdeen)   Manchester, May 11, 1826

To the *principle* of the plan you propose for the relief of Stonehaven[2] & of other
places similarly circumstanced, I can see no material objection. I think it would
have many advantages; & would constitute a kind of *garrison-duty*, in which some
of our veteran supernumeraries might be very useful, and, if they could but think
so, very happy. I fear, however, that it would not be found *practicable* to carry
it out to any considerable extent. There are a few cases in which it is now acted
upon; & but a few. For, generally, our Brethren, when compelled to become
Supernumeraries, incline decidedly to sit down in places where their families,
friends, or particular connexions reside; & are unwilling to spend their last days
among strangers. I have looked over the minutes; & do not find *one*; whom I
think we could persuade to leave his present abode for a place so distant, & especially so far *north*, as Stonehaven. The only chance would be to find, at the ensuing
Conference, if you can, a Preacher *just giving up* the regular work, & not yet
settled in any particular place, to whom your proposal might be acceptable. But
I am apprehensive that even this is by no means probable; unless you happen to
know of some preacher, who is a native of Scotland, or whose wife is so, or who
now travels in Scotland, that has an intention of retiring from the work into more
private life.

        I wondered that several of you sh[oul]d be so willing to pass, in the first
instance, from the climate of the West Indies to that of Scotland. To poor Bro[ther]
Davis,[3] it seems, the transition has been fatal. I hope, by God's mercy, *you* will
escape further mischief; ⟨some?⟩ fine weather may now be expe⟨cted⟩ I ⟨co⟩n-
gratulate you on your success with the City Council ...

1. John Shipman (1768-1853), Superintendent, Aberdeen Circuit, 1825-27. Served
   11 years in the West Indies.
2. Stonehaven possessed a Methodist Society and a Chapel from 1828-59. The
   plan of employing supernumerary ministers was suggested owing to the financially embarrassed state of the Scottish Districts and the poverty of many of
   the rural Societies.
3. Henry Davis (1779-1870), Superintendent, Dundee Circuit 1826-28. Missionary
   to the West Indies, 1821-25, where his health broke down.

28.   *To Joseph Entwistle*[1] (Glasgow)   Manchester, June 21, 1826[2]

After many earnest but fruitless efforts to make such arrangements as would enable
me, without *material* injury to my Circuit & Flock, to spend one week with you
in Dublin, I am now finally compelled, by an overpowering *sense of duty*, to
announce to you that I must, however reluctantly, deny myself that pleasure. One
of our new chapels was opened only last Sunday; it *demands* the best supply we can
give it; we have but three preachers till after Conference, to do the work of four; &
many important arrangements are yet to be made, & made forthwith, to which I
must personally attend. Our other new chapel is to be opened on the 16th of July;
& to its affairs also I must carefully apply myself, in order under God, to ensure its
success. Some very important changes, also, are just now proposed in our Sunday
School system,[3] which as they do not depend on myself or on the friends of my
Circuit alone, I cannot suspend or postpone; and about which I am *very anxious*. I

cannot absent myself, even for 8 or 9 days *successively*, while these discussions are going on. On these & *other grounds which I cannot enumerate in a letter*, I feel myself imperatively & conscientiously called upon to decline for this year a visit to our Irish friends ...

I hope you have had a pleasant visit to Scotland; & may God preserve you & bless you in all your future journies by land or by water, & bring you to Liverpool in health & peace ...

1. Joseph Entwistle (1767-1841), President of the Conference, 1825 (2nd time), Superintendent Birmingham Circuit, 1823-26.
2. This letter was written to Entwistle during his 1826 visitation to Scotland, & shortly before the Conference. Jabez Bunting was both Secretary of Conference and a Circuit Superintendent at this time, & this letter indicates the impossibility of trying to hold down two very demanding appointments.
3. The Sunday School movement had begun many years earlier with the establishment of schools often quite independent of Methodism, attended by children of all shades of religious persuasion. By 1824, pressures were building up for the establishment of Methodist Sunday Schools, culminating in the setting-up of a Conference Committee in 1826 and the adoption of the 'General principles & rules to be observed in the Management of Methodist Sunday Schools', approved by Conference in 1827. See *Early Correspondence* p.115-116 and 228: also Hayes (1976a) op.cit.

29. *From John Shipman*[1]   Liverpool, July 21, 1826
                                Scotland

As I cannot get an opportunity of conversing with you very conveniently and as I have written to you before on what I conceived would promote the work of God in Scotland, I take the liberty of writing a few lines on the same subject, which you may glance at, when you have a few moments to spare.

The plan of getting Supernumeraries you thought good, provided they could be prevailed on to accept of the offers made of £20 per annum, but you thought that none could be persuaded to go so far north. I have now Sir to state, that the Stonehaven friends authorize me to say, that they would even go as far as £40, provided a suitable person could be obtained, although but 17 members & all of them very poor, save two or three. To shew the feeling they have towards Methodism. They heard that Dr Clark[e] was to pass through the Town during the night — two of them stayed up all night to see him, & one, a Baker, had prepared two packages of Biscuit for us to eat by the way. Now I think that they really could not afford to give £40 a year, yet they might give £20. But as I fear that a preacher cannot be got on this plan, I would suggest that it would be well if you would move for the appointment of a Committee, to consider the state of Scotland, & whether any thing can be done to relieve it. I am of opinion that something might be done, & that something ought to be done to save our body from that odium which the present state of things is likely to bring upon our whole Connexion. We are suffering the reproach of *insolvancy*. We are not able to pay our just debts, & the Trustees of our Chapels are actually trembling for themselves & families, expecting to be thrown into jail. And their circumstances are known to both friends & foes. Our enemies triumph & our friends are altogether dispirited & stand aloof. Now as it was the unanimous opinion of our District Meeting that the state of our Chapels was the one great hinderance to our work in Scotland, I would wish a Committee to be appointed to consider whether any thing can be done to *relieve those in distress, if kept, & how* they can be supplied with regular preaching. And on the other hand, if

56

Plate 6. Wesleyan Chapel, Doune, erected 1844. Closed 1890 and converted into houses. Photograph A.J. Hayes, 1980.

Plate 7. Methodist Church, Stirling, erected 1844. Photograph A.J. Hayes, 1980.

Ridley sculp

MR JABEZ BUNTING Aged 25

Preacher of the Gospel

Plate 8. Mr Jabez Bunting aged 25. Engraving from Methodist Church Archives.

Plate 9. Rev. Jabez Bunting, President of the Conference. Engraving from Methodist Church Archives c. 1828.

sold for what they will fetch, how the loss, which will be very considerable, can be met. I would just observe to you, that whilst I am in Aberdeen that I am willing to act upon one of the following plans.

1st. If the Chapels in the Peterhead Circuit could be sold for what they would bring and the loss be provided for by Conference, that I would take these Societies & visit them on weekdays, & give them all the help in my power, although Peterhead is upwards of 30 miles from us, & I should have it mostly to walk.

Or 2nd. If it be continued as it now is, a Circuit with one Preacher, and the Missionary Committee would allow me two of their young men, which they wish to improve before they send them abroad, that I would take two & find them their meat & washing &c. so that they would only have to pay their quarterage; & I think that the benefit these young men would receive by having to preach to our Scotch congregations &c. would be worth this much. Other Missionary Societies are at some expence in training their young men, & I believe that no rational objection could be stated to it. And there are other places where board & washing might be had & several others employed. Or if the preachers in the Conference know of young men, who are expecting to be called out, who have private means of support, & would come on this plan, they obtaining a promise that their recommendations to travel, should be *first* considered in Conference. This would be an inducement to some to accept of this offer. And it must be kept in mind that there is generally no difficulty in finding food & lodging in a plain way, the difficulty is raising quarterage &c. Now these things I would wish a Committee to consider, that something might be proposed to Conference for its adoption.

Another matter I would like to have noticed, and that is, whether an alteration, as to the *mode*, & *frequency* of taking the Sacrament might not benefit our cause. The Independants[2] in Scotland have it *monthly*, so have we in England, but not in Scotland, here it is but at most quarterly. And whether the Church of England form accompanied by our usual extempore prayers might not be proposed. If the Conference recommended something of this sort officially, it would at least be treated with respect.[3]

But Sir, the time of the Conference could not be taken up with those lengthy discussions which this would require. I therefore merely state these things, to desire if you feel your mind at liberty to move for the appointment of a Comm-[i]ttee to consider the state of Scotland. Delicacy forbids me from pushing myself forward to propose any thing of this kind in the Conference. Many would view it as downright impudence in me. And yet I am very troubled in my mind respecting Scotland ...[4]

1. Shipman continued as the Superintendent of the Aberdeen Circuit for a second year. See also Letter No. 27.
2. i.e. Congregationalists.
3. There is clear evidence of the problem associated with trying to compress Methodist practice regarding Holy Communion into the pattern prevailing in Scotland.
4. This letter was written to Bunting during the 1826 Conference at Liverpool. It illustrates clearly the parlous condition of many of the smaller Societies, arising from massive chapel debts. See also Wesley Swift (1947) op.cit. and Ward, W.R. (1978) 'Scottish Methodism in the time of Jabez Bunting', *Scottish Church History Society Records* XX(1), 47-63.

30. *To Joseph Entwistle*[1] *(Bristol)* Manchester, February 3, 1827[2]

I owe you many apologies for the delay in answering your kind letter...

1. With very much pleasure should I visit you at your Missionary Anniversary. But it is *impossible*. This month I am engaged to Blackburn; in March to Halifax; in April to Oldham & Huddersfield; in May to Scotland; in June to Ireland ...

1. Joseph Entwistle, Superintendent, Bristol Circuit, 1826-29.
2. Partly printed in *Life* ii, p.224-225.

31. *To John McLean*[1] *(Salford)* London, August 2, 1828

... I shall be very sorry to lose you from our quiet & pleasant Circuit, so suddenly & so unexpectedly; and so, I believe, will all our friends in Town & country. This you will take into your consideration; and remember also, that it is possible there may, at this late period, be some little difficulty in obtaining a good supply, and still more, in satisfying our friends at first, that they are not injured by the change. If you can comfortably stay, I beg you will. But if, on talking with Mr Bell[2], & with Messrs. Wilde and Davies, as Circuit Stewards[3], or with any other leading friends, and on calmly reviewing your obligations to your mother and sisters, you finally deem it right to go to Scotland, tell me so, and I will do my very best for you, and for the Salford Circuit. Probably in that case, there may be an opening for you at Glasgow itself; as I believe there will be two single preachers stationed there with Mr V. Ward[4], who will be glad to have *you*, for one of his colleagues.

But allow me to press on you again *one thing* viz. That this removal must be your act and deed, and that you must tell our Stewards & Friends, that it is *yours*, acting from a principle of filial duty & obedience towards an aged and afflicted mother.

Write to me without fail, & give me specific & distinct instructions, in reference to your stay or removal, by the *very next post*.

1. John MacLean (1806-66), Preacher, Manchester (Irwell St.) Circuit, 1827-28. MacLean was stationed in Glasgow at the 1828 Conference. He had been a probationer in Bunting's household and regarded himself as, in a special sense, a protégé of Bunting. A violent Protestant Politician and an Ultra-Wesleyan, his mental balance was precarious. See also Letter Nos. 35,98,124,125,126, 127. See also *Early Victorian Methodism* p.187.
2. Alexander Bell, Preacher, Manchester (Irwell St.) Circuit, second man and in charge during Bunting's absence.
3. James Wilde, printer or gingham manufacturer, and Thomas Davies, cheese factor and provision dealer; the Circuit Stewards of the Salford Circuit in 1828.
4. Valentine Ward, Superintendent, Glasgow Circuit, 1827-29.

32. *From Valentine Ward* Glasgow, November 24, 1828

The above is a copy of a letter to me from Mr Cunninghame[1] which I lose no time in submitting to you for your consideration. Mr C. is so pleased with Mr Rickets[2] that he wished to engage him for the year 1829 — upon being consulted I remarked that Mr R's situation in reference to our connexion was such as would prevent him from making any engagement which would prevent him from being at the call of the President. Mr Strachan[3] has been here and at Stewarton. His health appears to me to be so much impaired as to render 12 or 18 months of comparative rest very desirable. The situation for which Mr C. desires him is just such as is likely to restore him. If you, Mr Strachan, his superintendent and Circuit think well of it, he might go soon after Christmas to Stewarton, and Mr Rickets, would, if

I mistake not, prove a very acceptable supply at New Mills[4] till Conference.

I wish I could inform you of the conversion of many souls. Of this however we ⟨are⟩ not permitted to boast at present. At the same time, it is a matter of gratitude that our congregation's weekly collections are decidedly larger than they have been for some years. The Seat Rents have also improved. May our Gracious Lord send us a gracious rain and make our wilderness as a fruitful field. We discovered some weeks ago that the rot had got into the floor of the Calton Chapel.[5] It became necessary to repair it, and with repairs we have connected some improvements. Our People have, many of them, done themselves great honour by their liberal contributions towards the expense ...

[Enclosed]

From William Cunninghame to V. Ward (Glasgow)   Lainshaw, November 20, 1828

In reference to what [passed] between us in conversation when I was with you in Glasgow I beg leave now to say that as it appears that the heart of Mr Strachan has in the good providence of God been directed towards the work in Stewarton and his health is scarcely strong enough for his present sphere of labour and requires at least a season of comparative relaxation it seems to me that if an arrangement could be effected under the sanction of the President of the Conference whereby Mr Strachan might be permitted to labour for the space of a year in Stewarton taking up his abode with us by hiring a house in the town that it might be of essential service to all parties. to Mr S. himself it might be the means under Providence of the complete restoration of health. It would materially ease my labour which is too severe and it might be instrumental in building up the infant church in this place which seems to be to be assuming an aspect more and more promising.

I am willing to allow a salary of £80 (eighty pounds) per annum which is more than most assistants get in the Church of Scotland, and I shall further allow any moderate sum for the expence of removing Mr S. and his family to Stewarton which cannot I presume exceed ten or twelve Pounds but if a pound or two more I shall cheerfully give it. Mr Strachan must out of his salary (if the offer be accepted and sanctioned by the President) furnish himself with a house here.

The first thing to be done I presume will be your sending a copy of this letter to the President who can consult Mr Strachan as to his inclinations and should he desire to accept the offer and receive the sanction of the President I will then lay the matter before our church without whose aquiescence I should not of course like to act and therefore till the Church is consulted I must hold the offer to be conditional.

I have understood that perhaps this arrangement if carried into effect may possibly be the means of bringing Mr Rickets more speedily into an active sphere of active duty in your Circuits. I have on this account made the proposition at an earlier period than I might probably done otherwise. I have not time to write to Mr Strachan being very much oppressed with work but I hope the present letter may satisfy him.

1. William Cunninghame of Lainshaw (d.1849), descendant of Adam Cunninghame of Bridgehouse, a cadet of the family of Copington. Well known for his piety, benevolence & writings. See Anderson, W. (no date) *The Scottish Nation* Vol.3 (Edinburgh).
2. William Ricketts (1801-75). At the time of this letter, Ricketts had just offered for the ministry, as in the Minutes for 1830 he appears as having travelled one year. He was received into full connexion at the 1833 Conference and was stationed as Superintendent of the Morpeth Circuit, 1833-34.
3. Alexander Strachan (1793-1865), Preacher, New Mills Circuit, 1827-29.
4. New Mills, Manchester.

5. Calton or Green Street Chapel, Glasgow. See also Letter No 34. The Calton Chapel in Glasgow was used by the Great Hamilton Street congregation from about 1821-52. See also Beckerlegge (1955).

33. *From Robert Nicholson*[1] Aberdeen, December 10, 1828

I have just rec[eive] d a Letter from the acting Trustees of the Peterhead Chapel, in which they inform me that they have had several persons applying to purchase the Chapel. All the offers however are very low £150 is the highest, until last week a person offered to give them £200. This they consider as much as it is likely to bring, but if it is sold for this there will be a loss of £300 occasioned by the sale of it, as the debt upon it amounts to £500. They therefore wish to have authority from you what to do, as if they sell for the sum offered, they have no means of paying the £300, & must therefore look to Conference to help them. A speedy answer is particularly requested, as the person who made the above proposal is a Shipmaster, & is very desirous of knowing whether his offer will be accepted before he sails, which will be in a few days.

As it respects the state of the Society at Peterhead, it is as I expected. When they found that they could not have a travelling Preacher[2] to supply every Sabbath, they did not wish for us to visit them, except once or twice in the year to administer the Sacrament as the congregation could not be kept up without regular preaching. 19 however still meet in Class, the rest have taken seats in other places of worship. I feel much for them. There are some pious Souls among them, & they are greatly distressed by the preacher being withdrawn.

If you have fixed the time when your purpose visiting this District, I shall esteem it a favour if you will mention it in your answer to this. It will be as well if you & Mr James[3] can make it convenient to hold Missionary Meetings in Dundee, Arbroath & Montrose on the Wednesday, Thursday & Friday previous to your coming here. Mr Stephens[4] did so last year & it was attended with good ...

[Endorsed] Ans[were] d Jan 9, [1828]

No authority to tell Trustees of Peterhead what they are to do, or to promise any sort of assistance or relief. No funds at my disposal. If you have instructions from last Conference abide by them. Even as to *advice* I am incapable of giving it.[5]

1. Robert Nicholson (d.1834 aet.57 of cholera), Superintendent, Aberdeen Circuit 1827-30.
2. At the Conference of 1828, the Travelling Preacher was withdrawn from Peterhead.
3. John James (d.1836 aet.46), Secretary, Methodist Missionary Society, 1827-32.
4. John Stephens (1772-1841), President of the Conference, 1827; celebrated for his conservative and authoritarian attitudes.
5. This episode marked the end of Peterhead as a separate Circuit (1817-28). It illustrates the Scottish predilection for having one minister attached to one church, rather than the typical itinerant system.

34. *From Valentine Ward* Glasgow, January 7, 1829

A considerable time ago I wrote you transmitting a communication from Mr Cunninghame of Lainshaw respecting Bro[ther] Strachan. It will oblige if you will, with as little further delay as possible answer that proposal. And should Mr Strachan's coming to Stewarton be deemed inadvisable, May Mr Ricketts engage with Mr C. till Conference, and May I tell him that in all probability sh[oul] d Mr R be removed then, he may be supplied for the following year with a Supernumerary or a Preacher from the list of reserve?[1]

Say also ab[ou]t what time we may expect you in Scotia, and whether you wish to meet the brethren here or in Edin[burgh]? our last meeting was here. Some of the Ministers and members of the Church of Scotland are desirous of obtaining our chapel in Tradeston[2] for a chapel of Ease or Parish Church. A correspondence has commenced on the subject. The Trustees met a few days ago, and after considering the matter Resolved. 1. That we have no such prospect of an increase of our Congregations & Society as would warrant us in keeping that chapel sh[oul]d an opportunity present itself selling it for its value. 2. That sh[oul]d the President &c. approve we would leave the value to be fixed by four competent men — two to be chosen by the intending purchasers and two by ourselves.

Waiting your opinion on this subject and requesting a letter as soon as convenient ...

[Endorsed] JB to V. Ward Ans[were]d January 9 [1829]

The prospect of a Methodist preacher leaving his proper work to supply an Independant Church is so novel & anomalous (& in my view so objectionable both in point of principle or expediency[)] that I cannot identify myself or my office with it. I can have nothing to do in the case either of Strachan or of Ricketts.[3]

I approve of the Resolutions of the Tradeston Trustees; & recommend if necessary a considerable pecuniary sacrifice rather than prolong present difficulties.

1. Preachers who had been received on trial at a particular Conference, but were not immediately wanted, were placed on a List of Reserve. If called out before Christmas, they were allowed to claim the privileges of those who had travelled the whole year, but not otherwise.
2. Glasgow Bridge Street or the Tradeston Chapel was opened in 1813 and then sold off in 1839 to the Railway Company. See Beckerlegge (1955) op.cit. and Wesley Swift (1947) op.cit. The parlous state of the Tradeston Trustees can be gained from the finances quoted by Wesley Swift. Erected by Valentine Ward at a cost of £6,200, the accumulated debt by 1839 was £5,500. The Chapel was sold for £6,000, leaving an outstanding debt of £5,000.
3. See also Letter No. 32. Bunting gives a very proper (and typical) reply to Valentine Ward's novel proposal. See also *Life* ii, pp. 248-249.

35. *From John McLean*[1]   Glasgow, February 18, 1820

... Since my removal from Manchester I have had ample time and occasion for regret. The advantages I enjoyed in your family were very great; and such as I may not expect again to be favoured with. If I had the time to live over again I flatter myself it would be better spent; but that is impossible; nor am I quite sure that my untrained and (I half fear) untrainable mind would still not *still* cheat me.

As it is, I thank God that I was ever privileged to live under your roof. Numerous as my defects *are*, they would have been still *more* numerous had I not received your valuable counsel and reproof; and I greatly lament that circumstances so operated as to remove me from them so soon ...

Our prospects at present are rather encouraging; we have had several awakenings of late; and a few conversions. There is unbroken union amongst the Leaders, and people; and a general expectation prevails that God is about to make bare his arm. May that expectation not be cut off.

You have been informed concerning the anticipated sale of Tradeston Chapel.[2] We hope it will take place though nothing has yet been done in the affair to set our minds at rest.

So far as we can learn their [sic] is peace, and a degree of prosperity over all our societies in Scotland. The intelligence from Aberdeen & Edinburgh is unusually pleasing. In the Metropolis especially the power of God's Truth has been blessedly exemplified by the conversion of sinners; and the quickening of his people. We hope for great things ...[3]

1. John McLean, Preacher, Glasgow Circuit 1828-29.
2. See also Letter No. 34.
3. This probably refers to the 1826 revival in Edinburgh and suggests a return to rather more stable conditions following the crisis of confidence. See also Hayes (1976a) p.96ff; Ward (1978).

36.   *From James Anderson*[1]   Hamilton, Sept[embe]r 25, 1830

I was glad to hear thro[ugh] my son, that you had arrived at Liverpool; but sorry to find that your recovery is not yet compleat.[2] I hope that the Lord will spare you to the world, & to the Church, fór many years, yet to come. It is now about a month since I left home, & have been to see many of my old friends in Mona. I am now in this place among my relations, many of whom live here. Since my arrival I have been very hoarse with a cold I got coming from Conference, and preached with difficulty on the Sunday evening; last week, however, the huskyness, which I felt in my throat & hoarseness gave way: & I was able to preach last Sunday morning and administer the Lord's Supper afterwards; and also to preach in the evening. As I find myself able to preach again with tolerable ease, I think of proceeding to Edinbu⟨rgh⟩ & Dunbar, & the regions beyond — to Stottencleugh in ⟨the⟩ Lammermuir Hills, in which a farmer lives who was ⟨converted⟩ to God, the last year I was stationed at Dunbar.

Last summer I was as far North as Inverness, O what a change in Methodism since I was there 39 y⟨ears⟩ ago! Then we had large Congregations, & lively societ⟨ies⟩ which are now reduced to mere skeletons; with a few exceptions; and others have become extinct. Buckie⟨which⟩ was first opened by the late Mr Doncaster[3] & myself, ⟨is⟩ the only place in the North that maintains its groun⟨d⟩. In those days we never consulted ease and conven⟨ience, our⟩ grand business was to do good; and to preach wherever ⟨we⟩ could find an open door — many a time have I traverse⟨d⟩ snowy hills, with a peice [sic] of dry bread in my pock⟨et and washed?⟩ it down by snow hardened in my hand. I assure you, I felt a great deal in witnessing this fearful desolation; and asked my self what can have been the causes of all this? and concluded that it must have been owing to the purchase or errection [sic] of Chapels with heavy debts upon them, which broke the spirit of the people[4] — fewer Preachers being sent out than formerly, in consequence of which the[y] could not have reglular [sic] preaching on Sunday — and Preachers being sent, who were never qualified to meet a Scotch audience, & who could be provided for *nowhere else*!!! A meloncholly [sic] proof of this I had in Inverness last year; the Preacher is Superanuated [sic] this year for *want of abilities*! When I look at the Preachers (with some worthy exceptions) who have been stationed in Scotland for some years back, & especially in the North; & compare them with those who were sent there in the days of yore — what a contrast appears! in olden time we could name a Hanby,[5] a Pilmore,[6] a Pawson,[7] and Atmore,[8] a Bogie,[9] a Johnson,[10] a Barber,[11] a ⟨Co⟩wnley,[12] a Newton,[13] &c.&c., some of whom were first rate ⟨ta⟩lent in their day. I am aware of the hackneyed remark that "little good has been done by us in Scotland"; but I believe that infinite good has been done in Scotland by Methodist preaching, the full extent of which will not be ⟨kn⟩own until the secrets of all hearts are disclosed.

When I shall be at home I cannot yet determine; ⟨I sh⟩all stay no longer, than I can be of use, more or less in a ⟨pub⟩lic way; and in this way I wish to do *all I can*, and as ⟨well?⟩ *as I can*. When the cold weather sets in, which generally ⟨hur⟩ts my *chest & voice*, it is likely that I shall be oblidged [sic] to ⟨giv⟩e up, although last winter I was able to preach a good de⟨al⟩...[14]

1. James Anderson, Preacher, Liverpool North Circuit, 1828-33.
2. See *Life* ii, p.222. This refers to a serious leg injury sustained by Bunting while attending the House of Commons on the Anti-Slavery Question.
3. John Doncaster (d.1828), Preacher, Inverness Circuit, 1791-93. Buckie Chapel was opened 1790-91, when Anderson was a Preacher in the Inverness Circuit.
4. See Letter No. 29.
5. Thomas Hanby (1733-97), Superintendent, Dundee Circuit, 1785-87. One of Wesley's Early Preachers, Ordained by Wesley to minister in Scotland, 1785.
6. Joseph Pilmoor (left the ministry in 1784 and returned to America), Superintendent, Edinburgh Circuit, 1779-80, 1783-84.
7. John Pawson (d.1806 aet.69), Superintendent, Edinburgh Circuit, 1785-87. Ordained by Wesley to minister in Scotland, 1785. Noted for his critical views on Wesley's approach to the Scottish situation, particularly in relation to the Administration of the Lord's Supper. (See Hayes (1976a).
8. Charles Atmore (d.1826 aet.66), Preacher, Edinburgh Circuit, 1786-87; Superintendent, Edinburgh Circuit, 1787-88. Ordained by Wesley to minister in Scotland, 1786.
9. James Bogie (1757-1837), Preacher, Glasgow Circuit, 1789-91; Superintendent, Dundee Circuit, 1791-94; Superintendent, Edinburgh Circuit, 1794-97. Ordained by Wesley to minister in Scotland, 1788.
10. Robert Johnson (d.1829 aet.66), Superintendent, Inverness Circuit, 1784-85; Preacher, Edinburgh Circuit, 1785-86; Superintendent, Aberdeen Circuit, 1787-89; Superintendent, Dundee Circuit, 1789-91. Ordained by Wesley (at Edinburgh).
11. John Barber (d.1816 aet.59 in his Presidential year), Superintendent, Inverness Circuit, 1789-91. Ordained by Wesley (at Glasgow) to minister in Scotland, 1788.
12. Joseph Cownley (d.1793 aet.70), Superintendent, Edinburgh Circuit, 1788-89. Ordained by Wesley to minister in Scotland, 1788.
13. Robert Newton (1780-1854), Superintendent, Glasgow Circuit, 1803-04; President of the Conference, 1824, 1832, 1840, 1848.
14. See also Wesley Swift (1947).

37. *From John MacLean*[1]   Leith, March 5, 1831

It is with diffidence I venture to intrude upon your very precious time; but trust to your well tried forbearance should you not deem the importance of the subject a sufficient apology. A few of our people in this circuit have lately been professing certain opinions which I think contrary to sound doctrine. One or two persons whom I greatly respect think that I am mistaken & contend that the views in question are not only scriptural but in perfect accordance with our standard works in theology.[2] On both these points I am at issue with them ...

They hold that in virtue of the death of Christ God is *now reconciled* to *all* men — that this fact ministers are commissioned to publish to the world; and that the belief of it brings men into a state of justification. In conformity with this they bring forward several passages of scripture, none of which in my opinion are to the point. They quote also from Mr Wesley and Mr Fletcher. From Mr Wesley's sermon on salvation by faith, especially that definition of the Church of England, in which forgiveness is held out as the object of faith, not the effect of it, "a sure trust and confidence &c."[3] I am happy to find that this definition of faith is erased from the last edition of his works, no doubt on his authority. The quotation from Mr Fletcher, is from the 52nd page of his "Address to earnest seekers &c" (last edition) where he represents Christ as saying "And now, I beseech thee, be thou (for one) reconciled to God for in me God is reconciled to *thee*, thy sin is covered and thine iniquity forgiven"... I cannot help viewing it as exceedingly unguarded (to say the least) though it certainly becomes very different when put into the mouth of Christ to a penitent sinner from what it is when uttered by a mere creature to *all men* indiscriminately. I know that you will forgive me for the trouble to which I am putting you; and as the opinions referred to are gaining ground rapidly in this part of the kingdom; and two of our principal leaders in this circuit profess to see no difference between them and the sentiments of the Methodist Conference as published in the works of Messrs Wesley and Fletcher ...

The points on which I respectfully solicit your opinion are the following:-

1. Is there any difference between saying that God is reconciled to the sinner, and that the sinner is forgiven?
2. Is it proper to say to ungodly sinners that they are already forgiven, or even to penitents?
3. Is remission of sins the object upon which faith lays hold; or does it take place after we believe?
4. Are forgiveness and justification two distinct blessings, so much so that the former may be enjoyed without the latter?

There is a mighty stir creating in all aparts of Scotland by the opinions above stated. It seems probable that a large secession will take place from the Kirk and other bodies, headed by Mr Erskine[4] and Rev. Mr Campbell of Row[5] ... We [?] Valentine Ward in this Circuit at present. His [?] in Glasgow has been beyond his expectations [?]. He has already raised £75 and goes back next week to preach and make a collection in the Rev. Mr Waters Chapel when he may calculate upon 15 or 20£ more. He manages (O'Connell like) to evade the proclamation against public collections by procuring dissenting chapels. Two ministers in Edinbro have promised him this indulgence.

There is nothing of particular interest going on amongst us here. The Church is likely to retain our chapel in Nicolson Square[6] for some time so that the trust will in all likelihood be put in most comfortable circumstances, but we have not had so many conversions as we desire. May God send a mighty effusion to the Holy Ghost. I expect to leave this Circuit at Conference; but where I shall go I know not ...

1. John MacLean, Preacher, Edinburgh Circuit, 1829-31.
2. Wesley's *Notes on the New Testament* and his first four *Volumes of Sermons*.
3. See *Book of Common Prayer*, Oxford, 1752 or Edinburgh 1756.
4. Thomas Erskine of Linlathen (1788-1870), advocate and theologian; became associated with Campbell of Row over the 'universal atonement & pardon through the death of Christ' — the Row Heresy for which Campbell was deposed in 1831 by the General Assembly. See *Early Victorian Methodism* p.xvii.
5. John McLeod Campbell (1800-72) Scots divine. Author of what became known as the Row Heresy. During his second year as minister of Row, near Cardross, Campbell became impressed by the doctrine of assurance of Faith and this led him to teach the 'universality of the Atonement'. This gave offence to his parishioners who petitioned Presbytery in 1829 and at the General Assembly of 1831, he was deposed after a hasty examination. After two years as a highland evangelist, he was minister to a fixed congregation in Glasgow from 1833-59.
6. This refers to the occupation of Nicolson Square by the congregation of the High Kirk of St. Giles, at the Town Council's expense. See Hayes (1976a).

The bearer Mr McPherson[2] has requested me to give him an Introduction to you. He has been here since he left his work near London. For some time he kept aloof from us but ultimately requested to be allowed to meet in Class. I wrote to Mr Marsden[3] whether it was according to Rule who replied that as Mr McPherson *left* our Work; was not expelled, I was at liberty to do as his conduct might warrant. He has met in Class but not as a regular Member. He has been in very destitute circumstances. Dr Chalmers and Dr Dickson[4] have contributed greatly to his support & at present he is expecting to be engaged with the New Episcopal Church.

We are increasing a little in this Circuit but under great embarrassment with the Leith Chapel.[5] We have thought of raising a *monument* to the memory of Mr Wesley in Musselburgh[6] where he first preached in Scotland. A small pious Society is raised there, & if a Chapel could be raised so as to give stability to our cause several persons would leave the Calvinists & come over to us — though heartily sick of Calvinism they can have no certainty of a permanent Church where our doctrines would be preached till we build a Chapel. A piece of Freehold ground can be obtained for 100£ and 300£ more would build a sufficient Chapel. A New Church has been built in Edinburgh by persons who hold shares of 10£ each & take the Seat rents for Interest. less or more — Some of our friends have suggested to me that 40 10£ Shares would build the Musselburgh Chapel & they are willing to relinquish all government of the premises — make the Chapel bona fide to the Conference — only reserving the Seat rents as Interest. No person could call in money — though they may transfer their Shares. I would be obliged by your opinion of this plan. The cause is prospering in Dalkeith.[7]

I believe our views on General Redemption are rapidly spreading in Scotland ...[8]

1. John Partis Haswell (1790-1870), Superintendent, Edinburgh Circuit, 1830-33.
2. Donald McPherson (left the ministry 1831), Preacher, Biggleswade Circuit, 1830.
3. George Marsden, President of the Conference, 1831 (second time).
4. David Dickson (1780-1842), minister of St. Cuthberts or the West Kirk, Edinburgh, 1803-42; Secretary of the Scottish Missionary Society and an indefatigable advocate of all benevolent & missionary work.
5. Leith was in desperate straits, owing to complications related to the Feu Duty on the Chapel and a large debt estimated at £4000. See Scottish Record Office (SRO) New Particular Register of Sasines 868,270; 869,33; 983,110; 1020,95; 1034,89; 1159,219; 1254,158; 1447,82; Register of Sasines RS27 2599, 42; 2683, 1868. See also M.C.A. Edinburgh District *Minutes; Fourth Report of the General Chapel Fund, 1821-1822.*
6. See also Hayes (1977b). Haswell was persuaded to put £100 of his own money into the ill-fated Musselburgh scheme. When the Chapel finally closed in 1847, he was still trying to get it back.
7. See also Hayes (1978b).
8. About fifteen months earlier, Haswell had written to his friend Mr S.H. Smith in Sheffield (December 6, 1830): 'The labour of this Circuit is only great for the mind— we are very little out of town, & when we are, it appears to very little good purpose. It is no easy matter getting a congregation — still more difficult to form a Society without a compromise of some of our peculiarities. It is a common notion that we must say nothing against Calvinism. My conviction is that Calvinism is the curse of the Country — it lies at the root of all their evils — Calvinism tells them that if ever they feel the motions of the Spirit God & good-

ness — it is proof enough that they are *elected* then they rest in the drawings of the Father & seem never to consider the necessity of the manifestations of the Son. It is no uncommon thing for persons to talk loudly of their election, even in a state of intoxication. A man wished to go into our last Lovefeast & when refused a Note and reminded of the necessity of sobriety "Ah Sir" said he "ye know there is nae perfection in this life" — I have been exceedingly mistaken in my calculations of the morality of the Scotch — Drunkenness and some of its attendant vices are more common and enter more deeply into the habits of the people than in England ... & yet their opinions place them in a strongly fortified Citadel. A Lady called upon me last Saturday wishing me to call upon here Husband who has lately begun attending our Chapel and as he wished to sit under our Ministry she thought it her duty to do the same thing though fully persuaded we were in error respecting General Redemption ... a long conversation finished by her assuring me that she would not quarrel with *her* God even though in his Soverign wisdom he should have determined to *damn* her Husband.

In reference to my own soul I have had serious depression of mind arising from various causes — especially from the low state of Methodism in the Circuit & the depression upon all our Financial affairs — Whether I may make head against the many discouragements time must prove but certainly if the same apparent indifference among the Leaders continue which has been too obvious in their financial embarrassments for the last five years, I cannot stay here longer than my first year but it is my intention to try to move them — I have offered to make the Circuit pay its way during my residence in Edinburgh if the Leaders will pay off by a private subscription the debt upon the Circuit Book of 160£ ... If my plans succeed we shall pay one-half next year.

Perhaps you may have heard of a new divisity scheme now making rapid progress in Scotland — called here the Rowe Heresy from the name of the place where Mr Campbell first propagated the sentiment to their scheme. Jesus died for all — *the world is in a state of pardon* — & *pardon* is the object of faith, not the Atonement — You were pardoned 1830 years ago — all you have to do is believe it — the sentiment is spreading especially among the higher classes. I have just heard that Mr Erskine one of their principal men is to preach in the House of an Advocate in the New Town today at 2 o'clock — the Churches are shut against them though they declare they do not separate from the Church of Scotland.'
See also Letter No. 37. Similar letters to S.H. Smith follow on August 16, 1831 and March 2, 1832 (See M.C.A.).

39.   *From Adam Clarke*[1]   Pinner, Middlesex, July 17, 1832[2]

When I had the pleasure of seeing you at L[iver]pool I spoke about *Shetland*, Mr Scott's[3] donation, and the £400 which I had from the Honble. Sophia Ward.[4] Lest I should not be able to attend Conference, I think it right to send an *Extract* from the Will, which was made at my request by the solicitor and to ask advice relative to the mode of settlement. These things will be best done while I am alive for I know that disputes *might* arise on some *points*, were I not consultable. Should I not get to L[iver]pool you cannot too soon give me your minds on the settlement of Mr S's money, because I have several to consult in order to their consent, who live at a good distance from each other — Bristol, Sheffield, Bath and London, & who must all concur. I mean the *Executors* and *Trustees*. Tho[ugh] I believe no money is likely to be paid till the *dead year* is up. If you order that the £400 shall be vested in Trustees for the repairs of the chapels, houses, etc. will it not be well to have two or three *Shetlanders* in the Trust? ...

1. Adam Clarke (1762-1832), President of the Conference 1801.
2. The holograph of this letter is at Drew University, Madison, New Jersey, U.S.A. The dates on this letter do not entirely coincide, but the subscription July 17, 1832 would fit the events more exactly than the earlier date. I have therefore placed it according to the later date.
3. John Scott of Vaila, Shetland. See Letter No. 24.
4. Sophia Ward. The title suggests a possible connection with the family of the Earls of Dudley, but no trace of a Sophia has been found in the main line of that family.

40.   *From William Constable*[1]   Tradestown Chapel, Glasgow, November 16, 1832

From the interest you so kindly took during the last Conference in my appointment I am led to hope that my addressing a few lines to you now will not be considered obtrusive ... I should most certainly have preferr[e]d Rochester to Glasgow & did at the time lament that most painful and mysterious Providence which prevented Dr Warren's[2] removal, but upon the whole I am led to hope that I am where Providence would have me be. I am happy to say that in the best things, we in this City are doing well. Since the Conference many scores have been added to our Society, & many more are enquiring what they must do to be saved. The first movement that we perceived was in the Prayer meetings: the attendance was better, & there appeared also more devotional feeling. Our congregations began to increase till at length in all the three Chapels,[3] tis no uncommon thing, after the Sunday evening preaching to hold prayer meetings until after 1 o'clock, when the people even at that late hour are very unwilling to depart. In almost every meeting from 15 to 20 penitents are found crying out for mercy and we scarcely ever close without some finding peace with God. This in Scotland is looked upon as a very extraordinary thing, & is not allowed to pass without much public animadversion. The good work however is happily going on, & our people on every hand are saying see what the Lord hath wrought.

Amidst this effusion of the Holy Spirit, & consequent prosperity of this branch of the Christian Church, there is one circumstance that weighs heavy on our spirits, I mean the tremendous load of debt with which our chapels are burden-[e]d in this City. The three estates are consolidated & the debt upon the whole is £14000. The interest is subject to an annual deficiency of about £120. We are at this moment at a most painful crisis & upon the decision of the Chapel Committe[e][4] which meets shortly at Manchester depends the fate of Methodism in the City of Glasgow. Just before the last Confer[enc]e a legal process was instituted against our Trustees to recover £2000 upon a Note which they gave to the late Mr Watson[5]: by vigorous efforts those proceedings were arrested till the decision of the Conf[eren]ce should be known. The Conf[eren]ce most kindly and liberally offer'd £2000 if the Trustees could raise £1000. The Trustees have done this. Mr Watsons Executors expecting that this Conference grant would have enabled them some time since to have met the bill commenced proceedings again last week & were determined to bring it into Court on the 11th Inst. We laid before them the printed circular, a letter from Mr Grindrod[6], & other papers intreating them to suspend the business till after the Com[mit]te[e] met in Manchester on the 26th Inst. They have listened to our solicitations & on the credit of the connexion have engaged to wait till the middle of December for one half of the debt & the middle of January for the other & our Trustees not doubting but they will receive the £2000 from the Com[m]it[t]ee have bound themselves to produce the Cash at those times. They are in nearly the same situation with two other Bills of heavy amount; & *have no resource now whatever but the Chapel Com[mit]te[e]*. The

Trustees here, are poor men, & they have issued promissary notes to the amount of £9000 & bonds for £5000. Upon promissary Notes they can raise no more — & they cannot execute a bond till the number of their Trust Deed is complete — & they cannot enlist new Trustees till two or three Thousand pounds of the debt is paid off — In fact the £3000 granted & raised when paid will place all our chapels in good circumstances — make it easy for us to get new Trustees — & then to shift securities. This with our present, & we hope it will prove continued, prosperity, will enable us to keep our Chapels & go on our way rejoicing. Meantime, we are tremblingly alive to the next meeting of the Com[mit]te[e] — & if — if — we should — fail — there — why then the law must take its course & Methodism [be] plunged into such disgrace that it will probably be nearly extinguished in this City ... I have applied to you in difficulty before, you have kindly met my case more than once, will you do us the kindness now to stand by us in the Com-[mit]te[e] ? Excuse my being so earnest in this business — it is not merely a case of distress — but a case of desparation [sic] — for if we fail in our supplies from the Com[mit]te[e] Glasgow is ruined ...[7]

1. William Constable (d.1845 aet.67) became preacher 1806. Superintendent, Glasgow Circuit, 1832-35.
2. Samuel Warren (1781-1862) remained a preacher in the Rochester Circuit until 1833. He was expelled from the Wesleyan Conference in 1835 over the affair of the Theological Institution. Founded the Wesleyan Methodist Association. Seceded to the Church of England, 1838; rector of All Souls, Ancoats, 1840-62.
3. In 1832, the Glasgow Circuit comprised the three chapels of John Street, Bridge Street (or Tradestown) and Green Street (or Calton). See Beckerlegge (1955).
4. The Chapel Committee was set up by the Conference of 1817, following the recognition that many of the new Chapels erected immediately following Wesley's death were embarrassed financially and that more relief was required in such cases than could be obtained in the circuits. See also Letter No 13.
5. James Watson of Bacup, near Rochdale, had loaned £2000 on a Promissory Note in 1817 towards the debt of the Glasgow Chapels.
6. Edmund Grindrod, Secretary to the Conference, 1832-33.
7. This letter indicates a time of much rejoicing for the progress of the work in Glasgow.

41. *From William Constable*   Glasgow, September 30,1833

... I will again trespass upon your patience by adverting for a moment to our Scotch concerns; & in doing so I am thankful to say our society in Glasgow is doing well. Our people are in a state of harmony & christian affection growing in grace & in the knowledge & love of God. Our congregations are gradually upon the increase & the work of the Lord prospers among us. There is however one fact that gives me deep concern. Twelve months ago our three chapels[1] forming a consolidated Trust Estate were sinking from 140 to 150£ per year. The Com-[mit]te[e] Providentially stepped forward & saved us from destruction by paying off thro[ugh] grant & subscription £3000. This has placed our chapels in a workable situation & the income & expenditure (600£ annually) are made to equal each other. Still the debt upon the buildings is nearly £11000 while a recent valuation by Architect is only £10150. This debt & valuation presents a barrier to any of our leading men becoming Trustees — & the consequence is our present Trustees, who in point of fact are only the shadow of what Trustees are supposed to be, have not the power to transfer securities in case of monies being called in. About 1000£ is now required by holders of promissary Notes & the Trustees a few poor men cannot command the money market, and none here will lend them the sum demanded; while the above quoted debt & valuation induces every one who has a little influence to stand aloof from the concern. If no monies were to be called in the Estate might struggle on but in proportion as securities requiring shifting the concern becomes embarrassed. The kindness of the Com[mit] te[e] has hitherto been our salvation, but the core of the disease has not yet been touched. Where to look or what course to take we know not. I have written to creditors begging them not yet to urge their claims & to Attornies to stop law suits till I really feel quite ashamed, & under the load which to me is indeed a heavy burden I have no small share of uneasiness. A lovely Prosperous Society — embarrassed Trusteees — improved & improving circumstances of a Trust estate — but all improvements overwhelmed with a load of debt, which might be managed if creditors did not call in their money — a Com[mit] te[e] whose kindness has been unparallel[e] d — but whose kindess has not fully relieved the case, the case being so tremendous as to be almost beyond the range of hope — these things give me feelings to which I can apply to name ...[2]

1. See Letter No 40.
2. In contrast to Edinburgh, where similar debts obtained, no help was forthcoming from the Town Council in the shape of a rent for any of the Chapels. See also Letter No 37; Hayes (1976a) and Wesley Swift (1947).

42. *From Abraham Watmough*[1] Dundee, February 14, 1834

With the advice of one of my brethren in this District, Mr Thompson[2] of Aberdeen, I take the liberty to lay before you a case respecting which we are somewhat at a loss to know what we should do ... and that you may be at no loss to judge of the case, I think it best to lay it fully before you in the the same manner and order in which it was brought before me, though it be rather tedious or long.

When I wrote to Mr Thompson, in September, respecting the financial District meeting, which I expected was to be held at Aberdeen, he informed me, by return of post, *that it had not been the custom in this District to have any financial District meeting — that the Chairman of the District had always divided the money to the best of his own judgement, till the spring District meeting, when any alteration which was then thought necessary, and could be agreed upon among the brethren, was made, and the business finally settled in this way.* He moreover intimated at the same time, that the manner in which the money from the Contingent Fund had been divided last year *had not been satisfactory*, and that my predecessor, Brother Nicolson,[3] had keep [sic] more of it than he ought to have done for his own circuit.

When we came together at Aberdeen, as a financial District committee, and were dividing the money, this subject was naturally brought before us, complaints about too much money having been kept at Arbroath were renewed, and the preachers themselves from Arbroath, did not scruple to allow, *that more money had been retained for that circuit than the circuit actually needed*; and moreover that the friends in the Arbroath circuit were not satisfied concerning the appropriation of the money which had been retained for its use out of the grant to the District from the Contingent fund. These things being stated to the Brethren present at our meeting they thought it advisable that the Circuit Books should be examined, in the first place, and then if it should appear necessary from the facts of the case, that a letter should be written to Brother Nicolson, simply to *request explanation* of any

69

thing which it might seem desirable to have further explained. Accordingly I examined the circuit Books, along with Messrs. *Kendall*[4] and *Hudson*,[5] the preachers now in the circuit, and a gentleman who was holding the office of the Arbroath *circuit steward*. These three brethren then stated to me that Brother Nicolson had been his own circuit steward, that they had no *regular* quarterly meetings &c., in the circuit, and that the following items, they conceived, to be objectionable and wrong:-

1. Board of Mr Nicolson's supply, during Conference	3. 0. 0.
2. Official letters	18. 6.
3. Affliction in Mr Nicolson's family	3.10. 6.
4. Mr N's travelling expences (*in the circuit*)	3. 4. 0.
5. Mr G's do. (i.e. Mr Grayham's, his colleague)[6]	2. 0. 0.
6. Mr Nicolson's removal	5.13. 7½
	18. 2. 7½

Other items in the Books were also pointed out as needing explanation: as

1. 'Travelling expences' (in the circuit) for the preceding year	10.17. 5½
2. Official letters for the preceding year	1.10. 0.
	30.10. 1.

Having put these items down in my letter to Brother Nicolson, I forwarded them to him telling him how they had been considered as objectionable by the Brethren, and by the friends in the Arbroath circuit, "especially as they appeared to have been paid out of the money granted from the Contingent Fund for the *Ordinary* expences alone of the Aberdeen District, and not for the *extraordinary* or casual expences of any one of the circuits" &c.

Brother Nicolson's explanation was to the following effect "The £3 for board was a charge of 10/- per week, for 6 weeks, for keeping or boarding the young man who supplied his places during the time he was away at the Conference. The 18/6 for official letters, he says, was for letters he received as Chairman of the District, which letters the Circuit of the Chairman was accustomed to pay" (I ought here to state, that *they also* paid him for his official letters at the *District Meeting*; so that he was paid twice over for them.) "The £3.10.6 for affliction was for *family medicine*, he says; that it was for the whole of the 3 years he was in the circuit, though only put down in the Book at the last quarter day; that his family consisted of 5 individuals; and that it was a reasonable charge for that time". There appears to have been no particular affliction in the family all the time. But he says, "I paid different doctors bills during that period, and frequently bought medicine without applying to them, to save expences. Affliction is always paid by the circuit, unless they are unable, when it is taken as an extraordinary to the District Meeting". Concerning the items for travelling expences the following are his own words to me. "You are well aware that it is the custom in our circuits to pay them if they can, if not the preacher has to pay them himself. Now I am nearer 60 than 50 years of age, and I found from repeated trials that I could not travel the circuit without injury to myself. I therefore was in the habit of taking the coach a part of the way; when the weather was bad I took it all the way. My colleagues did the same, though not to the same extent, for they were all young men in the vigor of life; and I can only say that the sums given in were all expended in that way. The sum of £10. 17. 5½ charged for the preceding year, was a sum, if I recollect aright, that remained after all others were paid at the quarterly meeting, of course disposable, and as we had received I think nothing for that year, for the expences of my past year on account of the smallness of the grant, so our steward agreed that the other preacher and I should divide it to make up, as far as it would go, our deficiencies for that year also, and this I know, we were left considerably minus after all. The sum paid therefore was not to me only, *my colleagues had their share of it too*. The sums you mention it ought to be noticed, were for *three years*, — this makes them not so considerable as at first sight they appear". The next item is that of £5. 13. 7½ for his removal to Shields. Brother N. expressed surprise that this item should be objected to, by saying, that "*I know it is the custom of every circuit to remove the family of the preacher to his next station*". This is all he says by way of explanation. And the case being now before you, and will be agitated again no doubt at our Spring District Meeting, in a greater or less degree, unless it can be properly disposed of in some other way, I should very much like your opinion upon the whole of the case, as we are mostly young brethren in this District, and I trust wishful to do right. To me it appears — and perhaps I ought to state to you my own view of the case, that, if wrong, your superior judgment may the sooner set me right — That whether or not the items would or might have been all claimed and paid in an *independent circuit*, they ought, in a *dependent circuit*, such as Arbroath, to have been claimed as *extraordinaries*, if claimed at all, and as such have been brought before the District and the Conference in the regular way, when the brethren would have judged of the circumstances of the case, and done what was right. As it is, it does appear to me, to say the very least of it that I can, that the business was done *very irregularly*; and Brother Nicolson being now out of the District, and being also doubtful whether the Conference will think we act right in entirely passing it over without its being noticed any further, I am at a loss what to do ...[7]

1. Abraham Watmough (1787-1863), Superintendent, Dundee Circuit, 1833-35.
2. Robert Thompson (1802-68), Superintendent, Aberdeen Circuit, 1832-35.
3. Robert Nicolson, Superintendent, Arbroath Circuit, 1830-33.
4. James Kendall (1799-1859), Superintendent, Arbroath Circuit, 1833-34.
5. Josiah Hudson (1805-59), Preacher, Arbroath Circuit, 1833-34.
6. Thomas Graham, Jnr (d.1845 aet.67), Preacher Arbroath Circuit, 1832-33.
7. See also *Early Victorian Methodism*, p.139.

43.   *From John M'Owan*[1]   Hull, December 4, 1834
Last week I sent to the Mission house, with your address, a box containing a silver cup sent to me by Mr Scott[2] of Stockholm for the benefit of the Miss[ionar]y cause ...

Accompanying it I received a letter from Mr Scott, requesting some information concerning the present state of the Connexion, of which he hears thro' the medium of the Advocate,[3] which is regularly sent to Mr Geo[rge] Stephens now a resident there. The exaggerations, misrepresentations, & falsehoods of that periodical have made him concerned, and having had no other communication since Conference except the September Magazine, he expresses an anxiety after more general information ...

1. John M'Owan (1791-1876), Preacher, Hull Circuit, 1833-35.
2. George Scott, D.D. (1804-74), missionary to Sweden, 1830-42. Converted in a love-feast at Nicolson Square, Edinburgh. Latterly Superintendent of Glasgow (John St.) Circuit, 1872-74, where he died.
3. *The Christian Advocate* — a savagely anti-Buntingite paper — was edited by John Stephens the younger, the brother of Joseph Rayner Stephens. See also *Early Victorian Methodism*.

44. *From Edmund Grindrod*[1]

Irwell Street, Salford, Manchester,
March 2, 1835[2]

... The Chapel Loan Fund Committee[3] have deputed me, Mr J. Fernley and Mr Cromer [?] to go over to Edinburgh, with authority to settle the affairs of the Chapel at Leith; and we shall, probably, take that journey next week. One of our objects will be to induce the Edinburgh Trustees to fulfil their former engagements and, for this purpose, we have sought the sanction of the President[4] to give notice to the Town Council to withold from the Trustees the rental of the Chapel, should they persist in refusing to advance the promised grant to Leith ...[5]

1. Edmund Grindrod, Superintendent, Manchester (Irwell Street) Circuit, 1832-35.
2. This letter was partly published in *Early Victorian Methodism* p.124-125.
3. The Chapel Loan Fund was set up in 1826 to relieve the Chapel Fund, by special efforts, from a part of the annual burden on it arising from the claims of those Chapels with large debts on them (*Minutes* 1826). See also Pierce, op.cit. p.632-637.
4. Joseph Taylor, President of the Conference, 1834.
5. This strongly suggests that there was some agreement by the Nicolson Square, Edinburgh Trustees to offset part of the Leith debt out of the rent paid by the Edinburgh Town Council (see Letter No. 38), but there is no evidence in the surviving accounts that this actually happened *or* that part of the rental was withheld. However, this tradition survives; See Hayes (1976a) p. 120.

45. *From Thomas Rought*[1]

Dumfries, July 16, 1836

I judge it needful in my present circumstances, to state to you the following particulars — I have been exceedingly ill, part of the time since I came to Scotland, & now, though much better, feel those infirmities wh[ic] h render me incapable of doing the work of a Circuit, even of this — Especially in the *Winter*. Therefore, however *painful to my* feelings, as I have now been engaged *41 years* in the full work I must humbly request to be placed on the *Super[numerar]y* list at this *Conference*. This appears to me like beginning the world, when one is just on the point of leaving it — The *Will* of the *Lord* be done.

I have nothing to begin this new *mode* of *living* with, but what I shall receive from the funds — I shall find some difficulties in the onset — I lost my property by the improper conduct of a son, who is now in a foreign land — But this I wish to forget.

I must say, and I hope you will pardon me, that I dont know any Brother, to whom I can so fully, without reserve, speak my whole mind as to *you*. I have stated my case, as far as I thought needful, (in a Letter, for I was not able to attend,) to the District.

If this request, should be approved by the Conference, I should wish to be set down as a Super[numerar]y at Stafford — there I shall be in the bosom of my family — I am not weary of the Great Work; but hope that I shall be ready at every call to do all I can ...

1. Thomas Rought (1772-1845), Superintendent, Dumfries Circuit, 1835-36.

46. *From Samuel Dunn*[1]

Edinburgh, October 7, 1836

As I am here a stranger in a strange land, you will excuse my writing to you so soon after the Conf[eren]ce on some matter relative to this Circuit. I entered on my work with a full determination to consecrate all my energies in endeavouring to save souls from death, and to strengthen the shakes and lengthen the cords of our

Zion; and during the few weeks that have elapsed, I have preached, met the Societies, held prayer meetings, and given the tickets with pleasure and profit to myself, and I trust, not without benefit to the people. But my heart has bled to see Methodism in such a languishing state, and sometimes I have scarcely known how to act.

The first Trustee meeting held since I arrived was last evening, and after talking for three hours, we ended where we began, though there were several important matters that called for an immediate settlement. I should remark, that I came here ignorant of the whole business connected with the Chapel. I found no instructions how to proceed, except a copy of the Resolution of the Com[mit]tee which sat during the Conference to consider the Edinburgh Chapel Case,[2] and no one called to give me the necessary information. I obtained, however, about a fortnight since, a copy of the Memorial of some of the Trustees for the advice of the Counsel, and from it and other sources have gathered the following particulars:-

The original Trustees who are still living, and who are *Infeft*, in the property are Jones, McKenzie and Hughes.

Those who at different times have been acknowledged as Trustees, but who have *not* been Infeft are *R. Anderson, Calder, Bladworth, J. Anderson, Turner, Lees,* Walker, McDonald, Mclean, Menzies, Walsh, Redpath, Austin, Danks, Gardner, Selby & Dodds. *Now observe* that of the first three Jones is still with us — McKenzie left in December, and Hughes, who lives in the country, *never* was a member.[3] Of the seventeen in the second class, the first six have joined the Association, the seventh was expelled many years ago, — the next three, though still in our Society, have expressed a strong desire to be released from the Trust altogether, the next six have *not* expressed such a desire, so far as I have heard, and Mr Dodds, the last mentioned, never was a member with us.

Perhaps you know that the Debt on the Premises is £2290, and the Annual Feu rent £62. But they have an Income, in addition to the Pew Rents of £60 from the Door Collections, something for the Schoolroom, besides £20, which they say the Circuit this year must pay for the House in which I live, so that the Trust, on the whole, is not in a bad state.[4]

Since I came, the gentleman who has a Bond of £2000, on the property, having heard that some of the individuals whose names are on it, wish to be released, has signified his intention of calling in his money.[5]

Also the Superior, as he is called, to whom the land belongs, has written to say, that if the Trustees refuse to purchase the Feu Duty, which he is anxious to dispose of, he shall offer it for public sale. He asks £1440 for it — would likely sell it for £1400. The Trustees are paying at present 3¾% for all the money on the Property.

And the Solicitor of the Trustees who have separated,[6] has informed us that they have given him instructions to proceed against us if they are not immediately released from their responsibilities.

Now here is the difficulty. The Trustees who are still with us will sign nothing — nor move hand nor foot, *before* they are Infeft; and Mr. Jones the only Infeft Trustee, now in Society, *objects* to it. He grounds his objections upon the expense that will be incurred, perhaps £40 or £50. But I think he has some doubt in his mind as to the *perfect* safety of the property if they were Infeft, and there may be a certain feeling on his part to have it entirely in his own hand. What then can be done ? The Counsel has given it as his opinion that they can *oblige* Jones to Infeft them. And I have no doubt but they would do it, if I were to appoint them. But can I do this conscientiously?

Here to you I speak in confidence, but plainly — I have examined the minutes for the last thirty years with reference to the Grants &c. to Scotland, and have endeavoured to take as favourable a view as possible of all that has come under my own observation — and am forced to the conclusion that Methodism here, has been everything but a failure. The late division here differs from those which have taken place in England. At Rochdale & Manchester I found that the separation of some, had done good to those who remain, it led them to examine the principles of Methodism more closely, to admire it more highly, and to determine to support it more liberally. But here, I fear, a large portion of those who remained, had the same feeling towards Methodism as those who left, though they did not think it proper to *resign* they laboured to the very last to keep the disaffected with us, and they still speak of them in terms far too favourable, while the rebels are doing all in their power to injure our blessed cause. But I must come to the Trustees who are still with us, and I have great pain in stating, that with reference to Methodism, I have not much confidence in several of them. I have tried as delicately as possible, to feel their pulse, but have discovered no vibration, nor have I heard in any of the meetings, any expression from them, that indicates any very warm feelings to our excellent system. But still what must be done? Do *you* think that there is no possibility of getting some noble minded Gentlemen in England to become Trustees, in case these persons *wish* to be released? Or, if they refuse to give up, but have no objection to a number of English Gentlemen being invited with them, cannot such be found? It is my free conviction that if this be not done, but the present Trustees be Infeft that the Preachers must not *calculate* on such peace, nor Methodism on very extensive prosperity. As I must call a Trustee Meeting again in a week any instructions from you will be thankfully received.

We held our Q[uarterly] Meeting last Thursday night, *commencing at 8 o'clock*. The income about the same as the preceding quarter — members 17 less — but as the congregations here are increasing and the attendance at the Prayer Meetings on Monday & Friday evenings, thrice as numerous, I am told, as formerly, I trust we shall have a shaking among the dry bones. We are greatly in want of a few active men — a Local Preacher and Leader, sent in his resignation shortly after I arrived, in consequence of his having embraced Socinian principles, and I have not yet been able to find a suitable person to take the Class.

The notorious Doctor[7] and Eckett[8] were down about a fortnight since *ordaining* two of the Dissentient Locals — one is gone to Barnsley, the other to Manchester. *Thomas Townend*[9] of Heywood (you will remember him) is appointed to be the minister of the Associationists in this City — *Breare*,[10] late of Shetland, has been ministering to them for some weeks past ... I *heard* also that I am honoured with the censure of the villianous Advocate. But none of *these* things move me, I have too many responsibilities trials & tribulations that come nearer home, and which make me tremble ...

[Endorsed]   London October 29, 1836

A friends opinion is as follows! (I can give none)
1. Let the Superior sell the Feu Rent if he likes. That will not alter our case at all.
2. *Jones* ought not to resist the Infeftment of the six willing Trustees, for the sake of the Expense, which is really a comparative trifle:
3. Infeoff the *Six*; & take all chances of the consequences.
4. Then *release* the others, & borrow the money.
No *English* Trustees can be obtained.
Suggest certainly advice of the Chapel Loan Com[mit] tee — or of Dr. Beaumont. As to Discipline, let all things remain for the present, as y[ou] r Predecessors left them, except in case of some *flagrant* wrong till you have obtained local knowledge & pastoral influence.

1. Samuel Dunn, Superintendent, Edinburgh Circuit 1836-38.
2. This was the aftermath of the Wesleyan Association Secession in Edinburgh in 1835-36. See Hayes (1977a, 1978a).
3. See *Edinburgh Methodism*, op.cit.
4. See *Edinburgh Methodism*, op.cit.
5. This was Mr Gerard, an Edinburgh banker. See *Edinburgh Methodism*, op.cit.
6. Robert Barclay Selby, Solicitor at Law. See also Hayes (1977b).
7. Samuel Warren, LL.D.
8. Robert Eckett (1767-1862). One of the leaders of the Wesleyan Methodist Association; President 1841. See also Letter No. 110.
9. See Hayes (1977a, 1978a).
10. Robinson Breare (left 1836), formerly Preacher, Berwick Circuit 1834-36. Joined the Wesleyan Association and opened the Wesleyan Association chapel in Edinburgh in July 1838. Received on probation by the Wesleyan Association in 1838. Disappeared from the Association 1841-42.

47. *From Samuel Dunn*   Edinburgh, October 21, 1836

I wrote to you a fortnight ago & have anxiously waited for an answer. On Wed-[nesda]y I received a notice that a Trustee Meeting would be held at half past eight that evening. During the day I troubled for the result. The object of the meeting was to take into Consideration the Proposal of certain individuals to have the use of our chapel two evenings in the week during the winter at 15/- per night for the purpose of delivering *penny* lectures to the lower orders on *Phrenology*. Think of my mortification when I found that such a proposal was entertained by persons connected with our blessed Methodism ... The *chief* objection was the *smallness* of the sum. I however, endeavoured to convince them that such a use of the chapel would be an awful desecration of it — a violation of the Deed by which they held it — and that never while I was in the Circuit should I consent to its being let out for any *such* purpose. Had the sum been larger, I fear notwithstanding that it would have been granted — when I certainly should have applied to the Bill of Chambers for an Injunction. Should I have acted Methodistically?

As yet I have done nothing towards the settlement of the Trust for the reasons assigned in my last, but I shall be *obliged* to do something very soon, though I hope not before I hear from you. Do again consider the peculiarity of my own situation — not having been in any Comm[it]tee which has sat on this difficult case:- nor received instructions from any one how to act:- and placed here alone without an individual with whom I can converse freely ...

There are also a few *other* points on which I shall be very thankful for your opinions:-

1. Am I to allow the door collections throughout the Circuit to go into the hands of the Trustees?
2. When collections are made for our Schools, and even for our Missions, is it right that the Trustees should deduct from the same, the usual Door Collections, and thus leave a mere trifle for our important Funds? In consequence of this, one of our best Friends, I am informed, on such occasions, refuse to give at all.
3. On Sacramental occasions, ought the Trustees to have all the collections, and the Poor have nothing?
4. Should I encourage persons to come to the Sacrament who are not members of Society? Those perhaps, who have long been accustomed to communicate with us, should still be permitted; though I have little doubt but such a practice has been injurious to our cause in Scotland.
5. Should I allow the names of persons who have commenced meeting in Class, to be introduced to the Leaders meeting for approbation or rejection?

75

6. Ought I to permit any member of a Leaders or Local Preachers Meeting, to bring forward an individual as eligible to fill an office among us, especially when I have not conversed with the person privately?

7. Is it not my duty to see that the Class Books are brought to the Leaders Meeting, and there to examine them?

Some of these questions may appear to you trivial, but you will excuse my proposing them, when you know that I have more than once been told, that I must not expect Methodism in Scotland to be the same as Methodism in England. The case with me is just this. There are some things here, which I think capable of improvement and which if not improved will greatly impede the progress of Methodism. I have not the least desire to be considered as a *Reformer*. To allow things to remain just as I found them is the road to popularity, with the officers of the Society — any attempt at improvement is viewed with suspicion and will be attended with some difficulty. So far therefore, as personal loss and honour are concerned, I have every inducement to go on, and *touch* nothing. But I am very desirous that our excellent system of discipline, should at least, have *fair play*, and I must, if I saw my way clear that, by the grace of God, no difficulties would prevent my walking in it. I look to *you* for advice, as one having authority.

Perhaps you know that my colleague Mr Barker,[1] who has travelled with *us* but three years, has been sent here as a single man, though he has a delicate wife and two children who have been born since he came into our work. He gave a pledge to the Conf[eren]ce he would support his wife and any children that might be born during his probation; but in consequence of family affliction, the little money they had at the time of marridge [sic] is nearly all gone. His circumstances evidently affect his spirits. I do all I can to help him. At the Q[uarterly] meeting though they allowed him *nothing* for coals, candles, washing, books, letters, travelling expences, but the bare £4 4/- they contended for above 2 hours that he should have but 12/- board. I thought, that in common justice, he should have 15/-, but it was only after I told them that my own should be reduced, that they consented. The Income just met the demands of my colleagues, when it was proposed that one of the members of the meeting should draw a Bill at four months on another member of the meeting, & get it discounted for me. But to this I objected not having any great liking for the "Bill Trade",[2] as well as to save 10/- expence, so I received not a penny, nor do I expect to get anything, before I receive the first Instal[men]t at Xmast[ide].

I preach in *this* chapel nine or ten sermons a month, meet two classes weekly, besides conduct on the Monday and Friday evenings, the public Prayer Meeting.

You will be glad to hear that the congregations are still increasing, and that I have got six *new* members to my classes, but do write immediately, and tell me how to act, especially with reference to the chapel Trust. No one knows that I have written to you; but since I have thus frankly consulted you, how can I move in it until I hear from you. Very little Methodist news reaches our ears. I trust that peace & prosperity, during the year, will increase throughout the Connexion ...

1. Francis Barker (1804-88), Preacher, Edinburgh Circuit, 1836-37.
2. The 'Bill Trade' was the taking up of loans (usually on chapels) on short-term promissory notes. See also Introduction p. 22 note 22.

48. *From Samuel Dunn*   Edinburgh, February 3, 1837

A period of such painful anxiety I had not passed through, since I entered on my itinerant life as during the three months that elapsed since I rec[eive]d your favour. A violent rheumatic attack of which I have been the subject the last two or three weeks has been bearable, but the "care of the churches" which has daily occupied my mind has oppressed my spirit. I saw with you that there was no probability of getting English Trustees,[1] and Mr West[2] to whom I wrote, being of the same opinion, I determined to take your advice, and do my utmost to get a settlement of the Trust. But after the many and lengthy meetings we have had, we came to nothing definite before last evening. A resolut⟨ion⟩ was then passed that a Deed of Infeftment be immediate⟨ly⟩ prepared. I shall rejoice if at the next meeting howe⟨ver if⟩ it be not rescinded. I will give you a brief statem⟨ent⟩ of what I have heard and thought. Mr Jones[3] the Infeft⟨ment⟩ Trustee has always strongly opposed the Infeftment of the o⟨ld?⟩ Trustees, and yet strange to say, always speaks of them, be⟨fore⟩ them, in the highest terms. *This* I have not been able to account for in any other way, than that he has thought by such a course, he should most likely prevent their Infeftment, and so retain the property, and with it, the honour and influence in his own hands.

The other Trustees, I speak generally, when called to act in any matter, have objected on the ground that they are not infefted; and *yet* when I have made the way plain, they have evinced no desire to be invested with the privilege, but have rather thrown difficulties in the way. This puzzled me again and again, beyond anything I had ever met with; and after the hours I have spent in considering the subject, this is the conclusion that has been forced upon me, that they have really no wish to be Infefted. To account for this may be difficult, but I have thought it possible, 1. That they dislike signing the Bond for £2000[4] which they must do if infefted. 2. Perhaps they do not wish the Trustees who have left us to be released, hoping that they will again return, and that, if I do not, my successor may, restore them to office; though these said Association[5] men, within the last few weeks, have had their bills and circulars about the City, denouncing the "tyranny" of the Conference! *Breare* is still with them. And 3. It has sometimes struck me, that they have shewn this indifference, that I might the more strongly urge it — perhaps, give directions about the Deeds and then the expense would fall on the Conf[eren] ce and not on them. The cost (I think about £30 or £40) of obtaining the Counsel's advice last year, because recommended by the President, they fully expect the Conf[eren] ce to meet.

One or all of these reasons, strange as they no doubt will appear to you will throw a little light on the conduct, which otherwise is to be inexplicably mysterious.

They have long since given up the thought of purchasing the ⟨Feu?⟩ Duty,[6] at least for the present; nor has the Superior[7] ⟨dis⟩posed of it to any other party.

The Agent[8] of the men who left us, has frequently written ⟨th⟩reatening that if they were not immediately released, he ⟨w⟩ould bring us into court. But they have been but threats.

Last evening, however, we were brought to a complete stand. Mr Jones, who had got the gentleman who had the Bond on the property, to agree to release the three separatists whose names are on it, on condition that the present trustees take their place, and, of his own accord, given directions to the Solicitor to draw up a Bond of Corroboration, brought it to the meeting for their signatures, when one and all refused to sign it. Their objection of course was their non-infeftment. I was therefore determined to bring the matter home, and asked, if they really wished it. — there was no way to escape, and it was carried that the writing be prepared. But as I said before, from what I have seen, I shall not be surprised, if at the next meeting, something turn up, that will set us afloat again. Both the Deed and the Bond require that the number of Trustees shall be at least eleven. We have at present altogether twelve; but I fear when we come to the point, that three or four if not more of these, will resist on being left out, and where to get one new Trustee, after looking through the Circuit I know not. A short time, however, will I think oblige them to determine one way or the other.

77

Leith Trust is in a most deplorable state, and as this is known abroad, the prejudice against the chapel increases. My settled conviction is, that it would be a blessing if anyone would take the whole concern for the debt that is on it, and what to do I know not. I can make very little of the 2 or 3 old Trustees. The Agent for Sir Tho[ma]s Munro[9] who has a bond on the property for £1000 complained to me very lately that the interest due in Nov[ember] has not been paid.

Of the six Trustees of the Musselburgh Chapel,[10] four have become our enemies, one is here, and Mr Haswell[11] is the other, so that I cannot with safety call a meeting, and yet the affairs of the chapel need to be looked into at once.

But I must proceed no farther with this dark picture, and yet painful as the disturbance is, I feel a little relief in having opened my mind freely to you on the subject.

By the blessing of God we had an increase of 20 to the Edinburgh Society the last quarter but the very general sickness has [tended] to thin our congregations.

At the Q[uar]t[erly] Meeting I accepted an invitation to remain a second year, on condition that they would give me their assistance in maintaining Methodism and that I saw a prospect of usefulness. But really if things do not [?] I think I shall be obliged to request a removal.

Our mission cause here was very low, but we made an extra canvas in the beginning of Dec[embe]r so that we are now above the preceding year. I have not heard when Messrs Atherton and Alder, the Deputation intend to visit us. [Will] you come at the same time? I think you will better serve the cause if you come alone. I shall be glad to hear when you have fixed ... I heard Dr Chalmers say a few days ago, that he would much rather send forth among a population that he served the assistance of the Church Extension Society, a band of Wesleyan Methodist Preachers, than a number of staunch buckram Calvinist ministers ...

1. Clearly, the possibility of getting Trustees from England to replace those Trustees at Nicolson Square, Edinburgh, who had seceded to form the Wesleyan Association Congregation was at least mooted. See also Letter No 50. Hayes (1977a, 1978a).
2. Frances A. West (1800-69), one of the Secretaries of the Chapel Committee in Manchester, 1834-53.
3. John Jones, bookseller & publisher, one of the Trustees of Nicolson Square, Edinburgh, who consistently opposed the seceders. See Hayes (1976a, 1977a, 1978a). Also Scottish Record Office (SRO) CS 239, ISK I&J 16/10 Jones v. MacKenzie.
4. This £2000 Bond was held by Mr Gerard. See *Edinburgh Methodism* op.cit. p.122.
5. i.e. the Wesleyan Association. The leading figures in Edinburgh were James MacKenzie, Robert Anderson, Johnathan Bladworth, Alexander Calder, James Anderson, Joseph Turner, John Leeds and Robert Barclay Selby, all former trustees of Nicolson Square.
6. See *Edinburgh Methodism* op.cit. p.106.
7. The superior was William Clarke, W.S.
8. Probably Robert Barclay Selby. See note 5 above.
9. Major General Sir Thomas Munro, K.B.Bart. Bondholder on the Leith Chapel.
10. The four Trustees were James MacKenzie, Robert Anderson, John Lees and Robert Barclay Selby. See Hayes (1977a). See also Letter No 38.
11. John Partis Haswell, formerly Superintendent, Edinburgh Circuit, 1830-33; Preacher, Birmingham Cherry Street Circuit, 1836-37.

49. *From James Rosser*[1] Aberdeen, February 28, 1837

You will greatly oblige me by favouring me with a little advice on the case of brother George Poole,[2] of Inverness.

It appears, from letters which I have received from the Stewards on the subject, that Mrs Poole has for some time been much addicted to drink, and under its influence, has conducted herself in a most outrageous manner. — That on Tuesday the 21st inst., after serious altercation between her and Mr Poole, she rushed out of the house into the street whereupon Mr Poole bolted the door, and has refused to admit her since: and has, also, published a notice in the Inverness Herald, that he will not be answerable for any debts which she may contract.

The Stewards write, "We have no charge to make against Mr Poole on the score of his moral conduct, doctrine or discipline". And yet they strongly urge his immediate removal from the Circuit. I wrote to them on receiving their first letter, offering the best advice I could, and stating that I had no power to act otherwise than as our Rules direct.

I have received a second letter, dated Saturday, the 25th inst., in which they say they had concluded to have a silent Sabbath, as it would not do for Mr Poole to occupy the pulpit. They decline the responsibility of calling a Dis[tric] t Meeting; but again urge an immediate change between Mr Poole and a Preacher in some other Circuit. They intimate that Mr Poole was not popular before, and state many things said by Mrs P. to his disadvantage, but add "We believe each and all of these foul slanders to be utterly false and groundless." — So that, with the exception of his having refused to receive her back, and having published the notice in the paper, neither of which they mention in the way of Charge, but merely refer to in their statement, there appears to be nothing brought against Mr Poole's personal character. And if it were found necessary it would be difficult to hold even a minor District Meeting on the case. I think there are only six Preachers in this District in full connexion, including Mr Douglas[3] & Mr Poole — Mr Douglas is at present in England, and will be for several weeks, so that there are but three besides myself, in full connexion, who could meet on the case. And even a Minor Dis[tric] t Meet[in] g owing to the great distance which the parties would have to travel would occasion an expense of from £15 to £20. And then no charge and no accuser! I am not aware that I should be justified, under these circumstances, in calling a meeting for the purpose of inquiry. And if a Meeting were called, it is, as I think you will perceive, doubtful whether anything could be proved against Mr Poole to warrant the extreme measures which they strongly urge. They seem never to have asked themselves what is to be done with Mr Poole, or what Circuit would be willing to make the change.

Inverness is about 110 miles from Aberdeen. If it had only been a moderate distance I would have paid them a friendly visit. But as it is, the expense would be at least £3 — and they give me to understand that they can bear no expense. Add to this I can ill spare the time and it is doubtful whether such a visit would be productive of much good. I shall be glad to hear on various accounts that you are coming into Scotland at your earliest convenience. I hope you will excuse me for having troubled you with this unhappy business ...

1. James Rosser (1791-1870), Superintendent, Aberdeen Circuit, 1836-38; Chairman of the Aberdeen District, 1836-38.
2. George Poole (1797-1847), Superintendent, Inverness Circuit, 1836-37. He was removed at the 1837 Conference and became a Supernumerary. His obituary calls him John Poole (*Minutes*, 1848).
3. George Douglas (1764-1853), Supernumerary, Aberdeen Circuit from 1829.

50. *To George Marsden*[1] *(Sheffield)*   London, March 24, 1837

I am on the point of setting out on a fortnight's journey, I have only a minute or two, to answer your kind letter, just received. I am very sorry that I *cannot* this year comply with the request of the Trustees of your Brunswick Chapel. It is literally absolutely impracticable. My long official journies, to North Wales, Edinburgh, Glasgow & Aberdeen, South Wales, and Cork, & then to the Leeds Conference, with other indispensable engagements & duties, leave me not a day, nor scarcely an hour, at my own disposal for six months to come, which I could devote to services on *the voluntary principle* ...

1. George Marsden, Superintendent, Sheffield (Norfolk Street) Circuit, 1836-39.
   Jabez Bunting was now President of the Conference (3rd time). The bulk of this letter is published in *Early Victorian Methodism* p.184.

51. *From James Rosser*   Aberdeen, March 30, 1837

I received your favour of the 24th inst. and beg your acceptance of my thanks for the advice it contains.

Having heard nothing more from Inverness, I conclude the parties have agreed to struggle on, at least till the Dis[tric] t Meeting.

Respecting a change with any Preacher in this District, I much doubt whether it could be carried into effect – I mean with the consent of the parties concerned – I should think Mrs P.[1] is at home, but I will endeavour to ascertain how things are going on, and do all in my power to prevent any evil which might arise from this unhappy business.

Now with regard to your visit to Scotland, I do hope and pray that, if possible, we may see you at Aberdeen. If I were to speak only of the personal gratification & benefit which I should derive I could easily fill this sheet. But I will not be selfish. I will altogether in this place shut out that consideration. – Such, Sir, is the respect which I bear you, and such the pleasure I should feel in complying with your request, that I would sacrifice such considerations as are merely personal, accepting the noble sentiments contained in your letter "Public interests should not be sacrificed to private feelings.."

It has already been stated by some in this neighbourhood, that you would not visit us, and I am sorry to say, I believe there are those, even in connexion with us, who would rejoice at such a disappointment.

Soon after I came to this Circuit, a Preacher, in connexion with the Association,[2] formerly a Local Preacher in this place and the son of a Member in the Aberdeen Society, who entertains the same views, came to deliver lectures on "Methodism as it was, Methodism as it is and Methodism as it should be." I acted with as much prudence as I could, but soon found that a spirit of dissatisfaction, which had been previously fostered, was gaining ground, and that a rupture was likely to take place. Several of our Leaders, with one of the Circuit Stewards at their head, seemed determined that the Class pence[3] should be discontinued, saying that it was a system injurious to the work of God, and one cause why Methodism did not prosper in Scotland. I understood the design, and calmly but firmly resisted, and refused to allow the matter to be discussed in the Leader's Meeting – at the same time informing them that if they wished it to be brought before Conference, it should be considered in the proper way and at the proper time. I was threatened for some weeks with a division, and an Association Preacher is now every day expected to settle in Aberdeen. As yet we keep together, all, of course, attending to Rule, but evidently not with the best spirit.

I thought it right to change the Circuit Stewards, as matter of course, at the usual time, the person referred to having been in office 4 years, and their being no *special* reasons to justify his continuance. The strength of parties was tried at our Quarterly Meeting, last Monday, when a considerable majority requested the continuance of myself and colleagues, none indeed, voting against it...

You must, if you please, come on Thursday May the 25th & help us, for a few hours, in our business on the Friday, and preach the introductory Missionary Sermon on the Friday evening — Then we must let you go on the Saturday. The time and expense will be well bestowed. The additional labour to yourself is the only question. Our good friends at Glasgow cannot complain, as you will be with them one Sabbath, and Mr Atherton & Mr Alder (whom we shall affectionately receive) are in themselves a host for Glasgow Meeting ...[4]

1. Mrs Poole, wife of the Inverness Superintendent. See Letter No 49.
2. The Wesleyan Association, established by Samuel Warren following his expulsion from the Wesleyan Conference in 1835.
3. The original rule of John Wesley was that every member of the Society should contribute at least one penny per week and one shilling per quarter towards the support of the travelling preachers. Since the weekly contribution was collected at the Class Meeting, the term Class Pence soon arose. See Pierce op.cit. p.70.
4. This letter illustrates the extent of the unrest following Warren's expulsion and the rapid spread of the Wesleyan Association.

52. *From Samuel Dunn*   Edinburgh, April 4, 1837
As the District Meeting cannot be very distant and as the friends here are comparatively few, they are getting anxious to know the time at which it is to be held. If you have therefore fixed, I shall feel greatly obliged by your informing me.

Since I wrote last, three of the then assumed Trustees, have resigned; and though not without great difficulty, I have obtained five new ones. An Attorney is now preparing the necessary Deeds of Renunciation, Assumption, and Infeftment, so that I hope in a few weeks, I shall see the termination of one of the most unpleasant and painful matters, with which I ever had to do.

I regret that I am not able to inform you of any great accession to our ranks ...[1]

1. See Letter No. 46.

53. *From Thomas Rogerson*[1]   Edinburgh, May 24, 1837[2]
I have thought it my duty to trouble you in this way with a knowledge of the circumstances of my case, because I was fearful when the subject might come before the Conference, the Brethren might suppose that I was acting as I ought not. The fact of the matter is, I would not wish to leave Scotland if I could by any means stay with prudence, but during the last winter my health was entirely gone, it was with the greatest difficulty I could attend to and of those duties which were imposed upon me, and I am fearful that another winter would render me altogether incapable of work, Mrs Rogersons friends also are most urgent that she should be nearer them. Her aunt with whom she has been brought up (she being an orphan) is extremely infirm, and is likely soon to be called away wishes us within a few days distance from her, so that if I could have a station somewhere in the Bath or Bristol Districts I should be obliged. Pardon me Sir for thus troubling you, I know that the Representative is the proper medium, but I thought it right just to communicate as much as this to yourself, that you might know when the case might be mentioned... There are other causes which would make a change desirable. Bro[ther] Garrett[3]

81

and self have felt most acutely the distractions which are at present prevalent in the Glasgow Societies. We love Mr France,[4] but are afraid unless something be done that Mr France will himself fall in the conflict, and that a terrible falling off will occur, the men being so very bitter in their spirit ...

1. Thomas Rogerson (1810-55), Preacher, Glasgow Circuit, 1836-37.
2. The date of the letter and the place of origin suggest that it was handed to Bunting at the District Meeting.
3. John Garrett (retired from Ministry, 1838), Preacher, Glasgow Circuit, 1836-37.
4. William France (1781-1850), Superintendent, Glasgow Circuit, 1835-38.

54. *From Samuel Wilde*[1]   Carlisle, July 8, 1837

I received yours in reply to mine, respecting the Dumfries Case. I wrote to Mr Hyde,[2] stating your proposal of a Minor District [Meeting] , and requested him to make choice of two preachers.[3] The Plaintives [sic] approved of the plan and chose two of the Brethren; but I am sorry to say Mr Hyde refused to comply with the proposal. I then considered that I had no alternative but calling a Special District [Meeting] ,[4] and this with great reluctance I did, which met at Dumfries on the 4 and 5 inst. We put Mr Pearson,[5] the agent of Morison's Pills on his trial before the Leaders, his case turned out to be worse than we expected, and we excluded him from Society. We then put Mr Hyde on his trial, he was charged with neglect of discipline, and contumacy, and after a patient investigation, he was found guilty, and with great reluctance we suspended him until the Conference. We were led to adopt this measure for the following reasons. He had rendered his character odious in Dumfries, by screening the pill man, and refusing to investigate his case; he had nearly broken up the society, and driven away the congregation, with his gross personalities from the pulpit. He denied an authority to put him on his trial; and we were quite certain that if we left him in the possession of the pulpit, he would introduce the matter to the congregation, and express his disapprobation of the whole procedure, and thus increase the evil already produced. We could not doubt but that he has for some time been labouring under some mental infirmity [sic] , or he would never have acted so strange a part as he has done, ever since he came to Dumfries. We allowed him to remain in the House until the Conference, with the express engagement that he will not in any way interfere with the Society or congregation. Brother Watmough[6] remains in Dumfries until after the next Sabbath, and then if you approve of the plan, Mr Coghill[7] from Wigton is to supply Dumfries until the Conference; and a young man from Whitehaven, who was recommended by our May District Meeting to be taken out to travel, is to supply Mr Coghill's places. We adopted this measure as the least expensive, but if you would rather send a supply, it will be quite agreeable ...

[Endorsed]   Ans[were] d July 10 [1837]

I sanction the plan for supplying Dumfries.[8]

1. Samuel Wilde (retired from Ministry 1853), Superintendent, Carlisle Circuit, 1835-37; Chairman of the Carlisle District.
2. James Hyde (d.1857 aet.80), Superintendent, Dumfries Circuit, 1836-37.
3. Parties involved in disciplinary disputes were required to choose two ministers each to act as members of a Minor District Meeting to try the case (*Minutes* 1793 p. 289-290).
4. The design of the Minor District Meeting was to avoid the inconvenience and expense of assembling all the members of a full District Committee for cases which might be determined by a less important jurisdiction and to engage as

few persons as possible in the investigation of such affairs as are of a painful nature. There was a right of appeal to the full District Meeting and also to the Conference. See Pierce op.cit. p.388 ff. In the Carlisle District Meeting minutes for 23 May 1837 appears the following: 'The only exception to this (the Question – Do all the Brethren approve of and enforce our discipline) is the case of Bro[ther] James Hyde of whom for the present we suspend expressing our judgment, it having been stated that he had omitted duly to enforce our discipline by refusing to investigate certain reports brought against one of the members of Society at Dumfries. The parties concerned agreed to endeavour to settle the whole case as amicably as possible with the aid of the Chairman & brother Heywood of Wigton, who were requested by the District Committee, to go over to Dumfries for that purpose & to report to Conference as they may find needful.' A Minor District Meeting followed on 4th July 1837. See MCA Carlisle District Meeting minutes.

5. Mr. George Pearson, Leader and Society Steward of the Dumfries Society; agent for Morison's Pills.
6. Abraham Watmough (1787-1863), Superintendent, Whitehaven Circuit, 1835-1837. The letter indicates that Watmough was brought from Whitehaven to supply Dumfries instead of Hyde, who was suspended from his duties.
7. Donald M.R. Coghill (1809-42), Preacher, Wigton Circuit, 1836-38. Coghill was sent to Dumfries until Conference, 1837, as a more permanent substitute.
8. Dumfries had been part of the Carlisle District for many years, owing to its geographical isolation from the remaining Scottish Methodist Churches.

55. *From Robert Thompson*[1]   Dundee, July 10, 1837

When I saw you at Aberdeen, I had not mentioned to our people in Dundee, that I had the slightest idea of leaving them at the approaching Conference, and that Mr Barr[2] might be secured. When I returned home I referred to it, and found that they would be greatly discouraged if I deserted them after struggling with them only 16 months, especially as during the next year our ex-friends[3] will have their new chapels opened and of course will make new attempts to injure Methodism.

After thinking and praying about the matter, I have concluded (that it shall appear right to my Fathers and Brethren) to remain another year, I may add, that I do this without reluctance, my heart is in it, and by the help of the "good spirit" I will do what in me lays to promote the cause of God in the form of Methodism as it is. There is one thing connected with this that I would urge, that Mr Talbot,[4] now of Paisley, be appointed to Perth, this will do well both for Perth & Dundee next year, as the change might be frequent, and at the end of the year Mr Talbot might be removed to Dundee for which he would be all the better fitted having been twelve months on the ground ...

1. Robert Thompson (1802-68), Superintendent, Dundee Circuit, 1836-38. He was continued at Dundee for a Second year.
2. Ninian Barr (d.1865 aet.71), Preacher, Whitby Circuit, 1834-37. Barr had previously been Superintendent, Dundee and Perth Circuit, 1828-30.
3. Daniel K. Shoebotham and a group known as the Shoebothamites or Shuffelbottamites had seceded from the Wesleyan Society in Dundee. See Cass, A.N. (1973) 'Developments in Dundee Methodism', *Journal of the Scottish Branch of the Wesley Historical Society* 2(2), 3-7; also (1974) 'Trials and Fortunes of Methodism as it was', *ibid.* 3(1), 22.
4. John Talbot (disappeared from the ministry c.1840), Preacher, Glasgow Circuit, 1835-37. He was not sent to Perth at the 1837 Conference, but to Tadcaster.

56. *From Robert Thompson* Dundee, July 9, 1838

When I saw you in Aberdeen last year, and referred to my leaving Scotland, you kindly requested me to inform you by letter, where I would like to go, and you would endeavour to serve me. The friends in *Halifax*[1] have requested me to travel with them next year. To do so I gladly consented, subject of course to the approval of Conference, and I have now to solicit your influence in securing that appointment. I do not attempt to conceal from you that I feel very anxious that the Conference would so far favour me, as to send me to that Circuit. I have now been nine years in Scotland. It was uphill work in Perth and Aberdeen, but the difficulties of the last two years and a half in Dundee have all but *crushed my spirit*. I can say that in the strength of God I have done my best for the connexion, I wish I had been able to have done it better. An appointment in England has now become necessary to reinvigorate me Methodistically. I most devoutly hope that you may see nothing in the way to prevent my going to Halifax. Then as to a supply for Dundee next year. If you could by any means spare Mr Ryan[2] of South Shields, he would be the very man. He has been three years in Scotland, *prefers* our Scotch work, and I believe would not only be able to establish our cause here, but also of hastening the period when "Shuffelbottam" will have to leave Dundee. Indeed I would not be surprised if Mr Ryan be sent that he should see "Daniel" fairly out of the Town. At the request of the President, I wrote to Mr R. but he informed me that he was engaged to go to Sunderland. In our Connexion you may find twenty men that would be willing to go to Sunderland, when you would be fast to find one suitable man, who would be willing to go to Dundee in its present circumstances. If you really cannot spare Mr Ryan, there is Mr Eggleston[3] now in Edinburgh, do send him. I am told the President has spoken to him on the subject, and that he does not object. I hear he is a very efficient brother. People say he is about to marry Miss Moulton, a niece of our excellent Representative Mr Roper,[4] now it is possible as Mr Roper knows the circumstances of Dundee that he might object to send his niece and her husband, but I hope you will not think that a sufficient reason why Dundee should be neglected. If I could have it my way I would say send Mr Ryan to Dundee, and Mr Egglestone to Perth. At any rate in justice to the noble cause of Methodism, and to vindicate its claims in the very face of the vilest radicalism, do the best for us you can. When Mr Heald,[5] of Pars Wood, was in Perth, we spoke of Ryan for that station, but a stranger to our Scotch work would do better in Perth than Dundee, and if a brother is to be sent to one of the places who has not been in Scotland before, he had better be sent to Perth. If Mr Moorhouse[6] of Banff could be persuaded to get married this Conference, he would do well for Perth. The Shuffelbottamites I understand are in trouble. They have opened their new Chapel it will seat about 1000, but they have seldom more than 400 present. This I am told is disheartening many of them. At their last half-yearly meeting they were £5. 0. 0 short, and at that time they had not entered on their new premises, which will cost within a trifle of £100 yearly. Say 1200 at 5 per cent *£60. 0. 0* - Ground Rent *£23. 0. 0* - Chapel Keeper *5. 0. 0* - Gass [sic] *6.0.0* - Insurance *3.0.0* which makes *97.0.0* - and the other three, if not more, will be needed for *sundries*. Then Daniel is to have £104. where they are to get 204 yearly I know not, nor do I believe they know. One of the first things they found fault with amongst us was the penny a week at the class, well, they have allowed class meetings to dwindle away almost to noth[in]g, but they have recently appointed persons to collect the penny a week from ev[er]y member. I understand they have now fewer members than when they first opened shop for themselves. They cannot last long. Only send us a good supply this Conference ...

1. Robert Thomson was stationed at Halifax at the 1838 Conference.
2. John Ryan (1811-88), Preacher, South Shields Circuit, 1836-38. At the Conference of 1838, he was stationed at Sunderland, 1838-41.
3. John Egglestone, Preacher, Edinburgh Circuit, 1837-38. He offered for the Mission field; became a Missionary in Australia from 1838; was General Secretary of the Australasian Missions 1858-63 and was President of the Australasian Conference in 1860.
4. Most probably James Rosser, Superintendent of the Aberdeen Circuit, 1836-38.
5. James Heald (1763-1873), Prominent Stockport Methodist: See *Early Victorian Methodism*, p.132.
6. Joseph Moorhouse (1808-91), Superintendent, Banff Circuit, 1837-38. See also Letter No. 55.

57. *From Ralph Wardland*   Glasgow, October 16, 1838

You are probably aware of my having undertaken, at the earnest request of the trustees & relations of the late Dr McAld, the Editorship of his mss. In this capacity, I am expected to prefix to the intended columns a brief memoir of our excellent and learned friend. I am aware of your intimacy with him, and from your being a member of a different religious body, you could not fail to have the best opportunities of observing, not only, in common with others the great general features of his mental and spiritual character, but especially one of its interesting *phases* — his Christian and ministerial *liberal*-mindedness. I have no title, my dear Sir, to ask of you a favour on *my own* account — although I am well-persuaded that, even if I had no other plea, you w[oul]d not refuse me, but the favour I now solicit, is one for which I have a plea you *cannot* resist — your regard to the memory of one whom I know you held in high and affectionate estimation. My request is, that you communicate to me your estimate of the Doctor's character, in whatever features of it, especially, struck you as most remarkably prominent & interesting; along with any such incidents, or letters, as might contribute to the proof and illustration of these. I need not, to *you*, enter into detail. You will at once understand what is wanted, and know what it is in your power, conveniently & with propriety, to communicate trusting to my discretion for the prudent use of any materials or laying me under such instructions as you may consider needful ...

58. *From Johnathan J. Bates*[1]   Edinburgh, May 23, 1839

I have long felt a desire to address you on the subject of Methodism in this Circuit, but hitherto various circumstances have prevented my attempting it, the principal of which circumstances have been the very great demand that is made on your time and attention from the different societies in the Connexion, and also my own want of familiar acquaintace with you to encourage the attempt. At present however, the hope that I shall be serving the cause of God in this circuit, is superior to every other consideration; nor do I think that in writing I shall be thought by yourself, to be acting improperly. I was exceedingly surprised and disappointed[2] when first hearing that I was put down for this circuit, but when I received the representative's letter containing the reasons for that appointment I was perfectly satisfied, and even grateful to find that I enjoyed the favour and confidence of my Fathers and Brethren in the ministry. Since my arrival I have endeavoured, in connection with my colleagues to do what I could for the promotion of God's glory and the good of his Church. I hope our labours have not been in vain, though our success is by no means such as to satisfy us. You are aware that we have raised towards the objects of the Centenary Fund[3] about £230, which to me is really surprising. We have not yet held a public meeting because I was quite satisfied *at that time*, it would have been impossible to have raised more money for the fund, & the attempt would have proved injurious to the minds of our Friends, & also to certain attempts then necessary for the improvement of the Circuit. Prior to my coming to this City the financial affairs of the Circuit had regularly gone back, so that a circuit debt of about £170 had been accumulated. At our second Quarterly Meeting we had just money enough to pay the young man his quarterage, the second preacher a portion of his, while for myself there was not a farthing. I laid the matter before our society, and the people very kindly responded to our appeal. We raised about £60 towards the circuit debt, and have so far increased the income of the circuit, that, at present we have been just able to meet the circuit expenses. I am quite satisfied however that unless some particular effort be made for Methodism in Edinburgh (and surely it will never be suffered to fail in this noble and beautiful Metropolis with its population of 162 thousand) it must either decline, or be *a greater annual expence*. By removals, backslidings, and deaths, our numbers are reduced to about 420, which at an average of 2/1 per member should raise about £43. 15. 0 per quarter; but if our members did not average with class-pence, ticket-money, & collections, more than 2/1 per member, we could not possibly go on even with our large grant. I merely mention this to shew that the members are doing all that they can. If the grant is continued (and we cannot do without every farthing of it) then we may go on with the present system so far as *the circuit is concerned*. But our chapel is in a very declining condition, as to its finances, and unless something be done to improve its condition the cause in this place must e'er long seriously suffer. I can truly say that I deeply sympathise with this people in their distress. They are respectful, kind, and affectionate; but they are not able to do great things or to surmount great difficulties. We have peace in our borders tho' in some individual cases we have had some painful calls for the exercise of discipline. I should have said that in consequence of persons having left the chapel the seats which they occupied have become vacant thro' which and other causes there was a falling off of £15 during the last year. Now I should like to see Methodism in this place rendered more efficient, independant [sic] , & respectable; and if possible I should like to see the annual grant of £138 saved to the Connexion. Now my dear Sir, I have thought a good deal on this subject, but possibly to you my thinking may not appear to savour much of mature judgment or of great experience,. Well, be it so, I will nevertheless shew my scheme. There is at present held by the Trustees a bond of £2000 – there are I think about £400 or £500 borrowed on Interest on the Trust property – there is also a fue [sic] which might be valued at £1400 or 1500 which in the form of a ground rent occasions the Trustees an annual expence of £62. You are aware that there are Baubee[4] collections made at the doors at every service, which collections the Trustees receive. Now if from the Centenary Fund (which through the Divine blessing has been, and I have no doubt will be more productive) a noble grant could be made to give to Methodism a respectable and permanent establishment in the Metropolis of Scotland, the sources now received by the Trustees might be appointed to the maintenance of the ministry & the annual grant from the contingent fund might be saved. I do not think that less than £3000 would fully accomplish the object. With that the bond of £2000 might be cancelled – the Feu might be purchased by taking about £500 more upon Interest on the property leaving about £900 as the whole expence of which the seat rents then would more than provide; the ground-rent of £60 would be saved and the Baubee Collections might then be appropriated to the Quarterly Board and such an arrangement made with the Trustees as would secure to the Contingent Fund the £138 per an[num] . I have now given you my plan merely as indicating my thought and anxiety for the welfare of Methodism in this city, where I should like to see it continue & flourish. I know I am not much versed in the finances of Methodism. and possibly my plan may be thought to be too opposed to some of the principles of our great system. I do not however advocate it, I only take the liberty of laying it before you; happy shall I be if it be the means of originating any scheme for our effectual relief. Without that, I see no alternative, but a continuance of the annual grant to the circuit and an annual grant to the chapel. All our official characters are in such circumstances as to be incapable of doing a great deal towards extraordinary expences and I have reason to believe that persons have been delivered from uniting a church fellowship & *even taking seats*, lest they should incur personal and pecuniary responsibility. I did hope to have had the pleasure of seeing you & conversing with you on the subject of Methodism in this place, but at present that cannot be. I believe Methodism is much wanted in this place & could we have two chapels in the city and spend our strength upon the inhabitants it would I think be better than distributing it among places which have not, neither are likely to repay with any amount of good ...

P.S. When I said that the chapel affairs had gone back £15 during the last year I meant £15 in addition to the former defficiency [sic] the whole amount of annual deficiency is between 40 & 50£ which is met by borrowing money on interest, & that is only a double increase of difficulties, in fact a quickened pace on the road to ruin.[5]

1. Johnathan J. Bates (1799-1883), Superintendent, Edinburgh Circuit, 1838-41. Bates tends to be somewhat pompous and verbose in his writings.
2. Bates's comments that he was 'surprised and disappointed' to be put down for Edinburgh suggests that Wesley Swift's contention that Scotland was regarded as a penal colony by many of the Preachers was justified.
3. The Centenary Fund was established in 1839 by soliciting private donations and public subscriptions from the Societies at home and abroad to commemorate the formation of the first Methodist United Society in 1739. The final report of the Fund in 1843 showed that £126,184 was raised, the bulk of which was spent on the Theological Institution, the Centenary Buildings, the Wesleyan Missionary Society, the relief of distressed chapels and for the support of supernumerary ministers and their widows.
4. See Letter No. 14.
5. At this time, the Wesleyan Association seceders had left Nicolson Square some three and a half years previously. The matter of the debt on the Nicolson Square Chapel had been significantly reduced by the Town Council rent, but the matter of the debt on the Leith Chapel was still largely unresolved. No wonder Bates's mind was exercised as to the best way to proceed to reduce the overall debt and the demands of the circuit upon the Contingent Fund.

59.   *From Johnathan J. Bates*   Edinburgh, July 31, 1839
... In our District Minutes a record is made respecting Haddington,[1] and I find the Stationing Committee have refused appointing a preacher to that place. I have thought that some attempt may be made to unite it to Edinburgh, and if so I think Edinburgh will be injured without Haddington being benefited. We have three preachers appointed to this circuit; but one resides at Leith, the other at Dalkeith 6 miles from Edin[burg]h so that I am virtually left alone in the midst of this large place & immense population. I can assure you that I am often ready to weep because I cannot find time to attend to things as I am expected, and as they require. No one can conceive of the labours and interruptions to which a Superintendent is subject in this city unless he is actually in the place; and unless the Preacher is first and last in everything Methodism cannot (humanly speaking) be maintained.

I hope, by a vigilant attention to the interests of the people, they are really improving in piety altho[ugh] our numbers are greatly diminished. I do not see how I can pay any efficient attention beyond the present circuit. And then as to help from local preachers I have very little to employ. We have seven places[2] and eight local preachers, three or four of whom are advanced in years and incapable of hard work and long journeys; besides the appointments for their own circuit keep them fully employed. The expence also is a matter of serious consideration. We cannot do with a farthing less than we received last year. If less be apportioned the declining state of the Society, which has been check[e]d, will be renew[e]d, and added to the declining state of the Chapel, which we cannot prevent, will hasten Methodism to a close in Edin[burg]h. Now the expence of visiting Haddington, if we had men to send, would be far greater than anything that would be raised. In fact the expence could only be met by grant from the Connexion. From all that I can learn it seems that a young man must be supported at Haddington or the place must be given up entirely; & most people think that to do the latter is preferable. I feel very anxious that it would be expended in this City, where it is immensely needed. I am quite sure that the religion and morality of the Scotch people are amazingly over-rated, while their wide spread Calvanism [sic] and their good opinion of themselves, do very much to prevent the spread of vital godliness. There is a good deal of practical preaching but not anything of a corresponding share of experimental and practical religion. Our good friend Dr Coldstream[3] often says instead of their religion leading them to God, they make a god of their religion. It is surprising also to observe what ignorance and what prejudice exist against the very name of Methodism; and yet a mighty friend of the Kirk said to me some time since he believed we were living it down. I do sincerely wish some thing could be done to bring Methodism more forcibly to bear upon the place & to make it a praise & a glory in this part of the earth. Our missionary meetings have done something to bring it before the public, & several respectable & popular ministers of the Episcopal and Presbyterian Churches have kindly assisted, and thus lent their influence to help us forward. Many pious persons believe it would be an awful thing for Scotland if Methodism were to be withdrawn ...[4]

1. The preacher was withdrawn from Haddington at the 1838 Conference. See Hayes (1977d) op.cit. Haddington had been united with Edinburgh up to 1812, but the then Superintendent, Samuel Kittle, was soon convinced that such a large Circuit was unworkable and for a number of years Haddington was combined with Dunbar in the Dunbar & Haddington Circuit.
2. The seven places referred to were Edinburgh (Nicolson Square), Leith, Dalkeith, Musselburgh, Portobello, Water of Leith (Dean Village) and either Prestonpans or Edmonstone.
3. John Coldstream, M.D. (1806-63), physician in Edinburgh; Secretary of the Medical Missionary Society — associated with the Evangelical Alliance. See also Letter No. 58.
4. This letter gives some idea of the difficulty of administering the Edinburgh Circuit.

60.   *To Thomas Chalmers*   Surrey Chapel Parsonage N.pl.[1]
                                                        April 5, 1840

You are probably aware of the deep & increasing feeling in the minds of many ministers & others in England, in reference to the great subject of Christian Union.[2] Too long had it been the reproach of those who are agreed in all the great rarities of the Bible that they have not manifested brotherly love & cordially recognised each

Plate 10. Rev. Peter Duncan, Chairman of the Edinburgh District, 1841-44;
Chairman of the Edinburgh & Aberdeen District, 1844-47.

Plate 11. Rev. William Lindley, Superintendent of the Aberdeen Circuit, 1842-45.

Plate 12. Rev. Adam Clarke, LL.D., FAS, Founder of Shetland Methodism.

*Plate 13. Rev. Valentine Ward, Chairman of the Edinburgh District,
1812-17; 1821-23; 1827-29.*

Plate 14. Rev. Samuel Warren, Superintendent of the Edinburgh Circuit 1827-30.
An arch opponent of Bunting and founder of the Wesleyan Methodist
Association, 1835.

other as the disciples & servants of one Divine Master. Denominational distinctions have alienated those who hope to dwell with each other in a blessed union through all ages. This ought not to have been so, nor is it necessary nor Christian that it should be so: moreover it has lessened true charity & piety in the church & presented Christianity to the men of the world in an unfavourable & unjust light. Are we to continue to deplore this state of things & to attempt no remedy?

A meeting was recently convened at the Wesleyan Centenary Hall in Bishopsgate Street where we had the great pleasure of seeing about 40 Ministers of various denominations all of whom desired publicly to express their Christian Affection for each other & to recognize each other as ministers of the Lord Jesus Christ. Among them we had your honoured coadjutor the Rev D. Candlish[3] who expressed in his own name & in the name of his brethren a strong desire for a close & affectionate Union of all Protestant Christians because it is scriptural & also because the state of Christendom urgently demands it. At that meeting a committee was appointed to prepare for a public meeting in Exeter Hall & it is now determined that such meeting shall be held by Divine permission on the 1st of June. We hope to have present on that occasion Ministers & private Christians of 10 or 11 denominations. Our object in now addressing you is most respectfully, but most urgently to request that you will meet with us on that spirit stirring & we hope eventful day. The meeting will be devotional & the assembly will be addressed by at least one minister or member of the different denominations then to be convened.

We think that the opportunity will be most appropriate for you to declare in the metropolis of Britain the Catholicity of the Scotch Free Church.[4] Your presence and Gods blessing will add greatly aid the cause of Christian Union so dear to your heart, & among all the services you have rendered to the Church of Christ, such a visit to London may in days yet distant not be reckoned among the least. We are fully aware of your many engagements & pressing duties: & that these will be multiplied during the next month: still we cherish the hope that God will give you strength of body, & move your heart to visit London to plead the message & the Catholicity of the Church of the Living God ...

1. The holograph of this letter is in New College, Edinburgh. CHA 4.
2. The Evangelical Alliance began as a result of lectures given in 1831-32 by Chalmers on Divinity and Church Government — 'The attention and the zeal of Christians have been vastly too much expended on the points on which they differ — now it is to be hoped that the sentiments they hold in common will be the objects of their ... regard'. In 1843 — the Bicentenary of the Meeting of the Westminster Divines — a book on Christian Union appeared by John Henderson. This led to a conference in Liverpool in 1845 and to the formal setting-up on the Alliance in Summer 1846 — partly as an Anti-Popish Association and secondly as a great Home Mission.
3. Robert Smith Candlish (1806-73), Scottish Free Church leader and Minister of Free St Georges, Edinburgh, 1843-73.
4. At this time, no organisation with the name of the Free Church existed. Could this have been a phrase used by Jabez Bunting to describe Chalmers and his party within the Kirk? This letter gives an indication of the extent of sympathy by the Wesleyan hierarchy for the infant Free Church of Scotland. Some of the sentiments expressed contrast sharply with others made by Bunting on other occasions.

61. *From Robert Day*[1]   Glasgow, April 13, 1840

The President[2] has informed me that he intends to spend June the 7th in Scotland, and expects that you, and Dr Alder[3] will accompany him, and so take Aberdeen, Edinburgh and Glasgow the same day and desires me to correspond with you, and Dr A[lder] on the subject. I have written to the President to ask him who is likely to visit Aberdeen, in reply he says "Perhaps Dr Alder may be prevailed upon to go to Aberdeen, for I fear my health will not permit me to under take the journey." You will greatly oblige me by conferring with Dr Alder on these points and favouring me with an early answer, as I am requested to correspond with Mr France[4] on the subject.

I suppose that it is your intention and that of the President to proceed from Scotland to Ireland to attend the Irish Conference ...

1. Robert Day (1794-1884), Superintendent, Glasgow Circuit, 1839-41.
2. Theophilus Lessey (1787-1841), President of the Conference, 1839.
3. Robert Alder, D.D. left the ministry 1853, d.Gibraltar, Dec 31, 1873; one of the Secretaries of the Missionary Society 1833-50.
4. William France, Superintendent, Aberdeen Circuit, 1838-40.

62. *From Samuel Trueman*[1]   Poole, July 28, 1840

Bro[ther] Currelly[2] is put down for Walls circuit in Shetland, he is very much distressed in mind in consequence of his appointment. They have 3 small children the eldest 5 years of age, the second 3½, and the third about 16 months, the youngest child is very delicate. Mrs C expects to be confined in the beginning of September. She is very timid of the water and in her present state could not undertake the voyage.

Currelly is not the man for Shetland. If justice is done to the work of God in Shetland, it will be by the appointment of zealous, devoted young men, that are living in the full spirit of their work. Currelly has not physical, and mental energy for that work. Bro[ther] C will do better in a little country Circuit at home, with a judicious superintendent that will set him an example of active zeal, and patient labour.

In consideration of Mrs Currelly's situation, the inconvenience and expense of removing his young family and Bro[ther] C's unsuitableness for the peculiar work of a Shetland Preacher, I hope you will use your influence and obtain for him an alteration in his appointment ...

1. Samuel Trueman (1790-1868), Superintendent, Poole Circuit, 1839-41.
2. Charles Currelly (1806-68), Preacher, Poole Circuit, 1838-40. In the event, Currelly's next station was not Shetland, but Chichester, where he was super-intendent.

63. *From Charles Currelly*   Poole, July 28, 1840

I hope you will excuse the liberty I have taken in writing you but as it is impressed upon my mind and that impression is strengthened by my knowledge (from what I have seen in the Conference) of the kindness of your disposition and conduct to a brother in distress I thought after much prayer I would yield to it. From my Representative Mr Dowty I learn that I am appointed to *Walls in Shetland.* You will not wonder at my dear wife and myself feeling very distressed in mind at so great a removal when I inform you that I have three little children the eldest of whom is just *five years of age* the youngest one and a half and so delicate that she can neither stand alone nor walk and is quite as much trouble as a babe of six months.

Mrs C's health in general is very delicate sometimes she cannot sit up many hours together in the day and quite expects to be confined in the beginning of September next. Her aversion to travelling by sea at any time is so great that the consequences would likely be very serious. Before Mr Dow.ty left for Conference I did not state the above as I thought he would then be anxious to keep me in this immediate neighbourhood and prevent him from getting for me a better circuit because it was a little farther distant — Since I have been here these two years past I have been studying closely and had it not been that my studies are much interrupted in this circuit by the length of time we are from home I should have consented to remain a third year as several of our friends wished among whom I am respected and useful. I hope Sir you will be so kind as to use your influence in procuring a change for me and get me appointed nearer to where it is likely I shall be comfortable and useful. Were it not for Mrs C's situation and that of the family I should not object for a moment to go anywhere to preach Jesus which is the delight of my heart I have thus freely and in confidence written to you believing in you I should find a father and a friend. No-one knows that I have written you. I have written to the President and my Representative on the subject ...

64. *From Robert Morton*[1]   N.pl. August 6, 1840

My mind is exceedingly troubled & cast down on account of not having a Circuit in England or Scotland.[2] My wife is subject to a spasmatic affliction in the stomach & sometimes she is seised [sic] with it in a most violent manner. We once travelled from Whitehaven to Liverpool in the Steam Packet & the sea sickness created such a violent pain she dare not encounter a sea voyage any more. Besides that our years seem to matter [?] against such an appointment as that of Shetland. And as the Brethren in the District meeting expressed a unanimous opinion in favour of my having a Circuit this Conference, I was led to hope that my Brethren in the Gospel would have made some way for me to have had a Circuit in England. But it appears the Stationing Committee were not willing to do that. Now it remains with the Conference to say whether I shall have any other appointment than that which is given me. If you will speak to the Conference in favour of me having an appointment in England perhaps it will be done. I shall have either to go to Shetland & leave my wife behind or to beg of the Conference to set me down Supernumerary either of which will be very painful to me. I have always been a Methodist ever since I knew anything of religion, & I trust I have the spirit of the work of a Methodist Preacher and am willing to go any where that the Conference in its wisdom might appoint, if it was not for this peculiar family feeling.

   During the last year I have been labouring regularly with the preachers in Wisbech,[3] & I think the Circuit is rising fast into circumstances to take a second married man. Mr Bond[4] can speak to this. I should have been willing to go to Shetland with all [?]

   I now have myself in the hands of the Conference, & will thank you to interest yourself in my favour if you think there [is] any thing fair & just in my request ...

1. Robert Morton (1785-1861), Superintendent, Patley Bridge Circuit, 1840-43.
2. He was not sent to Shetland. See 1 above.
3. He is recorded as a Supernumerary in the Peterborough Circuit, 1839-40.
4. Robert Bond (1802-87), Superintendent, Wisbech Circuit, 1839-42.

65. *From John Killick*[1] Arbroath, August 8, 1840

Knowing that you have some acquaintance with my brother at Newbury I am encouraged to address you in reference to my appointment. At present I believe I am down for Brampton in Cumberland.[2] I have sent a Certificate to Mr France our representative from the medical gentleman who has attended her for the last two years, stating that such is the critical state of Mrs Killick's health that a removal into the South of England is indispensably necessary to arrest the progress of disease & prolong her life ... I do hope for the sake of her who is so near & dear to me the Conference will kindly comply with my wishes. I am Sir able & willing to labour in any Circuit however laborious provided the locality is suitable to Mrs K's constitution.

1. John Killick (1808-86), Superintendent, Arbroath Circuit, 1838-40.
2. Killick was sent to Brampton as Superintendent 1840-42.

66. *From James Kendall*[1] Market Rasen, November 14, 1840[2]

Being called to Edinburgh a short time ago (as a witness in a trial of great importance) I was introduced by my friend the Rev Mr Guthrie[3] (Minister of Gray Friars) to the Rev Dr Chalmers who invited me to breakfast with him. Several literary gentlemen breakfasted with us. Our conversation though miscellaneous was interesting — and the subject of the Doctors letter to you, which accompanies this, formed no inconsiderable part of it.

The Doctor seemed pleased when I told him that though in our Connexion we gave no encouragement to remonstrances founded on mere whim and caprice, *reasonable* remonstrances received respectful attention from the Conference. Still the sole and exclusive *right* of appointing preachers was with ourselves etc., etc. The Doctor likes this and while paying all due attention to the 'powers that be' maintains (and as I think very reasonably), the right of the general assembly, or the local Presbyteries to regulate the appointment of ministers to parishes. But as it is not my intention to discuss so important a point as that contained in the Doctor's letter, I must satisfy myself with stating that the letter was given to me by Dr Chalmers unsealed, that I might read it, and acquaint you with our conversation.

I cannot tell Reverend Sir what are your opinions of the controversy in the Church of Scotland, but for my own part I *at present* incline to think that Dr Chalmer's opinions cannot easily be subverted. I moreover think that if we *as a body* we can help Dr Chalmers and the venerable Church to which he belongs, we *should* do so. I mean however to be prudent ...

1. James Kendall, Preacher, Market Rasen Circuit, 1840-41. Kendall's views on the Scots establishment should be compared with those on the English establishment referred to in *Early Victorian Methodism* p.59.
2. This letter was previously published in *Early Victorian Methodism* p.251.
3. Thomas Guthrie (1807-73) Scots evangelical, minister of Old Greyfriars, Edinburgh, 1837-40.

67. *To Thomas Chalmers* Wesleyan Mission House,[1] Bishopgate St.,
  London, January 23, 1841

Though, from pressure of indispensable business, I have not been able sooner to acknowledge your obliging Letter, received some time ago, be assured that I have not been in any degree indifferent as to its truly momentous subject. It appeared to me that *we* could best give a practical form & value to our unfeigned sympathy with the venerable Church of Scotland, in its present difficulties & struggles, by the instrumentality of our Wesleyan *Press*; viz. The Wesleyan Methodist Magazine, which is official, & circulates 16000 or 18000 copies monthly, and the Watchman Newspaper, which, though, not official, is weekly read by all our principal friends, & in *other* influential quarters. I therefore called on all the Editors of those Periodicals, had long conversations with them, & was pleased to find that their impressions substantially agreed with my own, and that they were quite disposed to render to your good cause such help as was in their power. I also introduced two of them to our common friend, Mr Hamilton of Cheapside, who gave them much information, & furnished them with various Pamphlets on the great question now at issue. I trust that the results will be acceptable & beneficial.

I have now respectfully, but earnestly, to request your kind attention for a few minutes to another subject. When I last had the honour & pleasure of seeing you in London, I mentioned to you the very strong wish, which the Committee of the Wesleyan Society had for many past years entertained, to be favoured with your invaluable assistance in preaching one of the Annual Sermons on behalf of their Funds. Their Anniversary being necessarily held in the last week of April, or first week in May, & your official engagement in Scotland being such as to prevent your visiting London at that time of year, you had more than once expressed your inability to meet our wishes, but had stated in the kindest terms your disposition to befriend us. I therefore took the liberty of asking the great favour of your recommending to us some other suitable Clergyman of the Scottish Established Church, to whom we might apply & of your permission to make respectful use of your name, or of your good offices, in order to give weight to such application. You were then pleased to say that I might write to you on the subject, when the time of exigency should arrive, and that you would be good enough to direct your attention on the matter. That exigency *now* exists in greater force & pressure than ever before. Our funds are quite exhausted; we are greatly in debt already; our expenditure annually much exceeds our income; our Missionary progress is arrested, though our calls & openings for usefulness are multiplied; and some new & powerful impulse is wanted, to extricate us from present embarrassments, and to enable us to re-commence a career, which God had condescended greatly to honour & to bless. Our usual practice has been to secure the services of One Minister, *not* of our own Denomination at our London Anniversary. This year we are in peculiar difficulties on that point; as not a few of our Dissenting Brethren in England stand aloof from us at present, being offended by our support of the Establishment principle in the recent struggles. We therefore venture to look for help in our emergency to some eminent and zealous & catholic-spirited Minister of the Church of Scotland; and anxiously hope that guided and aided by your counsel & influence, we shall not look in vain. Will you Rev. and dear Sir, do us this friendly & important service, by naming to us one or more individuals, whom you would deem *able*, & likely to be willing & at liberty, thus to aid the Cause of Missions as carried on by our section of the Universal Church of our common Saviour. What we should request of such an individual would be, to preach once in Great Queen St. Chapel, on Friday Forenoon, April 30th, & once in City Road Chapel on Sunday, May 2, and to take some part in our Meeting at Exeter Hall, on Monday, Mar 3 r[d] ...

1. The original of this letter is in New College, Edinburgh CHA 4.296.65

68. *From George Cubitt*[1]   Brunswick Place London February 1, 1841

Will you allow me ... to ask for five minutes of your time for me to report progress
on the Scotch Question[2] ... I have devoted all my exertion to the Scotch pamphlets
— a very large number of which I have on the table. I think I have all the aspects
of the subject before me. I increasingly feel that it has many difficulties, & will
require careful, & even delicate handling:- though, at the same time, I feel gratified
in the persuasion that our Wesleyan Position & Principles are such, as will enable
us to examine it honestly — with an impartial regard to the true interests of the
community.

I am of opinion that it is a subject that requires calm exposition — & the
total absence of rhetorical advocacy whether *for* or against. I think that there may
be a decided statement of the truth & righteousness of the case without severity
of censure against those who think differently — & that it may be, up to a certain
point mediatory, without obscurity or vacillation. I wish to be ready to let Mr
Nichol have it early in April ...

1. George Cubitt (1791-1850), Assistant Connexional Editor, 1836-42.
2. Throughout 1841, the constitution and difficulties of the Scottish Church were
   very fully reported in the *Watchman* which on July 21 (p.231) reprinted views
   of the Scottish Guardian on the non-intervention question. See also *Early
   Victorian Methodism* p.237.

69. *From George Cubitt*   London, July 21, 1841[1]

... I had therefore fixed to come to Manchester next Monday — when, last night,
I received a note from the "Elders and deacons of the Scotch Church, Regent
Square" — inviting me to dine, next Tuesday, with them and other friends of the
Church, at the London Tavern, to meet Dr Gordon.[2]

It seems that a Scotch Clergyman from Edinburgh, is to be settled over the
Congregation in Regent Square. His name is Hamilton.[3] Next Sunday Morning,
Dr Gordon is to preach there, and introduce Mr Hamilton to the Congregation.

Now, as we *have* entered into the Scotch question and as neither *yourself*
nor *Mr Beecham* are in town, I thought perhaps it would be important that some
of us should have the opportunity of seeing these good Gentlemen, and learning
from them the actual position of affairs, and there is no one else for it, but myself.
I attach importance to the subject thus, by hearing what these Gentlemen themselves say, and reflecting on it in my own leisure, I mean to obtain a more exact
acquaintance, with the ins & outs of the question, than mere books could give
me ... In a note which I have seen from Mr Burns,[4] (of Edinburgh, I believe) he
says that he has not seen in my article, "a single blunder, either in facts, places,
or dates." adding — "And that is saying a good deal for an *English* article".

I hope that what we have done will do Methodism good. The *Scottish Guardian*
has not only spoken favourably of the Review, of your & Mr Beecham's attendance
at the Meeting held at Exeter Hall, & of the labours of the *Watchman* in the same
cause, but likewise gives this important testimony to Methodism:

"Out of the Establishment, there is no body of Christians comparable to the
Wesleyan Methodists in numbers, in piety, & in zealous exertions for the spread
of the Redeemer's Kingdom. They have more than eleven hundred Ministers, whose
faithful labours have surrounded them with multitudes of attached adherents, full
of vital energy, in every city, town and village of England. They have long been
the salt of that land." — Speaking of the *Magazine*, and earnestly recommending
the July number, he says that it "circulates throughout their *whole Church*"

Under all circumstances, had I not better wait over Tuesday, & accept the
Invitation ...?

1. The bulk of this letter was published in *Early Victorian Methodism* p.266.
2. Robert Gordon, D.D. (1786-1853), Minister of the High Kirk, Edinburgh (now part of New College), 1843-53. Supported Chalmers in founding the Free Church.
3. James Hamilton (1814-67), Assistant Minister, St. Georges, Edinburgh 1838-1839. Minister of the Scotch National Church, Regent Square, London, 1841-1867.
4. Robert Burns, D.D. (1789-1869), Minister of the East Kirk, Perth, 1811. An associate of George Whitefield. A strong anti-patronage man; joined the 1843 Disruption and settled in Canada in 1845.

70.　*From Peter Duncan*[1]　　　　　　　　　Edinburgh, January 5, 1842

It is with no common feelings of reluctance that I trouble you with this letter, but your intimation in your last that it is doubtful whether we may expect you according to the arrangements of the last Conference compels me to write though it will not be necessary for you to reply.

It may be my weakness but I assure you that intimation has already cost me many a sleepless hour. My convinction is this, that our affairs in Scotland in general, but in this City especially, must undergo a thorough investigation, and right or wrong I cannot help thinking that those who would look at them with the most friendly eye are in general those persons who would be the most hostile to such changes as I have no doubt are essential to the continuance of Methodism here. I believe you are both willing and able to help us, but I cannot see how you can have time to acquaint yourself with our numerous concerns unless we are to be favoured with your presence. I would not however urge this for one moment at the hazard of injury to your health but allow me respectfully to submit whether your journey to Scotland might not be arranged as to beneficial in this respect rather than otherwise. — The sum and substance of the matter is simply this. Methodism in Scotland must be restored to its former state as established & left by Mr Wesley. If not an ineffectual struggle only will be carried on against the prejudices of the people which after spending thousands of pounds we must in the end give up. I admit that popular memory be sent and as was the case under Mr Warren and some others a horde of radicals may connect themselves with the Societies, and the "upshot" will be precisely what it has been before:- they will continue till they find that no form of Methodism can blend with radicalism, then after tearing the Societies they will leave us prostrate as we are now.

In this City we have some prosperity. Our increase of members at the Quarterly Meeting was 23, leaving 17 on trial; and between 30 and 40 additional sittings were taken at the late seat-letting. This however gives me but little comfort, for it is impossible to anticipate any such prosperity as will enable us to surmount our pecuniary difficulties. The chapel trust cannot work, and though according to the directions I received in Manchester, I stated our case several months ago to Mr Heald,[2] and subsequently to Mr West,[3] yet neither has sent me any reply — My predecessors have also allowed the Circuit to get into debt to the amount of £160, and although about £80 were raised nearly three years ago for liquidating it, yet during the past three years the income did not meet the expenditure by about £30 per annum, so that Mr Bates left a greater amount of debt than he found. Our house is also like a rag-shop, only there is but little in it, and what is most painful our poor people are exerting themselves far beyond their ability in the hope of seeing better days. They are all in better spirits than I am. They have entered very heartily into your juvenile Christmas offering[4] and if all the Societies do as well you will realise thrice the sum you anticipated.

95

Besides benefiting Methodism directly I cannot doubt but your visiting this place about the time of the General Assembly would be advantageous in another way. I know many of the Establishment Clergy would be happy to see you, and your friendship will neither do us nor themselves any harm. I have seen several of them and their kindness astonished me. I preached in the church of Prestonpans the other Sunday evening for our missions and spent the night at the Manse most agreeably. I have also been at a number of meetings in Ayrshire and the clergy in several places some of whom are on different sides in their church controversy, have lent their churches for Wesleyan Missionary Sermons. Do fix I beseech you to come and see us if possible...

1. Peter Duncan (1798-1862), Superintendent, Edinburgh Circuit, 1841-44.
2. James Heald, Parrs Wood, Stockport, See *Early Victorian Methodism* p.132.
3. Francis A. West (1800-69), Secretary, Chapel Committee 1834-54; President of the Conference, 1857.
4. In 1842, the Juvenile Christmas offering to the missions had raised an additional £5000 for the Methodist Missionary Society. See *Minutes* 1842, p.372.

71.　*To John Beecham*[1]　　　　　　　　　　Manchester, January 13, 1842[2]

I have just received your letter, &c of yesterday; but am really too unwell to be capable of thinking, much less of writing, to any good purpose about anything...

It is rather hazardous to affix one's signature to a document, which one has never read. I wish a *copy* of the request to Dr Chalmers had been sent me. But if it be simply what you state, and *you* approve of the wording of it, as committing us to *nothing more*, you have authority to append my name. I heartily wish that Dr. C may consent. It would be sure to do good.

... I have also given Mr Scott[3] for Mr Hoole,[4] a letter from Shetland with an order for £50, as missionary balance from that District, which, when he receives it, he will please to acknowledge in the usual form ...

1. John Beecham (1786-1856), General Secretary of the Wesleyan Missionary Society 1831-55.
2. Part of this letter was published in *Early Victorian Methodism* p. 270.
3. John Scott (1792-1868), Preacher, London (City Road) Circuit, 1842-43. President of the Conference 1843.
4. Elijah Hoole (d.1872 aet.74), Missionary Secretary 1837-72.

72.　*From Peter Duncan*　　　　　　　　　　Edinburgh March 25, 1842

I write to the President[1] by this post and submit the following plan of your visit for his approval, hoping both you and he will find it convenient, viz.

Sunday 29th May	Missionary Sermons in Edinburgh & Glasgow
Monday 30th	Glasgow Missionary Meeting at which you will both be expected
Tuesday 31st	A Sermon in Glasgow
Wednesday 1st June	District Meeting in Edinburgh, Missionary Meeting in the evening
Thursday 2nd June	District Meeting and Missionary Meeting in the forenoon & Sermon in the evening
Sunday 5th	Aberdeen.

I hope nothing will occur to prevent your accompanying the President. You may rest assured your presence was never more necessary in Scotland than it is now. I am quite certain our affairs must undergo a thorough investigation in order to their being placed on a proper basis. Excepting yourself and Mr Grindrod,

I do not know of anyone else who in those matters could be of any service to us. But I have been informed that he is seriously ill, and were it otherwise there are other things which render your visit most desirable and for which no-one can be your substitute.

The General Assembly commences its sittings on Thursday 19th May and closes on Monday 30th. Let me urge your being here as early as you can at least on the week beginning with the 22nd. I have mentioned to one or two of the clergy that we expect you with the President, and I believe they are almost as anxious to see you as I am. Mr Guthrie told me that if you came they will secure you a place in the body of the church, that you might not be annoyed by any pressing &c. I think this matter is of no little importance to ourselves, and you cannot but know, that in this no one can supply your place. The truth is, that if you cannot accompany the President, it will be of no use whatever to have any other person. The Missionary collections might be a little more but that little would be counterbalanced with travelling expenses. That, however, is but a trifle. We want Methodism in this country set right and I know God has given you the ability to do it & I believe the inclination also. On the subject of your visit I have just to observe that on the 29th May when the sermons will be preached in Edinburgh and Glasgow, we shall of course expect you to preach here.

We have finished our Quarterly Meeting and we shall have to report about 20 more members this year than the last. There would have been more but for an uncommon number of removals from Leith. The congregations are improving a little, but not much. But could our chapel affairs be adjusted, and our work established according to the old Scottish system, I have no fear of ultimate success in this city.

1. James Dixon, D.D. (1781-1871), President of the Conference, 1841.

73. *From Peter Duncan*   Edinburgh, April 5, 1842
I fear you think me troublesome but I cannot help it. I had yesterday an hours conversation with Dr Candlish, in course of which I adverted to our expectation of seeing you in Edinburgh along with the President. He had not heard of it before, but the moment it was mentioned he was evidently delighted, and instantly proposed you preaching in his church, for which he seemed uncommonly anxious. Now although I doubt whether your preaching in St George's Church will be felt by you as an additional attraction to Edinburgh, yet it is certainly such an opportunity of being serviceable to our poor depressed cause in this city as has never been presented before, and may never be presented again. I cannot help viewing this as a call from God and cannot but think you will see it in the same light. This is another service for which you cannot find a substitute.

Dr C. told me that his pulpit is already engaged for Sunday the 22nd May, but on the 29th when we expect you it is at liberty, but he desired me to write as early as possible that he might know your decision, I presume lest there might be some other application ...

74. *From John Tindall*[1]   Portadown, April 20, 1842
In the hope that your health & engagements will allow of you accompanying the President in his approaching visit to Scotland, I take the liberty of very respectfully soliciting the favour of your honouring us by spending an evening at least in Alnwick on your way thither & of affording us your aid at our annual Missionary Meeting. As often as it could be accomplished the services of the President and his companion have been secured by our Alnwick friends much to their gratification & much to the interest of the cause of Methodism & its Missions ...

97

This is the third week of deputation service in which I am now engaged in the North of Ireland ...

1. John Tindall (1827-91), Preacher, Alnwick Circuit, 1840-41. Son-in-law of the Rev. Valentine Ward.

75. *From Peter Duncan*   Edinburgh December 17, 1842

I am sure you will excuse my troubling you with this, but I have nothing to ask but your sympathies and prayers. We received notice yesterday that our law case[1] which was decided against us will be settled as to expences next week. The taxation of costs is appointed for Wednesday and the Trustees have received warning to be ready with the money by that time. We held a meeting last night and a long and sorrowful one it was, but we can do nothing for the truth is we have neither money nor credit. I have written to the President[2] and to Mr Heald, and indeed, with the exception of a few sleepless hours have been at my desk since 11 o'clock last night. If help cannot be obtained our poor trustees must be utterly ruined and our cause in this City will be entirely quenched? Our congregations of late have been rising, and no fewer than 32 additional sittings have been let at the late term. Though I suppose as I am a trustee ex-officio, I am equally liable with the others I feel their sufferings more than my own. They reflect on no-one and their the utmost attachment to Methodism. The spirit of the Society also affects me much. Though in the greatest poverty their contributions to the Worn-Out Preachers fund will average 8d per member and the late increase of congregation has diffused no common joy through the whole of them. I feel most of all from the fear that occurrences of a most disgraceful nature, will be brought before the public, but in which the people had no part only to resist them with the most determined opposition.[3]

I have had letters lately from Perth, Dundee, Aberdeen, Arbroath & Montrose and in all these places the congregations are increasing and their prospects such as many years have not intensified. In Perth, however, some of the troubles of last year[4] are not settled though the Society and congregation are prospering. I am under the necessity of going there on Monday, though the state of my health rather requires me to stop at home. My voice gets very little better and if it do not improve before Conference I fear I shall be under the necessity of sitting down for at least a year;[5] but I feel I am in God's hands and can safely leave all to him, but I have been more frequently unable to preach within the last four months than all the last twenty years put together.

I have only to request which I do most earnestly an interest in your prayers. My present depression is more than I can describe. I trust God will open a way for us though for the present all is dark.

1. The lawsuit relating to the Wesleyan Association secession in Edinburgh. See Hayes (1976a, 1977a, 1978a).
2. John Hannah, D.D. (1792-1867), President of the Conference, 1842.
3. This must refer to some of the activities of the Association in trying to discredit Wesleyan Methodism.
4. The troubles at Perth in 1841 concerned the departure of the Rev Joseph Sykes (1810-97), Superintendent, Perth Circuit in August 1842, without settling the manse rent and gas bill. See (1974) 'The Trials and Fortunes of Methodism as it was', *Journal of the Scottish Branch of the Wesley Historical Society* 3(1), 22.
5. i.e. become a supernumerary.

76.   *From John Beecham*   Wesleyan Mission House London
                                                      January 14, 1843[1]

I have just seen Mr Hamilton again and have copied on a subsequent page the para-graph in the petition which embodies the request to Dr Chalmers;[2] and which I think you will see substantially accords with the brief description I gave you in my last. I think I told you that the Duke of Argyll heads the petition, and that Messrs Plumptree[3] and Hardy[4] M.P.s had also signed it. Yesterday I find the Hon and Rev Mr Villiers, Rector of St George's, Bloomsbury;[5] the Hon and Rev Baptist Noel;[6] Rev Mr Beamish of Trinity Chapel,[7] Conduit Street, the Rev Mr Bradley of Clapham;[8] Isaac Taylor of Ongar;[9] and a few others have added their names. Mr Hamilton in-forms me that he and his friends have been anxious to select no more than a very select list of signatures, and I understand that they have now got nearly the number they wished, about 40 or 50 names. As he is very anxious to send off the petition today, I have ventured to avail myself of your kind permission and have affixed your name as well as my own.

I send you herewith a copy of *The Times* of this morning, containing the answer of Sir James Graham[10] to the Scotch Memorial etc. Mr Hamilton thinks that there is now only one course left; but is of opinion that the Memorialists will not separate from the Church before the meeting of the General Assembly, when they will make their act the *Act* of the *Church*, whatever that Act may be.

I very much regret to hear so poor an account of your health. I hope you will take all possible care of yourself and not give way to desponding feelings respecting your inability to do what you could wish. Thank God, I am feeling pretty well, and am endeavouring to clear our way as much as possible, by getting on with our foreign correspondence etc, and preparing for the next General Report ...

Extract from the Petition

We deem it desirable that the subject should now be followed up by a further course of lectures on the questions how far the dependence of National Churches upon the state for temporal provision is compatible with their independence in spiritual things: how far these two principles admit of being harmonized — and whether it is in their combined practical operation, that a well-founded exception may be entertained of most effectively accomplishing under the Divine blessing the great objects of religious establishments in the moral and religious instruction of the community.[11]

1. This letter was previously published in *Early Victorian Methodism* p.280.
2. In 1838 Thomas Chalmers had given a celebrated course of lectures in London, defending the principles of national establishments. He was now to be asked to define the limits of the rights of the state over the established church.
3. John Plumptree, M.P. for East Kent, 1832-47.
4. John Hardy (c.1773-1855), M.P. for Bedford, 1832-37; 1841-47.
5. Henry Montagu Villiers (1813-61), Rector of St George's, Bloomsbury, 1841-56; Bishop of Carlisle, 1856; Bishop of Durham, 1860.
6. Baptist Wriothesley Noel (1798-1873), leading evangelical and minister of St John's Chapel, Bedford Row, 1827-48; became a Baptist, 1848.
7. Henry Hamilton Beamish, anti-Tractarian controversialist; vicar of Kinsale and incumbent of Trinity Chapel, London, 1832-62.
8. Charles Bradley (1789-1871), incumbent of St James's Chapel, Clapham, 1829-1852.
9. Isaac Taylor (1787-1865), artist, inventor, and, as author of *The Natural History of Enthusiasm* (1830), *Fanaticism* (1833) and other works, celebrated as a lay theologian. On staff of the *Eclectic* Review, 1818, began a controversy with the Tractarians, 1839-40.

99

10. Sir James Graham (1792-1861), Home Secretary, 1841-46. At the end of 1842, following the decision of the House of Lords in the Auchterarder case, Graham had received a memorial from between four and five hundred Scots ministers threatening to resign their livings if they were further subjected to the jurisdiction of the civil courts in matters spiritual. On January 4, 1843 Graham had replied somewhat brusquely that the Kirk was demanding that her proceedings should be beyond the cognizance of the courts of law and was claiming the right to decide for herself what were spiritual matters and what were not.

11. This extract is preceded by a short paragraph briefly referring to the *fact* of Dr Chalmers having delivered a course of lectures on the Establishment Question; and it is followed by another paragraph, in conclusion, briefly disclaiming all *party,* and *political* motives, expressing also the opinion that the present state of the Scotch Church furnishes an additional reason for such a course of lectures as is now requested.

77. *From Robert Murray McCheyne*[1]   St. Peters, Dundee March 6, 1843

I am favoured with yours of 28th ult[im]o and I would have answered you sooner but was desirous of laying your request before my Eldership. I did so this evening and have their nearly concurrence in my undertaking the service you desire.

I desire always to gather assuredly that the Lord calls me before I can go anywhere with comfort. I trust he does so in this instance and therefore willingly comply with your desire.

You will kindly send me notice of the motion which I am to have the privilege of moving or seconding ...

1. Robert Murray McCheyne (1813-43), Minister of St. Peters, Dundee 1836-1843. Appointed 1839 as one of a Deputation from the Church of Scotland on the Conversion of the Jews. A saintly character, anxiously devoted to his ministry and a successful preacher of the Gospel. See A. Scott (ed.) (1925) *Fasti Ecclesia Scoticanae*. 5. Synods of Fife and of Angus & Mearns, 340 (Edinburgh).

78. *From William Robert Ellis*[1]   24 Chancery Lane London[2]
March 14, 1843

The London Wesleyan Ministers have recently given a public expression of their feeling in favour of the Scotch Church. Would it be advisable to give those of the general body of the Wesleyans who hold similar opinions an opportunity of making them publicly known to their Scotch Brethren? And if so what mode would be the best for such a purpose? A meeting of the Wesleyans friendly to the Scotch Church might be called, and at that meeting the true position of that Church might be explained, and resolutions passed approving of the determination of its ministers; and parties might be named who would receive subscriptions for its support. It is not improbable that such a meeting in London would be followed by similar meetings in the country. Or if it be thought inexpedient to risk such a meeting, might not circulars be addressed to such of the Wesleyans as may be supposed likely to give inviting them to subscribe; or may not some means be adopted enabling the Wesleyans to assist the cause as Wesleyans? If it be thought well to adopt any plan for such purpose is the present time for its adoption on the principle that *bis dat qui cito dat,*[3] and because the matter is now before the public mind? Or would it be better to wait until the ministers have actually left their livings? Or is the Wesleyan body too little informed or too little interested about the matter to make any attempt to elicit a public expression of its feelings towards the Scotch Church prudent?...

100

1. William Robert Ellis, equity draughtsman and conveyancer; d.1883 aet.76.
2. This letter was previously published in *Early Victorian Methodism* p.282.
3. 'He who gives quickly, gives double'.

79. *From William Vevers*[1]   Derby, March 14, 1843[2]

...I greatly admire your petition on Scotch affairs, and think with you that a
very heavy blow will be struck at the Establishment in this country. The time
has arrived when we as a body must distinguish between the Church and the clergy.
I am sorry to say that though in the towns a few of the clergy are tolerant, yet in
the country places they are our bitterest foes. They are certainly the greatest
enemies to their own Establishment ...

1. William Vevers, Superintendent, Derby Circuit, 1842-45.
2. Part of this letter already published in *Early Victorian Methodism* p.283.

80. *From James Beckwith*   Dundee, March 23, 1843

I perceive from the *Watchman* of this work that it was intended for the Rev.
Mr McCheyne of this place to preach one of your Anniv[ersar]y Sermons for the
present year. It becomes, however, my painful duty to inform you that Mr M'Cheyne
died this morning of Typhus fever, which has been raging in this Town for several
months. Mr McCheyne was undoubtedly a good young man, but whoever could
have thought of recommending him for the above occasion, I cannot conceive;
the intelligence of it here was perfectly astounding. As you will need a substitute
for Mr McCheyne, I would just mention the Rev. Jno. Roxburgh of St John's
Parish here, who is very popular and was selected by the last General Assembly
to preach before the Lord High Commissioner.

I think he would not object to serve you and as far as I can judge would
answer your purpose ...

81. *From Peter Duncan*   Edinburgh March 27, 1843

Some considerable time ago, I took the liberty of sending you a letter giving an
account of our painful circumstances in connection with the unfortunate law-suit
in which this Trust is concerned. I heard from Mr Newstead[1] that you felt a deep
interest in that matter which is the reason by which I am induced to write you at
present. This letter like the other requires no reply.

At the time I wrote you, we were warned that the account would be taxed
on a certain day, and that as it was likely the Lord Ordinary[2] would then "modify"
the expences we must be ready with the money. The account of the opposing
lawyers was presented for taxing. It amounted to £115, of which no less than
£35 was struck off.[3] We have been in fear that every day would bring us the decision
of his Lordship, but through mercy he has not decided yet, and the Court[4] rose
a week ago, and will not sit again until the middle of May, so that I have now the
expectation that it will be near Conference, before this blow can be inflicted. In
whatever way the costs may be modified, we shall not get out for less than £300.

Things are still looking up on the Circuit. We have had indeed a falling off of
numbers, arising from the failure of small country Societies, which in a great
measure consisted of English People, who have been forced to return home on
account of the failure of employment. In the City also there was a falling off of
numbers through the leaving of a number of very young people from the Sunday
School, whom I found on trial when I came to the circuit. But our number is
quite made up, and of a very different class of people though they are still poor.
The increase of the congregation is now visible to all. My highest expectations in

coming here have been realised at last and were it not for pecuniary embarrassments from which no increase can possibly be anticipated which can give the smallest relief, all my fears would be dissipated. In Dalkeith, our prospects were never more pleasing. The chapel there will hold about 240 people. A year ago, the evening congregation amounted only to about 40, but the chapel is now well filled, and indeed I have seen it literally wedged and of the most respectable persons in this town. In the forenoon and afternoon, the congregations have increased, more than one third. The number of members was 31; this quarter 42. Leith is very little improved, and I fear there is but little prospect of improvement which cannot be surprising to them who know its most melancholy, but disgraceful, history.

For the last two weeks my voice has been considerably better, though it is still very bad, but I have now some hope that by God's blessing I may be able to go on with my work. For some time I have been busy in collecting the accounts of our chapels in this country with the view of preparing for the Conference according to its resolution of last year,[5] but I intend to do nothing more than give a simple statement of facts, and leave others to say what ought to be done. I shall not ask for one farthing; but all may rest assured that the work here cannot go on fettered as it is with ruinous chapel debts. In England such debts are the result of imprudence at the very worst. I wish it could be said that imprudence is the very worst here, but it is not so and yet the innocent are the sufferers. If adequate relief can be given, well; if not, I shall ask to be withdrawn from a field in which the result can be nothing but defeat and disgrace.

I suppose by this time you have heard of the death of the Rev Mr. Cheyne of Dundee whom you expected at your Anniversary. His loss will be severely felt. I rejoice in your Petition to the House of Commons. It produced an excellent effect here. Indeed, the state of public feeling was never so favourable to us before, and if our fetters would only allow us to advance, we might yet see something worthy of Methodism, but I confess I have little hope, and the extinction of our cause seems to me almost as inevitable as the disruption of the established church...

1. Robert Newstead (1789-1865), Superintendent, Second Leeds (Oxford Place Chapel, etc.) Circuit, 1843-46.
2. The Lord Ordinary is a Judge of the Court of Session.
3. See Hayes (1976a). The final bill for legal costs paid by the trustees was £65. 0. 0.
4. The Court of Session is the Supreme Civil Court in Scotland.
5. In 1842, when dealing with chapel affairs, the Conference resolved that Schedule books were to be provided for each District in which the particulars of each application to the Chapel Fund should be registered and that the Chairman of the District be required to compare these Schedules year by year, & to see that proper local exertions were made for the relief of each case before being presented to the District Meeting. (See *Minutes* p. 380-389.)

82.   *From John Beecham*   Wesleyan Mission House
                                                          London, June 21, 1843[1]

I snatch a moment to write to you a few lines on Scotch affairs.

The deputation are evidently producing already a considerable effect. On Sunday morning Mr Guthrie preached, as I am told, a most powerful sermon in Mr Hamilton's church,[2] which was crowded with that very description of persons whom it is most desirable to interest in the affairs of the Free Church. Several *very distinguished* persons were present.

Last night he preached again at Woolwich. Tonight the first public meeting is to be held at Mr Burn's Church, London Wall; Patrick Stewart Esq. M.P.[3] to take the chair. I am going thither, and have made a half-promise to say a little on the occasion.

On Friday night, another public meeting will be held in Dr Leifchild's chapel;[4] and on Monday evening we are to have one at the Centenary Hall. On the subject of this arrangement I need not dwell, as Mr Farmer writes to you about it by this evening's mail.

The great meeting at Exeter Hall is to be held on Wednesday evening next, as was arranged when you were present at Mr Nisbett's.[5] The Marquis of Breadalbane[6] has consented to take the chair.

Now my principal object in writing is to convey to you the earnest wish of the Committee that you would endeavour to attend: a wish in which I most earnestly participate. Everything is going on most prosperously; but I feel it most acutely that at so important a juncture I am left so much alone. I am doing my best in a prudent way in meeting with and assisting our friends; but I should like for the honour of our Connexion, and for the advantage of the common cause, that you were with us; and I must beg of you, if you can do it consistently with your health, to get home in time to dine at Mr Farmer's, with our Scotch friends, on Tuesday, and attend the meeting at Exeter Hall the day after. If you could only move a vote of thanks to the chair, or say half a dozen words at any other period of the meeting, so that we might have your name mixed up with it, I am sure it would be of immense service. Do come if possible.[7]

The Marquis of Lorne[8] has sent his adhesion to the Free Church. I am afraid our friends Hamilton, Lorimer[9] and Burns will have to turn out of their churches shortly. I feel especially for them...

1. This letter was previously published in *Early Victorian Methodism* p.289-291.
2. Regent Square Presbyterian Church. See Letter No. 69.
3. Patrick M. Stewart, Liberal M.P. for Renfrewshire, 1841-46.
4. John Leifchild (1780-1862), minister of Craven Chapel (Independent), Bayswater, 1831-54.
5. Probably James Nisbett (1785-1854), bookseller and publisher; one of the founders of the Sunday School Union, and a Sunday school teacher at the Scotch Church, Swallow Street, 1803; for a time a follower of Edward Irving.
6. John Campbell, 2nd Marquis of Breadalbane (1796-1862), a strenuous supporter of the Free Church.
7. Cf. M.C.A. MSS Barnard Slater to Jabez Bunting, May 26, 1843: '... I hope my dear Dr., that you, or your dear William, or some person of character and name among us, will prepare to present, if possible on the first day of Conference, some suitable resolutions in reference to the deeply injured, but most spiritual and excellent, Church of Scotland, by way of sympathy etc... The free church of Scotland very much resembles the Wesleyan body now; and Dr Chalmers and Dr Hannah hold it appears to me very similar offices.' See also Joseph Lawton to Jabez Bunting, October 7, 1843.(M.C.A.)
8. George Douglas Campbell, Marquis of Lorne, later 8th Duke of Argyll (1823-1900).
9. Peter Lorimer (1812-79), minister of Riverside Terrace Presbyterian Church, 1836 till the Disruption, 1843. Professor of Theology at the new English Presbyterian College, 1844; Principal, 1878.

83. *From Peter Duncan*   Edinburgh September 30, 1843

... We have been scarcely able as yet to set fairly to work since Conference, but I am thankful to be able to say that we are not weary nor faint in our minds.

Our congregations in the City are better than I have ever seen them at this season. Mr Williams[1] has entered on his work at Leith with great spirit and both there and in this city he has been received with great cordiality. In Leith, I never saw more than 150 persons at the Chapel but Mr W[illiams] had twice that number last Sunday evening and several have begun to meet in class. It is certain that there has been no such excitement there for many years, so that I hope even there our labour will not be in vain.

I was much afraid that Mr Perks[2] would be much discouraged in Dalkeith exhibiting as it does such a contrast to the previous scene of his labours, but I am happily mistaken. He is delighted with his appointment and our truly excellent people there have given him a cordial Christian welcome. The Society in Dalkeith is a relic of the old Scottish Methodism and according to its numbers I have never seen its equal. There has been considerable improvement there as to congregations. We have nearly thrice as many who attend the chapel on the forenoon of the Lord's Day as we had two years ago, and we are still looking upward.

Our Financial District Meeting was held last week, and though we had some difficulty, owing to the reduction of the grant,[3] yet we had neither a murmuring word nor I believe a murmuring thought. The majority of the brethren are more than satisfied with their appointments. Their hearts appear to be in our work in this District & most of them would not exchange their stations for Circuits in England. We are all looking forward to a prosperous year...[4]

1. Thomas Williams (left the ministry 1854), Preacher, Edinburgh Circuit, 1843-1846. Probably stationed at Leith. See also Letter No. 85.
2. George T. Perks (1819-77), Preacher, Edinburgh Circuit, 1843-45; President of the Conference, 1873. Probably stationed at Dalkeith. See also Hayes, (1978b).
3. At the Conference of 1843, the Edinburgh and Aberdeen Districts were combined and the grant from the Contingent Fund was reduced from £620 to £579. See *Minutes* 1843.
4. This letter indicates a change of heart by Duncan after his depression in 1842.

84.   *From Peter McOwan*[1]   Bristol, January 27, 1844

... I am very sorry for the news you have received from Scotland; and I regret that a deliberate and unexaggerated conviction of personal unfitness for the services you assign to me, should have laid me under the necessity of adding to your embarrassment. My judgment still is, that the work "is too high for me" and that the credit & general interests of the good cause are likely to suffer, if I accede. But if no new light is shed on the subject, and if you are still shut up, I dare do no other than submit myself to God & you, to be led as a blind man, in a way that I knew not, trusting that He will make darkness light before me & crooked things straight.

You kindly profess a readiness to do anything in your power to meet my wishes in other points but after surrendering my judgment to you respecting the Wednesday evening services I feel disposed to leave the rest to your kind consideration. I may however state that if I preach twice on Sunday, which I do not decline, I may find myself under the necessity of requesting to be excused from taking any part in the *Monday* Meeting...[2]

1. Peter McOwan (1795-1870), Preacher Bristol, King Street Circuit 1842-44. Formerly Preacher, Edinburgh Circuit 1821-22.
2. Although the *Minutes* for 1843 fail to indicate that McOwan was included in the Missionary Deputation, this letter suggests that he was asked to participate in special services in some way, probably in his capacity as General Treasurer of the Schools.

85. *From Thomas Williams*   Leith, February 19, 1844

... In Methodism we are moving on in Scotch style.[1] Slowly our Congregations are increasing a little, but I see no prospect of any great increase in members. I preached four times yesterday: one in the open air on the Pier. I think it would be much better to give up Methodism in all the Country parts and confine it to the three Cities; or to separate Scotland in the same way as Ireland is from England. Some change must be made, we cannot go on much longer as we are ...

1. Presumably he meant slowly. This letter contrasts sharply with the optimism shown by Peter Duncan during his stay in Edinburgh, but Leith had more than its fair share of difficulties, financial and otherwise.

86. *From Peter Duncan*   Edinburgh March 21, 1844

... On the greater part of our circuits we are rather looking up. We shall have a small increase here, but in Edinburgh the occupancy of our chapel by Mr Guthrie's congregation[1] makes considerably against us; but we are poor and what can we do.

From all the Scottish Societies the tidings I hear are pleasing. There is peace and a degree of prosperity. In Glasgow they are still in a very painful state, and from what I can learn, a division is likely to be the ultimate result.[2] Something must be done for our cause in that city, but no man who knows the Circuit will I fear consent to go...

1. After the Disruption of the Church of Scotland in 1843 'Thomas Guthrie and his congregation sought refuge in the Methodist Chapel in Nicolson Square, and there he preached till his new church on the Castle Hill was erected'. See Guthrie Rev Dr. Thomas (1877) *Autobiography and Memoirs by his Sons* (David K. and Charles J. Guthrie), Daldy, Isbister & Co. London. Dr. Guthrie's congregation paid the Nicolson Square Trusteees £150 per annum for this privilege. See Hayes (1976a) p.142. The unsatisfactory nature of this arrangement is highlighted in a letter written by Peter Duncan to the Rev. John Hannah (then President) on 1st April 1843: 'I have thought seriously of the results to our work should we have to occupy the school below the chapel for our morning services. Several of our most respectable hearers and members could not attend on account of the excessive damp of the place, and such is my own state that I doubt if I should be able to preach in it at all. For the last six months I have only been able to go down to *close* the prayer meetings which are held there. I could not remain all the time, and only go down for a few minutes, more for the purpose of showing that I am not inattentive to their propriety, than for any thing else. I have had some conversation with the Trustees Stewards who strongly deprecate our return to that uncomfortable place, especially as this congregation after so long a collapse is beginning to rise, & though it must not be thought they would stand in the way of any arrangement which might be thought proper, there is another plan which if you thought proper to sanction would not I think be at all objected to and which would be productive of little or no injury; that is if both congregations could make their arrangements as to occupy the chapel at different hours. If Mr Guthrie's people would agree to this, which I daresay they would it would be far better for us in every respect. If so, were they to agree to give us only £100 per annum according to that figure instead of £150, I believe it would be no disadvantage to us even in a pecuniary sense. It is this therefore which I would recommend, and I think all our people can be very easily persuaded to submit without the slightest dissatisfaction to the little inconvenience a change in the hours of the morning service might occasion.

105

I think you will now be able to dispose[?] of the whole matter and to give your notice which as soon as I receive it I should see Mr G. and his people, and arrange accordingly. Should they object to the plan I have suggested above, you will be good enough to say whether we ought to go to the schoolroom and hazard the result. I do not believe that our people would make any obstinate opposition, though I cannot doubt but that the effect on our cause would be injurious. Whether any pecuniary advantage which might arise from so letting the chapel would be a compensation is of course very uncertain...'

2. This must refer to the events leading up to the division of the Glasgow Circuit into Glasgow West and Glasgow East in 1851. There is strong circumstantial evidence to suggest that there was much dissatisfaction between the two main Chapels, John St and Green St. The Calton Chapel organisation was ramshackle in the extreme; no regular Leaders Meeting minutes being kept before 1860. In addition the majority of the Green St Trustees had either died or moved from Glasgow by 1844, leading to great complications when the Trust finally came to be renewed in 1850. No direct evidence survives, however, as to the precise reasons underlying the division. See Glasgow Circuit Records, City of Glasgow Record Office.

87. *From Peter Duncan*   Edinburgh, August 23, 1844

On Monday morning I received a letter from Mr McLean intimating by your direction a wish that if possible I should proceed to Londŏn. I sincerely thank you for this other mark of the interest that you feel in our poor cause in this District. You may rest assured that it was a painful disappointment to myself as I expected great advantage from your instructions in the present state of our work. I had made up my mind to remain in Birmingham until Wednesday, but a letter from home received a few minutes before I received that from Mr Maclean hurried me from Birmingham the following morning. I can now only look forward to your visit which I believe will be considered a great blessing ...

88. *From Peter Duncan*[1]   Glasgow, September 2nd, 1844

I arrived in this City on Friday evening & preached yesterday morning in John Street, and in the other place in the evening. From many of the people I received a hearty welcome, but on my returning home in the evening I found the enclosed note [missing] with which I trouble you. I have never seen the writer to my knowledge, but I understand he is a young married man, a clerk in a warehouse. He is an Englishman and but a very few years resident in this City. He was made a Leader and [?] by Mr Heys,[2] and I have been told he has been very busy in endeavouring to get up an opposition to my coming to Glasgow. Should he write you and you should notice his letter, I respectfully submit whether it might not be for the good of this poor and long-distracted Circuit to give the writer kindly advice, but I leave the whole matter with you.

1. Peter Duncan, Superintendent, Glasgow Circuit, 1844-47; Chairman of the Edinburgh & Aberdeen District, 1844-47.
2. Robert Heys (1791-1857), Superintendent, Glasgow Circuit, 1841-44.

89. *From William Lindley*[1]   Aberdeen, October 15, 1844

It is my painful duty to inform you that the Revd W[illia]m Wears[2] has written to the Trustees of the Long Acre Chapel, Aberdeen, refusing to comply with the order of the last Conference, by which, he was required to remit to them, the sum of £16 10/- being money he took from the Trust-Concern, "without their knowledge or consent".

106

The Trustees are certainly much annoyed by Mr Wears' conduct. Hitherto letters from myself, from the Trustees, from the Chairman of this District, as well as, the order of the two last Conferences, have failed to lead Mr Wears to refund the money. But the Trustees, request me to say, that in making this Communication to you, they have the fullest confidence in obtaining redress ...

1. William Lindley (1809-90), Superintendent, Aberdeen Circuit, 1842-45.
2. William Wears (1778-1869), Superintendent, Aberdeen Circuit, 1841-42.

90. *From Peter Duncan*   Glasgow, November 18, 1844

From what transpired after my first coming to Glasgow I have thought you would wish to know something of this long agitated circuit. The feeling of hostility to myself was far more inveterate than I ever imagined. That however is now almost extinct as far as I can learn while I have conceded nothing.

But the work is far from being accomplished. There has long been a leaven of discontent and disaffection, in this circuit, which has been much increased through the broils and quarrells [sic] of the last three years.[1] Till this be effectually removed nothing like permanent prosperity can be expected. Should God give me influence enough to neutralise this and restore a proper confidence in our ministry I shall ever feel thankful for coming to Glasgow. I am quite sure however that this will require some time, but this is an object I never lose sight of.

I have with as much caution as I could intimated the necessity of dividing the Circuit, by separating the greater part of those country places from the City which lie between it and Edinburgh.[2] There is in that District a field of usefulness which Scotland has never presented to us before. We have already 500 members there, and the division I contemplate would bring two additional ministers (a married and a single) on the ground. If this can be effected it must be done without any help from the Contingent Fund and would save Methodism in this part of the country. The greatest pecuniary difficulty would be in the city but my friends have assured me that if I can effect that change money will be forthcoming. In mentioning this I expected great opposition from the country, but it has not been so. All are desirous of seeing it accomplished. There are however many difficulties in the way, and I am alternately the sport of my hopes and fears respecting it. Indeed, I never had so much depression to struggle against before. The feeling which has been evinced with reference to the Worn-out Ministers Fund, and other connexional institutions is lower than I ever witnessed. There is so much soreness also about the financial state of the circuit. Three years ago they had money in hand, but now they are considerably above £100 in debt. Everything depends upon the restoration of a proper connexional feeling. While there is any hope of that I shall consent to remain in Glasgow, but if that cannot be restored I shall remove. My health also is not good, and my wife has been ill almost since our arrival & has been confined to bed for the last month. So that we have had discouragement enough.

I am happy to say that the person whose note I enclosed to you is now in a very different state of mind. It is true that their prejudices have not operated favourably on our cause here, but I have found them to a great extent aware of that and seen them ready to sacrifice their own peculiar feelings for the good of the cause. I have found however some of the Irish (who are the majority) very different. A number of them have been excessively insolent far beyond anything I ever saw and our Scottish members while they make no complaints of there [sic] English brethren, complain loudly of the insults they receive both publicly and privately from many of the Irish, and I have heard of several who on that account have [been] driven from us to other places where they may worship in peace.

107

I know not whether Mr McLean[3] has written you, but they are getting on well in Edinburgh. I was thankful for the increase of congregations I saw there for several months before I left, but it was nothing compared with what his success has been ...

1. See Letters No. 88 and No. 103.
2. The Airdrie and Stirling Circuit was separated from Glasgow in 1845. See M.C.A., Edinburgh & Aberdeen District *Minutes*.
3. John McLean, Superintendent, Edinburgh Circuit, 1844-46. It is clear that the tide had turned for Methodism in Edinburgh.

91. *From John MacLean*   Edinburgh, November 28, 1844

I have deferred writing; with the design of discharging so important a work leizurely [sic] and at some length; but the stress of circumstances deprives me of my gratification & compels me in haste & brevity to make my first communication to you from the North. I have this morning learned from Mr Hoole that Mr Freeman[1] is coming down; and write especially to request that you will be so kind as to send Dr Alder along with him. We shall get the great Hall of the Free Church at the Cannonmills; and I think by the blessing of God you will be able to do something for the Gold Coast Mission to which so many of the great here are very favourably disposed; but the presence of Dr Alder is all but indispensable. His style of speaking takes amazingly with our Edinburgh magnates; and he is besides personally known to many of them. As we have agreed to delay our next meeting to the close of the year this comes quite opportunely & I hope will be productive ... We are quite happy here; and God has already given me to see more fruit than I had all the two years I was in Lambeth; but the thought of being so entirely separated from honoured & beloved friends whom we cannot hinder from growing old is sometimes depressing...

1. Ambrose Freeman (1794-1857), Superintendent, Bishop Auckland Circuit, 1843-45.

92. *From William Lindley*   Aberdeen, December 4, 1844

At the urgent request of the Trustees of our Chapel in Aberdeen I take the liberty of addressing you again on Mr Wears' case. Not having heard anything either from yourself or Mr Wears in reply to my letter to you on the 15th of Octo[be]r, the Trustees have become exceeding uneasy, and I have found it impossible to pacify them without troubling you with a second letter on the subject.

Perhaps I may be permitted to say in apology for the uneasiness of our Trustees, that they live in Inverury,[1] 16 miles from Aberdeen; that they never worship in the Chapel themselves, having a chapel at their own place, which they attend; that they have no connection with Aberdeen, excepting as Trustees, which makes them responsible for a debt of £830, the interest of which is raised with considerable difficulty; that the case has been in agitation more than two years; that their number is only three; and that they are far advanced in life.

When Mr Wears wrote the Trustees refusing to obey the order of the Conference, which was officially communicated to him, the letter having been signed by Dr Bunting as President, & Dr Newton as Secretary, I thought myself, *in duty bound, at once to let you know*... For the sake of our Trustees, who really need the money, I shall be most happy if you will favour me with a word in reply ...

1. The Inverurie chapel was closed c.1916. See Wesley Swift op.cit. See also letter No. 95.

93. *From John Maclean*   Edinburgh, Postmarked December 13, 1844

I have been engaged all the afternoon getting up an account for the Watchman &
have only time to say that last night I received a bank note for £100 for the African
Mission from a friend who chose to be unknown. I have some suspicion that the
good Moderator Henry Grey[1] is the donor; but dare not breathe this except to
you in a whisper...

1. No Moderator Henry Grey appears either in the records of the Church of Scotland
   or of the Free Church. Could this possibly have been Andrew Gray (1805-61),
   Free Church leader and Minister of the West Kirk, Perth, 1836-61? See letter 96.

94. *From Peter Duncan*   Glasgow, December 28, 1844

I have a disagreeable affair to lay before you, but I shall not trouble you with the
details.

I have received a letter this morning from Mr Lindley of Aberdeen, stating
that Mr Wears still refuses to pay the money he owes to the Trustees of that Chapel.
You will remember he was ordained by the last Conference to return that money,
but as he writes Mr L. informs me that they are resolved to apply to a civil court.
I cannot wonder at their resolution as Mr W. has treated them with an insolence
and vulgarity disgraceful under any circumstances, but I shall write to entreat
their patience a little longer though I confess I am aggrieved [?] to do so.

As this affair has been before the Conference which had decided it, I have
judged it my duty to apply to you which I do with great reluctance knowing your
numerous engagements. If I have done wrong perhaps you may be able to tell me
how to proceed.

I would mention that the amount of money in question was £16 10/-. Mr W.
before a Committee at the Sheffield Conference acknowledged the debt & engaged
to pay it. Why he now refuses I believe no one can tell. I hope any appeal to a civil
tribunal on the part of the deeply injured Trustees will be rendered unnecessary
but it certainly will be made unless Mr W. obey the order of the Conference.
I am grieved to say it but instead of giving them any satisfaction his letters have
been marked only by artful equivocation & insult. I hope it will soon be settled.
P.S. In a few weeks I shall have to write you relative to your visit which I sincerely
hope nothing will occur to prevent. Our poor Circuit is gradually improving but
it will require some time to diffuse a proper spirit throughout the whole ...

95. *From Peter Duncan*   Glasgow, January 29, 1845

I hasten to acknowledge the receipt of your letter on Mr Wears' business. I am
sorry for the trouble you have had, and especially grieved to perceive that he has
treated you too much in the same manner as he has treated the Aberdeen Trustees.
I am however bound to say that I have strong doubts as to his sanity and that
if I believed him perfectly sane any complaints should be presented in a very
different form and involve charges of a very different character.

I cannot bring my mind to trouble you with the details of this affair. It will
be sufficient to say: That the Trustees of the Aberdeen chapel reside in Inverury;
that Mr Wears kept both the Trust and Circuit books; That he had £16 10/- in
his hand, with which he indeed debited himself in the former, but took credit on
the other side for furniture to that amount. It was affirmed that no such furniture
was ever procured. The case was investigated at Sheffield. Mr Lindley produced
the Trust book before the Committee. Mr W. then brought out a list of articles
of furniture which he had paid for. Mr L. then produced another (the Circuit)
book but before it was opened Mr W. said "Oh, are those articles there? if so I

am mistaken". The Circuit book, and his list were then compared, and it was found that every article had been paid for from the *Circuit Funds*. He at once acknowledged the debt and engaged immediately to pay it which I reported to the Conference and thus the business ended for that time. I was afterwards astounded to find he had written a long letter to the Trustees, refusing to pay the money and hence our complaint to the last Conference. I have only to add, that there is not one material sentence bearing upon the case in his letter to you, but what I pledge myself to prove to be absolutely & flagrantly untrue.

I feel thankful for the hope you have given us of seeing you in Scotland and pray that nothing may hereafter occur to prevent it. But cannot you remain longer than you propose? I do not ask this on account of business, for the District Meeting will not require your presence more than two days, but if you could remain the usual time, I believe your visit would not only be conducive to the good of our poor cause but also to your own health & comfort ...

The week you appoint for the District Meeting will suit us well, only it would be better to commence on Wednesday instead of Tuesday which I trust you will sanction. Should you be able to remain two Sabbaths with us we shall expect of course that way will favour Glasgow with the second but if you cannot may I venture to look for a sermon any week night you may find convenient.

I am quite certain the time proposed for holding the Missionary Meetings will be a great improvement, both in the Northern & Southern parts of the District, namely in October. You will be kind enough to settle whether we may expect the deputation appointed at the last Conference to come along with you at the District Meeting, or whether their visit will be delayed until autumn.

I expect we shall have much to submit at the District Meeting for your counsel & advice, not on the nauseous subject of chapel embarrassment, for all we intend to say on that will not occupy many minutes, but upon matters purely ecclesiastical ... Your visit will be an important era in our most painful ministry...

96. *From John Maclean*   Edinburgh, January 30, 1845[1]

... I was mistaken in supposing the donor of the £100 to be Mr Henry Grey. It was from a member of my own class, a lady who has joined since I came to Edinburgh. Don't enter it from a Dissenter; but a Friend by J. MacLean ... I am not without hope we shall get our heads up in this place after all, but we have been all but extinguished during the last six or eight years. The Free Church with the exception of some recent demonstrations on Calvinism, of which we take no notice, is thoroughly friendly. I have preached in some of their principal pulpits & they are pleased to pronounce me *sound*, which is about the highest compliment current in these regions. The effect of this must in the end be favourable; and if we conduct ourselves discreetly and maintain our interest in the Divine regard I feel confident our position in Scotland will in a few years be improved. I don't think we are called upon (for the present, at least) to extend ourselves beyond our existing stations. The Free Church seems to be God's elected instrument for evangelising Scotland; but we occupy an important position here notwithstanding; and the Free Church will herself be the better for our presence & efficiency in this country. We keep up to its proper height the standard of experimental Godliness, abate the severity of Calvinism, moderate hostility to the residuary church & from our known friendship for the Church of England (which I trust in God we shall never sacrifice) we are a sort of breakwater to the ferocity of their anti-episcopal wrath. Above all we are increasing the amount of living Christianity & thus promoting the Glory of Christ ...

1. Part of this letter was published in *Early Victorian Methodism* p.315.

97. *From John Maclean*   Edinburgh February 6, 1845[1]

I received yesterday through Dr Alder the *order* of the President to put myself
in immediate communication with Mr Guthrie, which I accordingly did, and found
to my great satisfaction that he had just written to the Mission House accepting
as I expected your invitation. He did this I am well assured with the most perfect
cordiality, and will I doubt not render you good service ... The controversy on
some points in debate between different sections of the Calvinistic churches in
this part of the kingdom seems to extend. Dr Candlish's letter which you have
doubtless seen has called forth two or three pamphlets; and some here think that
we should make our voice heard; but I think otherwise; and being in some power,
I hope I shall be able to restrain both their tongues & pens. The extreme volun-
taries on the one hand and the Established Church on the other are exceedingly
anxious to set us & the Free Kirk by the ears; but I hope we shall *all* become
more united. I don't think this controversy will do us any harm if we keep out of
it & just preach our own precious soul-saving Gospel.

I wish much you would write me a few lines ... and as I am in a new and
rather responsible situation, I feel in need of such counsels as I know you can
give. I have to preach next Lord's Day one of the Jubilee Sermons for the London
Missionary Society in conjunction with Dr Candlish & that in the chapel of one
of the strongest Calvinists on these parts, so we are not breaking any bones by
this controversy...

What moving times we live in! Is this increased grant to Maynooth likely to be
succeeded by any more specific recognition of Popery by the state, or is it intended
whilst it quiets Ireland rather to ward off that? I can't give up my confidence in
Sir Robert Peel yet; but he would need (as our Scotch proverb says) 'a *lang* spoon
that sups wi' the Deil'.

1. Part of this letter was published in *Early Victorian Methodism* p.318.

98. *From John MacLean*   Edinburgh March 24, 1845

... Yesterday and today brought us the first taste of spring which we have had
this season. The winter has been long, severe and very trying to persons of delicate
health. We have had many deaths. The crepe has not been removed from my hat
for the last two months. Several of our best people both old and young have
been taken, but they have all died in peace — some of them were remarkably
favoured in their last moments. I have myself had hard work to keep on my legs:
but by the goodness of God I have been able to keep to my work. Yesterday was
the day appointed by the Commission of the Free Church for Diets on the subject
of popery. Mr Guthrie being from home I preached for him in the afternoon &
gave a lecture on Popery to our own people in the evening. Hearing of my intended
lecture the Committee of the Free Church sent a notice to Mr Guthries Congregation advising the young people to attend my service in the evening. The consequence was that young and old came and we had such a congregation as our
people have not seen for twenty years, Many were glad to get standing room in
the aisles, and not a few went away. I was greatly assisted, maintained my self-
possession from first to last; and I could see was enabled to make a deep impression.
You will laugh when you read this; but you will not attribute it to vanity. I have
always hoped that God would enable me to rise above the sneaking and embarr-
assing nervousness with which for some years I have been troubled and hampered
in my public work; and my hopes are not being disappointed. I pray that I may
not get too bold and constrain the Lord to throw me down again. We have had
several very remarkable awakenings lately — our people are becoming more devout;
and getting better principles put into them. They are a worthy people; but just

think of the succession of Superintendents they have had since good Mr Grindrod left & you will not be surprised that they have much to learn, and some little to unlearn. The Warrenite Association[1] is breaking up. Their preacher has come over to us & twenty or thirty of the best of them; old friends of my own[2] who never would have left; had Methodism not been betrayed by the man who was sent here to be its guardian.[3] I pray you, dear and honoured Sir, let us have sound men sent here and Scottish Methodism will do you good and not evil. We must have no equivocal character — no man who comes for his own popularity more than the credit of the Conference. I would rather have the worst radical that could be picked up out of the small residuum of the Warrenite clique, than one of the modern few who affect to run with the hare and hunt with the hounds. You can do with them in England, for they are a supple bending race; and will not break violently out of the traces, but here they would play the very mischief with us. I am much favoured with my colleagues. They are men of the right stamp; genuine Methodists. Mr Duncan has been very poorly & sometimes low during the winter; but I trust is now better — he is a noble little fellow; has some capital principles in him as deep as Metternich, but he has not had the advantage of sufficient intercourse with our leading men. His plans are a little too popular for my taste; and a little too Scottish. We are working harmoniously together however, and I am not without strong hope that a little of my toryism, sweetening and sanctifying his Whiggism will make him just what the Chairman of Scotland ought to be. I attended a bible meeting in Dr Bennie's[4] Church (established) last week. I don't think very much of Bennie; he has acted so inconsistently; but knowing him in former years, and wishful to preserve myself, though so deep in the Free Church, from any imputation of direct hostility to the establishment, I was glad to accept the invitation of the Secretary, a Free Churchman, and so I went — It was a cold affair. Margiall[5] was there and Bennie in the Chair, which with a Cameronian Minister,[6] made up nearly the whole concern, speakers & hearers. There were no Free Church ministers present. It is perhaps too soon to expect this even on such an occasion as a bible meeting, but I was glad I went. Bennie laid hold of me with both hands on parting, although I was very guarded in letting out any thing that might seem to indicate any lurking kindness for the residuary. The Free Church is apparently God's Elect instrument for the evangelisation of Scotland. The Lord is evidently with them, and I look to great days of revival ere long. Marzialls is making a good impression in Edinburgh. He preached for Dr Candlish yesterday, and is to be I know not where else in the course of the week.

1. See Hayes (1977a).
2. Maclean had been previously stationed in the Edinburgh Circuit in 1826, and again in 1829-31.
3. Samuel Warren, Superintendent, Edinburgh Circuit, 1827-30.
4. Archibald Bennie (1797-1846), Minister of Lady Yester's Kirk, Edinburgh, 1835-46. See F. H. Scott, D.D. (ed.) (1915) *Fasti Ecclesiae Scoticaneae* 1. Synod of Lothian and Tweeddale (Edinburgh).
5. This is probably William Marshall (d.1860 aet.47), Minister of Leith United Presbyterian Church, 1839-48.
6. Descendants of the Covenanters, named after Richard Cameron, one of their earliest and most energetic leaders. Ultimately became the Reformed Presbyterian Church.

99. *From John Simon*[1]   Inverness, March 25, 1845

I am anxious to know whether or not there is any connexional movement contemplated by us in reference to Sir R[obert] Peel's intended augmentation of
the grant to Maynooth. Would you have the kindness Dear D[octo]r at your
earliest convenience to give me the requisite information on this subject. I have
been waiting to hear something officially on the point, but have not heard anything in that way yet.

Your attention to this, truly, to provide me right [?] as the Superintendent
of this Circuit in which no steps whatever have been taken in the matter, will
Dear D[octo]r be esteemed a favour.

1. John Simon (1802-61), Superintendent, Inverness Circuit, 1843-45.

100. *From William Lindley*   Aberdeen March 27, 1845

Some time ago, Mr W[illia]m Smith, who then lived in Aberdeen, informed me
that he had engaged you to be his guest, in the event of your coming to Aberdeen
Missionary Meeting. You may be aware that, since then, circumstances have transpired which have led to Mr Smith's removal from this place. I therefore beg most
respectfully, to say that I fervently hope this circumstance will not in the least
influence your arrangements with reference to Aberdeen ...
[Endorsed] Ansd. (Neg.) Apl. 2, 1845

101. *To William Lindley*   London, April 2, 1845

I thank Mrs Lindley & yourself for your very kind invitation to Aberdeen; which
however, I am sorry to say, there is no *possibility* of my accepting.

I have to go officially to North Wales, South Wales, and Ireland, as well as
to Scotland. My visit to the last-mentioned place, must, therefore, of absolute
necessity, be very brief and hurried; and be limited to Edinburgh & Glasgow.
Under other circumstances, had health as well as time permitted, I should have
rejoiced to extend my journey as far as Aberdeen.

The Edinburgh District meeting, I *think*, must be held on Wednesday &
Thursday, May 28th & 29th — But you will, of course, hear from your Chairman
something definitive soon.

I understand that your September Financial District Meeting decided (I
think, very properly) that the Missionary Meetings at Edinburgh & Glasgow, at
all events, if not elsewhere also should in future be held in *October*. Dr Newton
highly approved of this change; relinquished all idea of accompanying me & Mr
Beecham to Edinburgh in May, & reserves himself for Scotland in October. I
think it would be best to have *all* the Scottish Miss[ionar]y Anniversaries at the
same period, that is, in *the same month of October* as this saves both time &
expense. Dr Alder, I understand, & possibly another, might there join Dr Newton;
they would probably gain access, in connection with a somewhat extended effort
in Scotland, for our Mission[ar]y Fund, to some Pulpits of the Free Church not
open to us in May. For myself, at all events, I must of necessity confine myself
to Connexional matters, in common with the District Meet[in]g. If you *cannot*
have your Miss[ionar]y meetings at Aberdeen & in the very North, in October,
but must have them in the spring, then I must return very soon after the Edinburgh Dis[tric]t Meet[in]g, to be ready for Wales & Ireland, & Mr Beecham, with
perhaps Mr Maclean, must go on in the following week to Aberdeen for this year ...

I wrote to Mr Wears, as you requested, & received a very unsatisfactory
answer, which I sent to Mr Duncan who will take the proper official steps to
bring the matter before the next Conference, for full ajudication [sic]. *I* have no
jurisdiction in such a case ...

113

102. *From William Lindley*   Aberdeen, April 8, 1845

.... We are ... sorry to find that there is "no possibility" of your visiting Aberdeen whilst we remain here.

In obedience to your order, I have communicated to the Chairman and the Edinburgh Super[intenden] t, my views, relative to the most fitting time for holding the Miss[ionar] y Anniversary, in Aberdeen and the "very north". My decided opinion is that to hold *all* the Scottish Miss[ionar] y meetings in October is, on several important grounds, *very desirable*. Certainly, October would suit Aberdeen, *much better* than the usual time, and as to Inverness, Banff and Dundee, October is about the usual time of holding their Meetings. Hitherto, the period of holding our meetings in Aberdeen has generally been found inconvenient, it being about "term time", when rents are paid & many people engaged in changing their residences . . .

103. *From Peter Duncan*   Glasgow, May 13, 1845

I can hardly express how severely I felt the disappointment occasioned by your last letter. When I look indeed at all the circumstances you mention I am forced to be of your opinion that it appears to be the "divine will" you should not be absent from London at present. I must confess that your engagements are momentous compared with any thing our poor discouraging cause in Scotland can present, and therefore, though with much pain of mind, I submit. I had been calculating much on your counsel with reference to the affairs of this most perplexing Circuit respecting which I scarcely know what course to take, or what to recommend.

We have several large societies between Glasgow & Edinburgh which must go down unless pastoral oversight can be obtained.[1] There are difficulties in the way of dividing the circuit yet divided it must be if we are to maintain our ground in any place, within its limits... The factions amongst us are indeed a feeble minority, and unable to make any disturbance, yet unless my successor were conversant with our affairs I fear they might again occasion annoyance, and our best men who unfortunately are not qualified to manage in a storm, would certainly quit...

... I feel embarrassed and scarcely know what to do. I cannot however close this note without indicating how happy we shall be to see Dr Alder again amongst us along with Dr Beecham. He knows our affairs well, and what the work here requires, while none more ardently longs for its prosperity...

1. See Letter No. 90.

104. *To John Maclean*   London May 21, 1845[1]

I write in the District Meeting & under severe & continued illness, to trouble you with a small commission.

Six numbers of the *Witness* are announced, as to commence on Saturday next, containing the usual reports of the Assembly's approaching proceedings. The price is 2/6, but must be paid *in advance*. Do me the favour of ordering them to be regularly sent to me, as published, addressed to me at 30, Myddelton Square, Pentonville.

Be assured I am exceedingly mortified at not being able to get to Scotland, as I wished. The first cause of abandoning the idea was the Maynooth Struggle. But it is well I declined; for I am quite unable to travel, & cannot venture out of my house at all at night. Excuse brevity, I can write no more...

1. The holograph of this letter is at Drew University Library, Madison, N.J., U.S.A.

I presume the deputation to our District will inform you respecting our late meeting in Edinburgh.[1] With the exception of a painful occurrence connected with this Circuit last year it was on the whole a comfortable meeting.[2] They originated a conversation relative to the importance of our work in Scotland at present, and it was thought that our effort ought to be increased, and that the present aspect of Scotland warrants the hope of success. A resolution was accordingly entered on the minutes to that effect, strongly recommending an increased number of Ministers. This unexpectedly brought out a plan which had been for two or three years in my own mind which I have several times spoken of to Mr McLean, and on which I had fondly calculated on your advice.[3] I submit the following sketch of it for your consideration, provided your numerous engagements will allow you time for that purpose. Should you be able to look at it and to give us your counsel I doubt not but it will be conducive to the prosperity of our work in this arduous District.

FIRST. Ministers ought to be appointed to the following places or most of them should be given up.

Airdrie where we have a chapel and 139 members.

Kilsyth &
Kirkintilloch two chapels and 184 members.

Stirling & two chapels and 76.
Doune

Paisley & a hired chapel & 180
Renton

Wallacestone a chapel and 176 members.

SECONDLY A native ministry must generally be employed in Scotland. There are many reasons for this measure which I cannot here specify. In order to carry it out I should recommend that for the future no young man taken out of Scotland should have any claim on an English Circuit. Not that any interchange should be absolutely prohibited as in Ireland, but interchanges to be regarded as special cases to be regulated by the Conference.

THIRDLY The incomes of ministers in Scotland ought to be stipendiary. The minimum for single men not residing with their Superintendents to be £60 pr. annum, and for married men £75 exclusive of a house and children's allowances.

The allowances for married men will appear to you excessively small, and I frankly confess that for myself they would not suffice. But let it be considered that this scale will only apply to natives of the country not yet taken out and from what I know of Scottish habits I have no hesitation in saying that such allowances will be sufficient to keep them as comfortable as our ministers in England. It must also be understood that this scale does not apply to the principal cities. But in such places the allowances can be greater.

FOURTHLY. A yearly grant from the Contingent Fund should be made in the same way as that to Ireland.

From the year 1812 to 1841 exclusive a period of thirty years the grant from the Contingent fund for ordinaries has averaged upwards of £720 pr. annum. When I came it was £746 and now £461. I think it ought to be reduced to £300, but Scotland to have its own yearly collection which at present amounts to about £60. Claims for extraordinaries to remain as at present.

FIFTHLY. Scotland should be divided into three Districts the Chairman to be General Superintendent.

I should strongly recommend Berwick and Dumfries to be added. The addition of the former would occasion no additional connexional expense whatever, and

115

the latter only a few shillings. But should those dependent circuits be added £50 or £60 must be added to the grant, but that would lessen instead of increasing the expense to the Connexion. On this plan the Edinburgh District would have nine ministers, Glasgow eight or nine, & Aberdeen seven. I think the Shetland District ought to be appended but we could have nothing to do with it financially.
SIXTHLY. There ought to be an "Annual Meeting" of ministers in Scotland, the President of the Conference or his deputy to preside.

At this meeting the appointments of each succeeding year ought to be drawn up, and presented to the Conference — there to be confirmed or altered on the same principle as the Missionary Stations. Young men having finished their probation ought to be ordained by the President in connection with this meeting. I also think its powers ought to extend to expulsion, only in all cases allowing an appeal to the Conference. Two representatives only in general should attend the Conference.

Such is the brief outline of a plan which has long been in my mind. I am sensible there are difficulties in the way, and also that it will require some time to carry it out. I must however be understood as recommending it or something similar *only* upon the supposition that it be the judgement of Conference that we should endeavour to perpetuate and extend our system in this country. To do this on our present plan is absolutely impossible, but could we obtain a willing and efficient ministry I should have no fears as to the result. I cannot blame brethren for being reluctant to come to this District nor can I wonder at their in general desiring to leave it as soon as they can. But such a state of things can never be conducive to prosperity, and I confess that unless some such plan as I have suggested be adopted, better at once to give up our smaller places and confine our labours to a few of the principal cities. Indeed if the Edinburgh chapel cannot be relieved I am of opinion the whole ought to be abandoned. It is impossible to suppose that our work can prosper there while the chapel is burdened with an enormous debt *for which every member in Society is liable*; and it is the opinion of all I know that if Methodism cannot be kept up in Edinburgh it must fall throughout Scotland[4] ...

1. The deputation to Scotland for 1845 was the President of the Conference (John Scott 1792-1868), John Beecham (Secretary of the Missionary Society 1831-1855) and J.M. Bunting (d.1866 aet.61, Preacher, 8th London (Islington) Circuit, 1843-45).
2. See Letter No. 90.
3. Not all Duncan's suggestions were adopted immediately, but at the 1845 Conference Airdrie was separated from Glasgow and four year later the Stirling and Doune Circuit was separated from Airdrie. In 1850, the Glasgow Circuit was divided into Glasgow West (John Street) and Glasgow East (St Thomas's — Green St or Calton). See Beckerlegge (1955) op.cit.
   The other suggestions were not adopted, but are perhaps the first mention, which became increasingly common after Bunting's death, of the need for some form of Scottish Conference. There was still a failure to realise that Methodism was to remain a small sector of the Christian Witness in Scotland.
4. Duncan's contention is curious since the debt had been reduced from approximately £5700 in 1816 to £2400. By 1845, it consisted of the £2000 bond, together with £400 in small amounts. Not until 1862 was the debt finally cleared. Perhaps Duncan had a congenital dislike of chapel debts. See Hayes (1976a).

106. *From John Maclean*   Edinburgh, October 30, 1845

We have this afternoon returned from our long tour.[1] Dr Alder is just writing
Mr Hoole; and I write one line to say that I shall send you a longer account soon,
than I have now time to give. It has altogether been an intensely interesting &
exciting journey. The impression made by our meetings & sermons is I believe
such as you would wish. In some things we have been disappointed. In one or two
places there seemed to be a holding back on the part of some of our Free Church
friends; but this was only apparent not real. The utmost & most cordial kindness
was shown to us by I may say all. The most signal failure happened in my own
case in a secession church at Inverness — I preached as well as I could. I believe
the Lord helped me & I thought the people were much impressed; but alas! the
entire amount of the collection was 17/6. So much for voluntaryism. It is but
a thin pasturage — the minister seemed very kind and hearty, but his people showed
but little in their giving.
   One meeting in the Free Church was very interesting. Culloden[2] took the
chair. We visited Culloden house; but of the particulars I must inform you afterwards ... Dr Alder ... has been working most nobly. I never heard him speak better
than at all the meetings ...

1. The Scottish Missionary Tour of 1845.
2. Duncan G. Forbes of Culloden (1821-97), great-grandson of Duncan Forbes
   of Culloden (1685-1747), Lord President of the Court of Session, to whose
   labours more than those of any other man was it due that the 1745 Rebellion
   was a failure. See Tayler A. and Tayler H. (1937) *The House of Forbes* (Aberdeen:
   printed for the 3rd Spalding Club).

107. *From Peter Duncan*   Glasgow, November 5, 1845

I should not have troubled you with this painful communication, only I learned
yesterday that you had been informed of the case of my esteemed friend Mr
Maclean & knowing that it will give you great concern, and believing that you will
be desirous of obtaining all the information I can give I write without delay, and
you will perceive at once that this is for yourself only. I think not to have written
so freely to any other person. (Mr Macleans health has been deteriorating for some
time and on Monday it was necessary to put him in an asylum, he having become
violent. Future efficiency can hardly be expected.) ... I cannot tell how I feel
under this painful stroke. Our Missionary Anniversaries are just over, and there
has been nothing like them in Scotland before. In this City our Collections have
been considerably more than doubled besides donations to the amount of £150.
The influence has been graciously felt by our people, and it has been general
throughout the District. In Edinburgh the congregations were rising, and in that
city the earlier and better days of Methodism seemed to be in fact returning.[1]
But our harps are again on the willows...[2]

1. This suggests that the appointment of Charles Clay to the Edinburgh Circuit
   was a Conference appointment to cope with Maclean's illness. On the other
   hand, both the District minutes and the Conference Journal (M.C.A.) remain
   strangely silent on the matter, the latter merely referring to 'Affliction — M'Lean
   (Edinburgh) for severe personal affliction. £28. 8. 0'
2. Psalm 137.

108. *To John Maclean*   London, November 22, 1845

I had of course heard of your affliction, which greatly distressed me; and, ever since I received the intimation of it, you have been the daily subject of my sympathising thoughts and earnest prayers ...

But you must not, under the influence of your characteristic & constitutional ardour be in too great hurry to return to your wonted labours. Let *Patience* have the perfect work; & follow implicitly the Counsels of your medical advisers. Would it not be well, so soon as they shall deem it proper, to *change* for a while the scene of your late tribulation for the society of your old English Friends & Associates?

I congratulate you on the many interesting occurrences and gratifying success of your late Missionary tour, in company with our esteemed friend, Dr Alder. He, as well as the President, returned from Scotland highly pleased & satisfied with their visit. We have been extraordinarily busy here since the Conference. In the last two months, we have out-fitted, ordained, & sent forth, *twenty* missionaries to various foreign stations; besides the same number of missionaries' wives & wives elect, children & schoolmasters. Surely this will prove even to *your* satisfaction, that we are not, as a Committee, *much* lacking in that "faith" which you have so often & so zealously inculcated upon us as our duty. The results of the meeting at Liverpool are likely to be very great. Many clergymen of the English Establishment have signified their approbation and adhesion. It is a wonderful movement; good, at all events in itself & its immediate influence, − and, eventually, I hope, good in its consequences. The four provisional & sectional committees appear to be active. That for London & the South has persuaded me, in conjunction with Mr Bickersteth,[1] Dr Leifchild, Dr Steane,[2] & Mr James Hamilton, to become one of their Honorary Secretaries. Sir Culling E. Smith[3] is our Chairman. This is for the present an onerous addition to previous demands on my time. But my health, in spite of various remaining infirmities, cóntinues, through God's mercy to be very much better. I enter on the winter with more agreeable prospects, in that respect, than for some years past ...

1. Robert Bickersteth (1816-84), Bishop of Ripon, 1845-50. Minister of St. Johns, Clapham: popular evangelical preacher.
2. Edward Steane (1798-1882), Baptist minister at Camberwell, 1823-44: joint pastor with John Burnet of the Baptist Chapel, Southampton St., Camberwell. Died at New House Park, Rickmansworth, Herts. 8 May 1882. See also Swaine, S.A. (1864) *Faithful Baptist Men*. p.282; see also Letter No.116 where his name is rendered Sleane.
3. Sir Culling Eardley (1805-63), religious philanthropist, only son of Sir Culling Smith. Founded the Evangelical Alliance, 1846.

109. *From John Maclean*   Glasgow, December 1, 1845

... I left the asylum last Tuesday with the intention of spending a few weeks at Burnt Island; but when I arrived there I found the house so small & close, (being an attic) that in my nervous state I thought if I remained I should be suffocated. I therefore left with Mrs Maclean the following day; and came direct here to the house of Mrs Renwick a widowed sister of my own, where I am quite retired seeing no one but the Doctor & my relations ... [J.B.'s letter came to him as life from the dead, but he could not add to J.B.'s burdens by accepting his kind invitation to stay at Myddelton Square.]

I rejoice that the Evangelical Union is succeeding thus far; and especially that you are getting some of the established clergy to join. I was afraid we should be in danger of splitting upon that rock; but God is able to harmonize all elements even the most apparently antagonist. I thank you heartily for the news you sent me ...

110. *From George Scott*[1]   Peterhead, June 4, 1846

As you are a great friend of the East, I now address you from the most easterly point of Her Majesty's dominions in Britain, and furthermore tell you that there will be a vacancy here next Conference. Nor do I think there would be any greater presumption in inviting you to fill it than in Banff asking Dr Adam Clarke to labour in that Circuit.

Your enclosures were immediately forwarded to Sweden with a request that Miss Selmer[2] would put herself in direct communication with the Secretary. I shall let you know the result when I hear. Have you consent to go to Conference? Can we get near each other there? I am it may be said ordered to go, and it is possible that the by no means delightful burden of Representativeship may oppress my shoulders. Will you give me, will Mrs Scott allow you to offer me half of your bed during the Alliance Conference?[3] Your enthusiasm in regard to the Alliance Movement sets me on fire, and reanimates my spirits since there are few standing by me on this question of your temperament. And yet we have gracious meetings even in cold granite hard Aberdeen. We have not yet come before the public except in the delightful concert for prayer which took place in the first week of the year, but our Local Committee now numbers 25 Ministers of 6 Denominations, and some 12 respected laymen while additions are made at every meeting. I had the high privilege of hearing the discussion on the question in the Free Church Assembly up to the time of B[rothe]r Candlish's reply but it being then ¼ p 12 I felt for my Gaius and withdrew. The Gibsonians will surely now be satisfied 311 to 7 is a tolerably conclusive "testimony", that strange man (Gibson)[4] preached not very long ago in John Street Wesleyan Chapel, Glasgow. Our Church was often and always *kindly* referred to during the debate and Gray[5] of Perth made a capital hit: "Our deputations met with much kindness and liberality from the Wesleyan Methodists in England. Mr Gibson's church is in part built by their contributions, does he intend to raise a new cry of — send back the money". We had a conversation on the subject of the Alliance at our District Meeting. Your old friend Williams[6] was the only one who had serious difficulty on the ground of being brought into Alliance with R. Eckett.[7] I am fully persuaded not only that we are right in the sight of God who heartily unite with this mighty movement, but that in Scotland especially there is good policy in actively engaging. Great shakings may be expected in Scottish theological matters, and if we have wisdom to be quiet and mind our own business, standing forth as the abettors of evanglical catholicity, without compromise — the friends of *all* the enemies of none, we shall in the natural course of events increase in power and influence, and by God's blessing in numbers too. Come & help us. We want gifted men of deep piety. The "testimony" of Methodism in favour of spiritual mindedness, and Christian fellowship is more than ever needed, and I conscientiously and strongly fear certain tendencies in favour of a *respectable* Scotch Methodism, a Methodism without the Communion of Saints which if yielded to will be the cutting of Samson's locks, and we shall become quiet, weak, formal & carnal as any of the petrified Presbyterians around us. Indeed given even our most ordinary Brethren who are pious folk but without intelligence and gumption in the Spiritual Father, the children will right or wrong seek pasturage elsewhere. In this place during the past year several persons in good circumstances have been brought to God under B[rothe]r Baylis[8] but they have gone and joined the Independent Church. This is trying. But this kind of work has always been going forward in Scotland, and

119

a glorious account in favour of Methodism will be opened at the great day. Our District Meeting was, Mr Duncan said by far the most harmonious he had attended in Scotland. Poor McLean present all the time, he is much better, but still shattered in body & mind. We all agreed not to oppose anything he might say, lest he should be injured. He insists on going to Conference, tho[ugh] several of his Brethren entreated him not to think of it. Our total number is 32 below that for last year though Aberdeen is 35 up. Yet there are many encouraging circumstances, and if the tendency above noticed be watched against all will be well. Three candidates were recommended. But of these you will hear in the examining Committee. My man is of course a nonsuch, shew him kindness for my sake when he comes, take him near if you can and cheer him, he is unfeignedly diffident tho[ugh] an A.M. His Grandmother lived here, a Methodist of 75 years standing yet able to attend all the means, she has walked in "perfect love" three score years & then. By the way if you wish to return any of my books Mearns[9] will take charge of them. None of you Englishers are to covet your neighbour's preacher, for should M. be accepted he must be allowed to labour in Scotland, and I am really ambitious of superintending his improvement for at least a year.

In what black pot has the "private correspondent" cooked his mess. There is always some new devilry schemed to cause discord among Brethren. I suppose each Minister has got a copy, when one has come so far North as Aberdeen. It is sure to work mischief. Oh how tremendously busy the accuser of the Brethren is just now, to hinder if possible the successful advancement of Christian Union. He will as usual overshoot his mark. I was delighted to hear Earbank,[10] Drummond[11] &c. referring to the great services rendered by Dr Bunting in the Alliance Movement, they went so far as to say that much of the consistency if not the very being of the Movement was owing to the wisdom, long suffering, brotherly kindness & charity of that eminent servant of God. I felt proud that Methodism had been able to present such a contribution, and thankful that many Ministers of other bodies would have an opportunity before his departure of knowing Dr B. better than they had done. No wonder therefore that Satan should thrust home at his standard bearer. We are not ignorant of his devices ...

I am fully satisfied that the Lord has chosen my inheritance for me in Scotland, & though there are pecuniary privations as compared with London & Manchester Circuits, yet we have much reason to be thankful. My back is in a much better state than when I left Gravesend ...

1. George Scott, D.D., Superintendent, Aberdeen Circuit, 1846-48.
2. The identity of Miss Selmer remains unknown.
3. The Evangelical Union Conference of 1846.
4. James Gibson, D.D. (1799-1871), Free Church polemic. Became minister of one of the Glasgow Free Churches, 1843; Clerk of Glasgow Free Presbytery; Professor of Systematic Theology in Glasgow Free Church Theological College from 1856.
5. Andrew Gray (1805-61), Free Church Leader and Minister of the West Kirk, Perth from 1836-61.
6. Thomas Williams 1 (left the ministry, 1854), Preacher, Edinburgh Circuit, 1843-46.
7. Robert Eckett (1797-1862), President of the Wesleyan Methodist Association, 1841, 1846, 1847. President, United Methodist Free Churches, 1858.
8. Edward Bayliss (1814-89), Preacher, Aberdeen Circuit, 1844-46.
9. William Mearns, M.A. (1821-1911), received on trial at the 1846 Conference; received into Full Connexion, 1850. Preacher, Arbroath & Montrose Circuit, 1846-47; Superintendent, Dunbar and Haddington Circuit 1847-49; Super-

*Plate 15. Rev. Samuel Dunn, Superintendent of the Edinburgh Circuit 1836-38.
        Another arch opponent of Bunting and one of the founders of the
        Wesleyan Movement, 1849.*

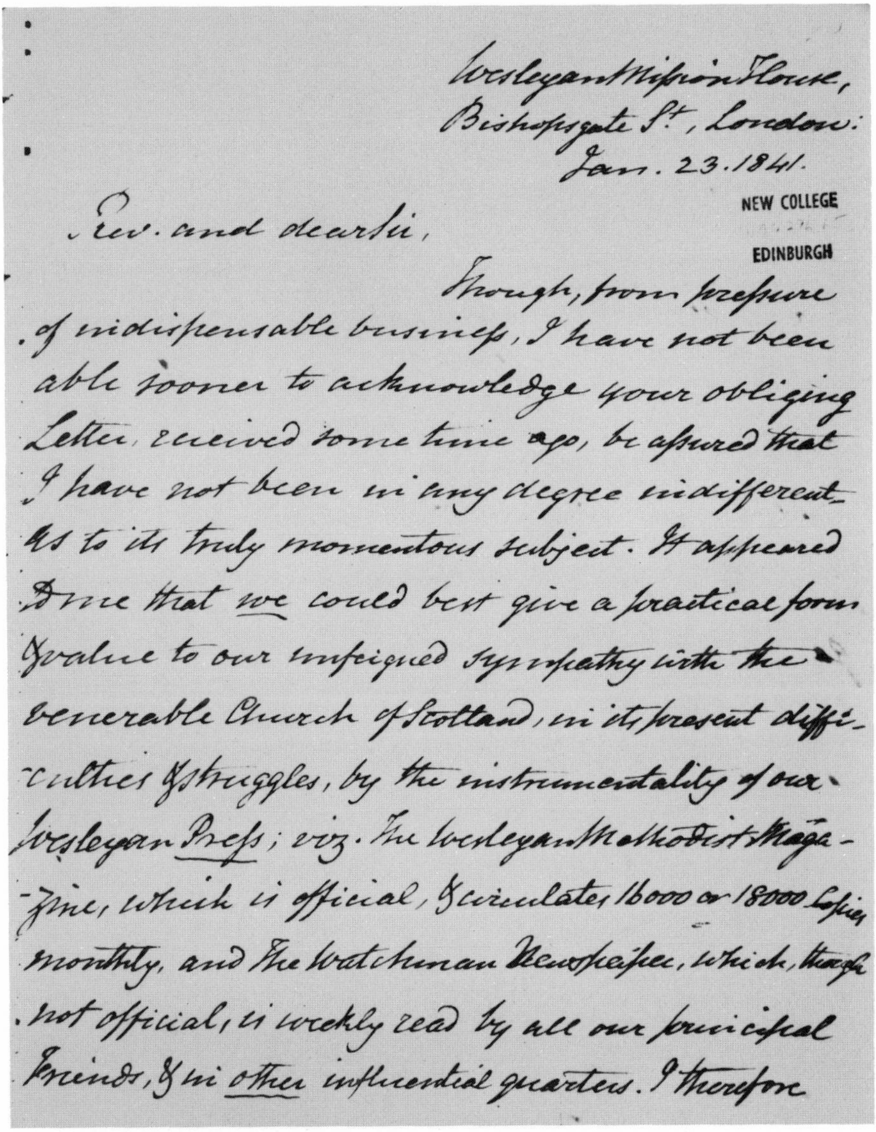

Wesleyan Mission House,
Bishopsgate St., London:
Jan. 23. 1841.

Rev. and dear Sir,

Though, from pressure of indispensable business, I have not been able sooner to acknowledge your obliging Letter, received some time ago, be assured that I have not been in any degree indifferent as to its truly momentous subject. It appeared to me that we could best give a practical form & value to our unfeigned Sympathy with the venerable Church of Scotland, in its present difficulties & struggles, by the instrumentality of our Wesleyan Press; viz. The Wesleyan Methodist Magazine, which is official, & circulates 16000 or 18000 copies monthly, and The Watchman Newspaper, which, though not official, is weekly read by all our principal Friends, & in other influential quarters. I therefore

Plate 17. *Facsimile of first page of Letter No. 67 from Jabez Bunting to Thomas Chalmers, London, 23 January 1841. Original in New College, Library, Edinburgh.*

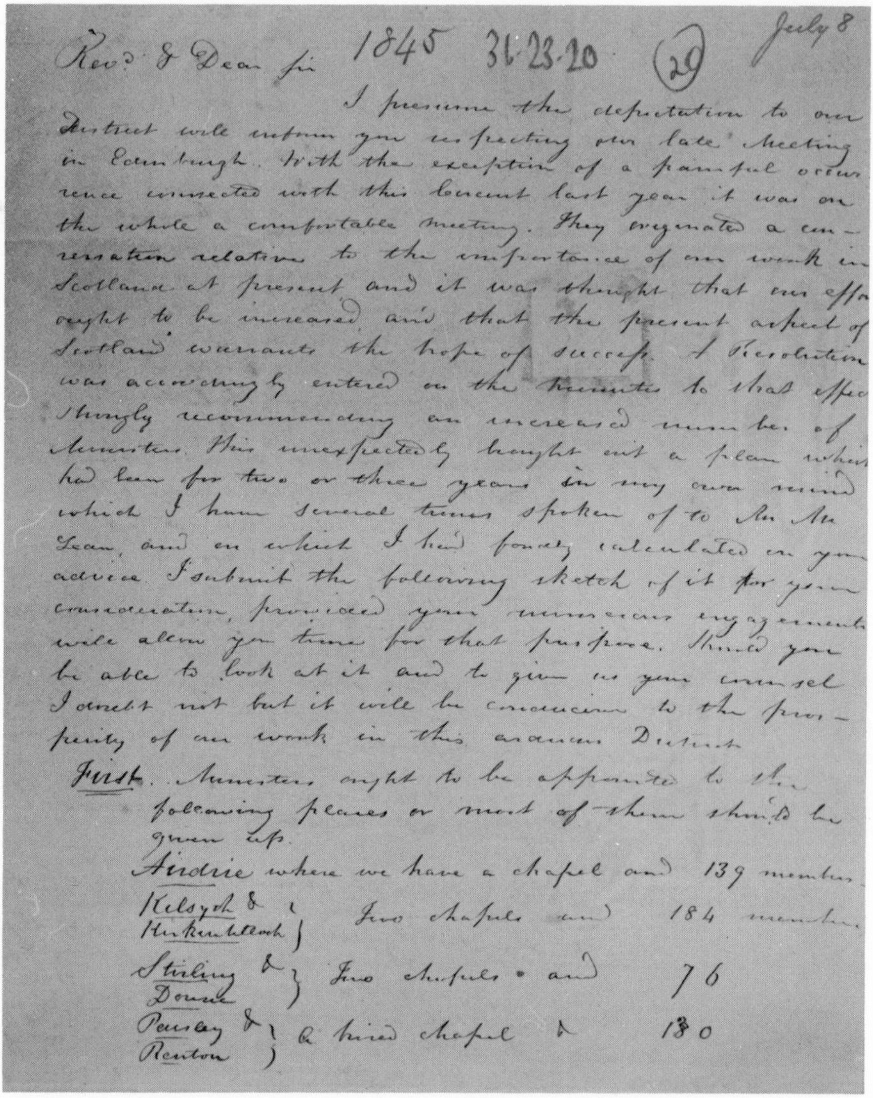

Rev⁰ & Dear Sir   1845   31.23.20   (29)   July 8

    I presume the deputation to our
District will inform you respecting our late Meeting
in Edinburgh. With the exception of a painful occurrence connected with this Circuit last year it was on
the whole a comfortable meeting. They originated a conversation relative to the importance of our work in
Scotland at present and it was thought that our effort
ought to be increased and that the present aspect of
Scotland warrants the hope of success. A Resolution
was accordingly entered on the Minutes to that effect
strongly recommending an increased number of
Ministers. This unexpectedly brought out a plan which
had been for two or three years in my own mind
which I have several times spoken of to Mr Mc
Lean, and on which I had fondly calculated on your
advice I submit the following sketch of it for your
consideration, provided your numerous engagements
will allow you time for that purpose. Should you
be able to look at it and to give us your counsel
I doubt not but it will be conducive to the prosperity of our work in this arduous District

   First. Ministers ought to be appointed to the
     following places or most of them should be
     given up.
     Airdrie where we have a chapel and 139 members
     Kilsyth &
     Kirkintilloch } Two chapels and 184 members
     Stirling &
     Doune } Two chapels and 76
     Paisley &
     Renton } a hired chapel & 130

Plate 18. Facsimile of first page of Letter No. 105 from Peter Duncan to Jabez Bunting,
8 July 1845. Original in Methodist Church Archives.

intendent, Greenock Circuit, 1849-50; Preacher, Stirling & Doune Circuit, 1850-51.

10. The identity of Mr Earbank remains unknown.

11. Henry Drummond, M.P. (1786-1860), politician; one of the founders of the Irvingite church.

111. *From Peter Duncan*   N.pl or d., [Post-marked Glasgow, September 8, 1846]

I can conceive that after what transpired at the last Conference you will be desirous of learning how matters are going on in Glasgow.[1] On my return I saw no appearance of any disturbance whatsoever. We have had a few Leaders' Meetings all of the most peacable description. The letter from the Conference was addressed to "Mr Thomson & Friends". [2] He invited the writers of the letters to tea and read the communication. He says all were in the best of temper but some of the few disaffected who headed the movement remarked that they must try to get a lay representation in the Conference, but there was no sympathy, and he could see that were they to attempt anything there would be no union.

The Calton concern is doing well. Notwithstanding the gown, pews are still being let, and since the reopening of the chapel the rents have increased from between £14 and £15 to between £22 and £23 and the usual collections from 10/- to 15/- per week. The congregations are larger by about one-third.

I am quite of opinion that whether the gown be laid aside at the Calton or not is a matter of perfect indifference. I would not contend for it for a moment, and were it necessary could discontinue it without any injury to myself either personally or officially for all I know I had nothing to do with obtaining it. But to give up anything to the clamour of a few who are disaffected to our whole system is another matter especially as it would disoblige the best and most efficient friends we have in the whole district.

I am convinced that there need be no difficulty whatever in extending our work in Scotland. There is a wide field and little or no opposition but what we create ourselves. My mind is however almost made up to quit at the next Conference. I have neither strength nor spirits to bear the annoyance from year to year on the part of a few who know nothing about our affairs, and who while here painfully demonstrated by the results of their efforts their utter incompetency to manage them. Enough and more than enough has been witnessed during the last five years, to show that Methodism wrought in the spirit and with the machinery appointed by Mr Wesley in 1785 possesses an admirable adaptation to the state of things here. But it is not to be denied that there are a few officials who retain a predilection for the semi-Pelagian squabbles of other times, and for the chartist-like 'simplicity' which they thought belonged to Methodism. In such a state the interferences at the Conference must operate injuriously, and though I am as willing and as desirous of remaining in the District as I ever was, yet I believe while such interferences are continued it would be utter madness to look for success. I incline at present to think that the little time I have remaining may be more usefully spent elsewhere; but I cannot be certain what the year may bring forth.

I trust that your efforts at the Conference and afterwards at the Alliance will not prove injurious to your health. I have not yet given up the expectation of your visiting Scotland, nor can I give up the impression that such a visit would be the means of placing our affairs on an unmovable foundation ...[3]

1. This refers to the publication of the Fly Sheets, the first two numbers of which had appeared in the Spring of that year. See Gregory, B. (1899) *Sidelights on the Conflicts of Methodism*. London.

2. This is probably Richard Thomson or Thompson (d. c 1850), one of the last suriving Trustees of the Calton (Green St) Chapel who latterly (c 1849) moved to the Isle of Man & died there.
3. The optimism of Duncan regarding the spread of Methodism in Scotland in this letter should be contrasted with his earlier opinions just after he had first arrived in Edinburgh (See Letter No.70).

112. *From Thomas R. Jones*[1]   93, Green St., Calton, Glasgow,
                                                                July 6, 1848

... I will ... take the liberty to state one or two things concerning myself which this opportunity gives. When I found myself down for Glasgow last Conference, I thought it strange that a minister in his 13th year should be sent to the miserable makeshift establishment to which this Circuit has recourse to order to provide itself with the labours of a 2nd minister. I however was willing to come, if the Contingent Fund would account me as a £40 man, thus bringing up my stipend to something approaching the Superintendent's, who received £125 per annum. You Sir, were pleased to say, when I spoke to you last Conference on the subject, that in consideration of my standing, I was entitled to some such consideration, and refered [sic] me to Mr John Scott.[2] Mr Scott was pleased to express himself in a similar manner, and referred me to Mr Duncan to introduce my case to Committee. I left the Conference before the Committee sat, and learnt afterwards that £10 was all that was allowed me.

When I got here I found things much worse than I had been led to expect. I came to understand that Mr Duncan had obtained from the Conference to allow the Circuit "a newly married man", instead of the usual family man, whose allowances were fixed at £80 per annum, while the Superintendent's were £115. Then since the Circuit could not afford to find him a house, one was allowed rent free by the Calton Chapel Trustees. This is the house I now occupy and out of which I have been trying in vain to get since I came here, but have been equally unsuccessful with my two predecessors who made a similar attempt. The house is miserably *damp* and I and my family suffered severely in consequence, during the whole winter. It is besides in the lowest possible neighbourhood, and surrounded by every conceivable nuisance. We are kept awake often night and day with the machinery and thumping of a Brass Foundry not a dozen yards in front of our whole house. When I have appealed to the Circuit stewards to change my house, they say they do not find a house for the preacher, and as they have no means of taking one for him they are glad that the Trustees will find him a house at all. When I have applied to the Trustees to find me a more suitable house they tell me, it is the only one they have to spare, and they have nothing else to offer. When I applied to Mr Moore[3] as the Superintendent, he advizes [sic] me not to rashly change my house and thus to come into collision with the Circuit (as, he says, Mr Ludlam[4] did) and so with one and another I am still in this place. Mr Moore has in the meantime managed to change his own house and get a much better one.

When I first came I also asked for an equalization of salary with the superintendent minister, and to this they *agreed* at first, but Mr Moore was also dissatisfied with the amount allowed him so that all that was done, was to give us £10 each additional making mine £90, and his £35 more.

I have to pay not certainly Rent but everything else — Rates (Police, Poor, Water &c.) — Coals — Gas — in short everything else — so that the £10 allowed by Conference has done very little for me. The friends hope to get a "newly married man" at Conference, and thus I am set afloat again at the mercy of this economizing system ...[5]

1. Thomas R. Jones (1810-83), Preacher, Glasgow Circuit, 1847-48; Minister at the Calton Chapel.
2. John Scott (1792-68), Superintendent, 8th London Circuit (Islington, etc.) 1848-51.
3. Roger Moore (1790-1881), Superintendent, Glasgow Circuit, 1847-49; Minister John Street Chapel.
4. This is surely a misrendering of Duncan, for no Ludlam appears in the Minutes or in Hall.
5. This letter shows the parlous state of the Glasgow Circuit in 1848.

113. *From Thomas R. Jones*   93, Green St, Calton, Glasgow,
                                               July 11, 1848

I had not intended writing to you again, but fearing that I have not made myself sufficiently understood in regard to the affairs of this circuit I hope you will bear with me in sending you this 2[n]d communication.

You are aware that we appear on the minutes as the Glasgow & Paisley Circuit. I presume Paisley is thus entered with a view to its being Methodistically worked, and under a conviction of the importance of the place, as a scene of Wesleyan Missionary Home operations, containing as it does some 50,000 inhabitants. But to enter Paisley in our Minutes on our present plan of supplying it is, to my mind, not useless merely, but positively injurious. Without a resident minister, with a Church of only 30 members very poor, and with an income of not more than £5 per annum, it surely ought not to be published to the Scottish world, as a sample of the Methodism of Circuit Towns in Scotland.

Accordingly, at our last District Meeting Mr Moore proposed that Paisley should be dropped altogether from our Minutes. To this, however, I ventured to object with a lingering hope that something might yet be done for Paisley worthy of the Town and of Methodism. As it is the Sabbath supply is almost exclusively by Local Preachers. We ourselves visit it on the Lord's Day about once in half a year for the purpose of administering the Sacrament of the Lord's Supper, and once a month only on the week night. The Local Preachers get some 20 or 30 persons to hear them, and there is but little prospect of increasing the number of hearers unless we can provide for Paisley in another way. I have been there on a Sabbath and we have had some 90 or 100 hearers, and have been told that all that was wanted to raise Methodism in that Town, was a Resident Minister. Several respectable persons would immediately join, if like other Churches they had a Pastor of their own living & moving among them.

What I should like to see would be the formation of *Paisley and Greenock* into one Circuit, taking (from Glasgow) Dumbarton and Campbelton, into the Paisley Circuit. These two places would furnish perhaps £5 additional income and with a push probably £20 per annum might be raised from the 3 places. This would not do more than pay House Rent & Taxes & perhaps the Circuit's proportion to the Children's Fund. Greenock supports its own Minister. The Salary of the Paisley Minister must therefore be provided by the Contingent Fund.

Now what I have to propose is this, that if the Conference would send me to Paisley, and make me a grant of £90 for my support, with £40 towards furnishing a house *immediately*, I should be willing to undertake the charge of it, and should have no fear in the course of a few years, of placing it if not in an independent position at least in a fair way to independency.

But perhaps the present embarrassed state of the Contingent Fund might lead the Conference to hesitate about taking such a step. I am persuaded it would eventually be the most economical course that could be adopted. But if that cannot be done then I would venture to propose another expedient.

You are aware that in Glasgow we have two chapels and that a minister resides in connection with each, who according to Scottish form is regarded as the Pastor of *his own Church*. On one question, these two causes widely differ, viz. the vestment question. At *my* Chapel the Gown & Bands are regularly worn: at John St. Chapel (Mr Moore's) Bands as well as Gown are altogether discarded. On this question the two causes will never agree, and there is consequently a jealousy one of another which hinges on this marked distinction, and which prevents that oneness which is so desirable between places linked together in the same Circuit Town. *Our* people would gladly separate from John St., and their only difficulty would be the support of their minister. To secure a lasting harmony, to prevent all undue and oppressive influence excited by the larger over the smaller cause, and to promote healthy rivalry, I would propose to divide the Glasgow Circuit into two, viz. Glasgow West (John St.) and Glasgow East (Green St. Calton).

In the formation of these circuits I propose retaining two ministers in Glasgow as at present, but as superintendents of the *separate* Circuits. Then to each circuit let there be attached two ministers, a married & a single man. Let the John St. young man reside in Paisley & change regularly with his superintendent. The Greenock Preacher could change as at present with the John St. Circuit. As it regards the support of the 2nd preacher in that circuit as a single man, I believe there would be no difficulty. The present Circuit Steward has often said to me and to others, and he made the remark again the last quarterly meeting, that if Calton were cut off from them they would readily support a married and single man. I believe they would do this for the sake of the separation and would gladly welcome an appointment in that form if made at the next Conference.

As regards the other Circuit it is plain, that it would not be prudent to make Calton a Circuit of itself, with only one minister in it. What then is to be done? The course I would propose in the formation of the Glasgow East Circuit is this. As *Paisley* is only 7 miles by railway from Glasgow, so *Airdrie* is only 7 miles from Glasgow, and by railway too. Paisley is on the West side of Glasgow and properly belongs to John Street, while Airdrie is on the East side of Glasgow, and in the event of a conjunction, would properly and geographically belong to Calton. Now why not unite Airdrie with Glasgow East, just as Paisley would be united with Glasgow West? The single man would reside at Airdrie as at present, and change regularly with the Calton Preacher.

Now this Plan while it would meet the case of Glasgow East would also greatly advantage the present Airdrie, Stirling & Doune Circuit. That Circuit is now a very unwieldy affair. The Superintendent, has resided at Airdrie, quite at one end of the Circuit (he is a single man) about 20 & 30 miles from Stirling and Doune. His connexion with these latter places has been merely nominal, the management of them being chiefly in the hands of his colleagues resident in those towns. Now by taking Airdrie & its immediate dependencies into union with Glasgow, Stirling & Doune with their dependencies would form a very manageable Circuit for Two Preachers as at present. The *House* is at Stirling which place would become the Circuit Town. The apportioning of places might be so arranged as to give to Stirling its proper quota of support. The Doune minister is supported by an endowment. The Airdrie minister's salary and the proportion of the Children's Fund from that part of the Glasgow East Circuit would be raised among themselves as at present.

The only matter of doubt would be the maintenance of the Calton Minister. A year ago the Society was about 110, and the income about £40 per annum. *Now* the Society numbers 180 members (taking with us a country place we should number 200) and the income the last quarter reached the average of £60 per

124

annum. There would then be £60 to begin with. My present salary is £90 from the Circuit, and £10 from the Contingent Fund. Now if the Contingent Fund would make the £10 into £20, thus guarranteeing [sic] me £80, I would risk the other £20, assured that our leading friends on this side would not abandon me. But there would still be the quota to the Children's Fund due from 200 members which we should have to raise additionally, making about £10. Now this also I should have no fear of raising provided we could have *our Chapel to ourselves.* It now stands on the principle of an united Trust, so that whatever surplus income it makes, is transferred to the benefit of the other Chapel. There is on this chapel a mortgage bond of £400, and could the place be surrendered to us with this liability only, we should be able to form a new trust, and any surplus income would come to the benefit of the Circuit. My impression is that the United Trust Committee would consent for the sake of a separation, and then I have no doubt in a short time we should be without any grant at all.

But in the event of such an arrangement taking place as would form this into a separate Circuit in Connexion with Airdrie, it would be necessary that we should have £40 allowed us towards furnishing a house for the Calton superintendent. The house I now have adjoins the Chapel & is a miserable shift, being so damp that myself & family were ill, all the winter, and I myself nearly lost my voice. I complained to the Circuit Stewards, but they said they could not help me as the Trustees found the house. I complained to the Chapel Committee, but they said they had no other house for me. I complained to the Superintendent, who, though he has secured himself in the possession of a most eligible residence of late, has recommended to be *patient!* I cannot at all understand how this Circuit sho[ul]d have been allowed a 2[n]d. Preacher on an *inferior* rate of salary without at the same time engaging to provide a suitable house and furniture withall. This house which I now occupy is as near *bare* as can be, and we cannot do anything towards furnishing it as matters stand at present. If however the Circuit were divided, I am persuaded the Friends on this side would do all they could to find me another house, and with £40 for the Contingent Fund we should get it decently furnished.

I am leaving this Circuit, I am persuaded, because it is annoying to the Circuit Stewards and chapel committees, and Leaders Meetings, to be told their duty in references to the creditable support of the ministers resident among them. Still on behalf of *my own people* in the Calton I have everything to say that is kind, and of this I am fully convinced that they would gladly hail my reappointment to this Circuit. It is only however in the event of a division were that practicable, that I would wish it. Otherwise I should prefer going at once to Paisley and doing my best to raise it ...[1]

1. The proposals to divide the Glasgow Circuit were implemented at the 1851 Conference. See also Letters No. 103 and 105.

114. *From Roger Moore*   Glasgow, December 27, 1848

Thinking you would be pleased to see how your long & true friend, the Rev Dr Newton,[1] was received at Glasgow, and feeling somewhat indebted to you for the D[octor]rs visit by your asserting it to be the duty of the President of the Conference to visit Scotland:- for your gratification and as an expression of my gratitude I have forwarded to you by this day's post the Examiner of Saturday. At the last Evangelical Alliance Preachers Meeting I was glad to hear John Henderson Esq of Park[2] say that you had stated if the Glasgow friends would have the next Alliance Conference in Glasgow, if spared you would visit us. I have no doubt Glasgow will respond to the request of Mr H[enderson]. As one who has always highly esteemed you, I pray you may not only be spared to fulfil your promise to the Alliance, but long spared in life for the sake of our beloved Methodism ...

1. Robert Newton, D.D. (1780-1854); President of the Conference, 1848.
2. John Henderson of Park, in the Parish of Erskine, Renfrew; a local laird; elder son of John Henderson.

115. *From Robert Harrison (late of Mold)*   Tyndrum, January 5, 1849

I have presumed to trespass upon your valuable time for a few moments in making a small request which, if it can be granted will be a source of much gratification to me and family in these distant Highlands. The request is this: To receive monthly, a copy of the Missionary Notices Newspaper, directed to *Robert Harrison, Tyndrum, Perthshire* N.B. I have been a member of the Wesleyan Missionary Society for many years, and have paid my subscription of 21/- for 1848 to the Rev[eren]d W[illia]m Exton[1], Glasgow together with £10 which I received from one of our Scotch Nobles, which must appear under the name of "A Perthshire Hace(?) Churchman" I was the more pleased to receive it as being the first fruits of my efforts in behalf of our Glorious Mission Cause in Caledonia. I am not now at liberty to name the Nobleman but am free to inform you that I am at present Manager of the Mines belonging to the Marquess of Breadalbane[2]. I live among the Grampian Mountains on the boundary of Argyleshire far away from my much loved Methodism. But thank God I carry it in my affections as well as enjoy the saving influence of its ministrations on my heart. "May they prosper that love thee". We have no direct communication with Glasgow for 8 months in the year, except by post; and the receipt of the Notices would be a rich treat. I hope you will not deem this an intrusion on my part. I did intend sending the money direct to the Mission House but I thought that the sum, small as it is, would help appearances in favour of our Scotch friends whom as it regards Missionary efforts are far behind ...

1. William Exton (1815-91), Preacher, Glasgow Circuit, 1848-49.
2. John Campbell (1796-1862), 2nd Marquis of Breadalbane; M.P. for Okehampton, 1820-26 and for Perth, 1832-34. Advocated non-intervention during the Auchterarder Case. A considerable benefactor of the Free Church.

116. *From Thomas Farmer*[1]   George Hotel, Glasgow, October 15, 1849

I only received your letter this morning from Mr Henderson[2] too late to admit of my returning an answer by this mornings post, having however received a notice of the meeting on the 17th from Mr Keeling[3] and made him acquainted with the circumstances which would prevent my attendance. I can only now regret afresh that my arrangements for accompanying Mrs Farmer & my daughter to Edinburgh on the morrow & to attend the annual Missionary Meeting there on Wednesday, will render a compliance with your wishes on my part Impracticable. At the same time, I wish to assure yourself & the friends who may assemble at Didsbury, that I feel deeply interested in the question to be brought forward by Mr Heald,[4] and am thankful that he has had his attention directed to the *means* of making the income adequate to the annual expenditure. If I had known what those means were, which he proposed to recommend I should have felt it to be a duty to consider and with due deference to the Council to offer an opinion, I can however now only express a hope that the wisdom that is profitable to direct may be given from above. For I very sensibly feel that the embarrassment in the funds of our several Institutions operates prejudicially upon the general interest of the Connexion. The allusion made in Mr Keeling's note to the existing arrangement between the Committee of the Missionary Society & the Institution leads me to infer that possibly some new arrangement may be proposed in reference to the loan of part of the Endowment Fund. On this head, as Treasurer of the former, it is my duty to urge upon the meeting the necessity for the continuance of the loan on the present reasonable terms or not to give notice for the repayment for at least 6 months to come. I need not add my reasons for this course as you are so well acquainted with our financial difficulties in Bishopsgate Street. The grant by the Centenary Committee of £500 towards the erection of a chapel at Richmond cannot, I think, with any degree of propriety be withheld, should it continue to be thought desirable to carry out the arrangements made for its execution.

I am pleased to think you have derived benefit from your sojourn at Buxton, although I sincerely regretted your absence from the Alliance conference. The attendance of members was thin, & the number of our own body much smaller than I either anticipated or wished for the interests of the Alliance or for a fair representation of our feeling towards its main object, the promotion of the love of the brethren. Your son Mr Percival[5] will have informed you of the letter written to the Conference by Mr Osborn,[6] its spirit was good & the language unexceptionable, but I am disposed to question whether, (after *it* had passed into the hands of the Chairman & been read in the Council) it has accomplished any good end in being made the subject of remark in the Conference seeing that Sir Culling Eardley[7] declined reading it there. The public meetings were very numerously attended, & pervaded by a seriousness & spirit of devotion that was felt to be very cheering & profitable. There was a great reluctance manifested by almost all parties to the introduction of the subject of finance & I could scarcely obtain a hearing till the last hour of the Conference. Although not satisfied with the result, I hope measures will be adopted at the early & next meeting of the Council in London more seriously to take up this point.

Evangelical Christendom is not in a very encouraging position, but I am entrusted with the views of Mr Henderson & Mr Wilson[8] who met me in company with Dr Sleane[9] & a new arrangement will I hope be the result to insure its continuance.

1. Thomas Farmer of Gunnersbury (d.1861 aet 70), the most prominent Methodist benefactor in the South, and a leading promoter of the Theological Institution.
2. See Letter No 114.
3. Isaac Keeling (1789-1869), Preacher, Stockport North Circuit, 1849-50.
4. James Heald of Pars Wood, Stockport. See Letter No 56.
5. T. Percival Bunting (1811-86), a Manchester solicitor, second son and biographer of Jabez, and a great lay defender of his constitutional policies. For many years a member of the Committee of Privileges.
6. George Osborn (1808-91), Superintendent, 5th Manchester Circuit (Oxford Road), 1848-50.
7. Sir Culling Eardley Smith. See Letter No 108. Also *Early Victorian Methodism* p.366.
8. J. Gilchrist Wilson (left the ministry 1864), Preacher First London Circuit, 1849-52.
9. See Letter No 108.

117. *From William Horton*[1]   Edinburgh, September 13, 1849[2]

...The entire press of Scotland, so far as it has yet spoken, is against us. At least I know of no exception. In the United Presbyterian Magazine there is a very bitter article. The Free Church Magazine, too, which came out on Saturday last, has a short notice of the "Wesleyan Schism", though comparatively moderate in its tone.[3] I have solicited Dr Begg[4] to write a leading article for the Witness, on the right side. He has the proposal now under consideration. He told me that Dr Candlish is studying the question. I have sent a copy of my Pamphlet to each, and to other leading men of several denominations. I shall be glad to put into Dr Candlish's hands the President's work, as soon as it is ready.

I greatly regret that we shall not have the pleasure of seeing you in Scotland this autumn — and more especially so as the hindrance lies in the state of your health. I trust your proposed visit to Buxton will, by God's blessing, prove beneficial ...

1. William Horton (1800-67), Superintendent, Edinburgh Circuit, 1847-50.
2. Part of this letter was published in *Early Victorian Methodism* p.382.
3. This letter refers to the aftermath of the Fly Sheets episode and the expulsion of Dunn, Everett and Griffith at the 1849 Conference.
4. James Begg (1808-83), left the Church of Scotland at the time of the Disruption. Minister of Newington Free Church, 1843-83.

118. *From William Horton*   Edinburgh October 20, 1849

I think I was not sufficiently explicit in my former Letter.

The Sermons which we propose to publish are to come out in monthly numbers, and in a cheap form. Each number is to contain about two sermons and to sell for two pence. The object is to shew the people of Scotland what Methodist Teaching really is, and to supply our own people every where with choice edifying sermons for their reading. Hogg of Edinburgh, and Mason of London, are to be the Publishers. It is only by an extensive sale that the project can be made to pay its own cost.

There is one special reason why I am solicitous to be favoured with a sermon of yours as early as possible. The 12 numbers of each year will form a very handsome and cheap volume. Each Volume will be dedicated to some eminent lay gentleman of our Connexion. The first volume is to be dedicated, by permission, to Thomas Farmer, Esq. I am particularly desirous for this reason that the first Volume should contain a sermon from your pen. If possible, I think it should stand foremost in the series ...

119. *From William Horton*   Edinburgh October 27, 1849[1]

... I send you by the same Mail which will convey this, a copy of the Free Church Magazine for this month — published last week. The article on the Wesleyan Conference is from the pen of the Rev W.G. Blaikie[2] the Editor. He applied to me about a month ago for information on the subject, having previously read my Pamphlet. I found he was solicitous to ascertain the true character of the *Fly Sheets*. I lent him the first number, and very gladly communicated to him all the information he sought. He candidly admitted that the short notice which appeared in the Free Church Magazine for September and which was decidedly opposed to the Conference, was premature. He has this month, you will perceive, got nearly right.

Dr. Candlish has given forth no "deliverance" yet upon the question. Nor have I yet had an opportunity of seeing him. But I am told, I think on good authority, that, in conversing with a friend, Dr Cunningham[3] said most explicitly that the Conference was right; that in its power of inquiry it possessed an advantage over the Free Church; that the Presbyterian system in Scotland sprang up during a period of great political excitement, and largely partook of the political element; that this has always hampered them; but that Methodism arose as a purely spiritual system, free from all political entanglements, and based solely upon New Testament principles.

128

If these are Dr Cunningham's sentiments, I should rejoice to have publicity given to them. But he may not think it expedient to make an open declaration of them. It appears to me that the leading men of the Free Church entertain more favourable views of Methodism than they think it right to express. They know that such views would be found to clash with the stupid prejudices which generally prevail in Scotland in regard to us. A change however in the right direction is unquestionably in progress. We are becoming better known, and more respected. And the day will yet arrive when we shall receive from the Free Church and the other Churches of this country, expressions of friendliness more satisfactory than any thing that has yet appeared ...

1. Part of this letter was published in *Early Victorian Methodism* p.388.
2. William Gordon Blaikie (1820-99), Scots divine. Free Church Minister of Pilrig 1844-68, Editor of several journals, Professor of Apologetics & Pastoral Theology, New College, Edinburgh, 1868-97.
3. William Cunningham (1805-61), Free Church controversialist. Professor of Church History, New College, Edinburgh, 1845; Principal 1847.

120. *From William Horton*   Edinburgh, November 14, 1849

I have written another small Pamphlet, — in a tone of friendly expostulation, — "addressed to those members of the Wesleyan Methodist Church who are seeking to effect certain changes in its Polity and Laws".[1] The Manuscript I sent yesterday to Mr Holgate,[2] requesting him to submit it to the examination of the Publication Committee. If they think it is not required, I shall lay it aside without hesitation and without regret. But if they think it should be published, I should deem it a great advantage to be favoured with any suggestions which you may think it expedient to give me, before going to press.

The first No. of our series of Sermons is to come out with the January Magazines. I am happy to say that the following brethren have all engaged to contribute — Arthur[3] — Lomas[4] — Steward[5] — Chettle[6] — Gregory[7] — West[8] — Prest[9] — Hurt[10] — McBrair[11] — Barrett[12] — McAfee[13] — and I think I may add W.M. Bunting[14] ... It would be an immense benefit to hear your Sermon on Justification by Faith in the Series. Would you be kind enough to give us permission to print it? It would thus be read by multitudes who have never seen it in its present shape ...

1. This pamphlet refers to the Wesleyan Reform Movement.
2. Israel Holgate (1798-1858), Preacher, First London Circuit, 1847-50; Secretary, London Book Committee, 1847-50.
3. William Arthur (1819-1901), Preacher, 6th London Circuit, 1849-50; Secretary of the Missionary Society.
4. John Lomas (1798-1877), Superintendent, Second Circuit, 1848-51.
5. George Steward (became preacher 1829, retired from the ministry 1853) became the most intelligent apologist for Wesleyan Reform.
6. Henry Hurlburt Chettle (1809-78), Preacher, Halifax Circuit, 1848-51.
7. Benjamin Gregory, D.D. (1820-1900), Preacher, Rochester Circuit, 1849-51.
8. Francis A. West (1800-69), Superintendent, Huddersfield 2nd Circuit, 1848-1850; President of the Conference, 1857.
9. Charles Prest (1806-75), Superintendent, Hull West Circuit, 1848-51. A staunch Protestant politician.
10. Joseph Hurt (1791-1861), Preacher, Bristol North Circuit, 1848-51.
11. Robert Maxwell McBrair (left the ministry, 1856), Preacher, Nottingham North Circuit, 1849-50.

12. Alfred Barrett (1808-76), Preacher London Islington Circuit, 1843-46; one of the principal theorists of the ministry.
13. Daniel McAfee (d.1873 aet.82), Preacher, Dublin South Circuit, 1849-50.
14. William Maclardie Bunting (1805-66), eldest son of Jabez Bunting by his first wife, Sarah Maclardie. Travelled 1824-49 when he became a supernumerary on grounds of ill-health.

121. *From W. Macleod (?)*   Dalkeith, February 7, 1849
Pardon me for not having replied before this time to your letter of the 23rd ultimo.

I deeply feel the brotherly love manifested by your committee, and the high honour which they have conferred upon me in making the request which you my very dear Sir, have conveyed in so kind a manner to me. It is just because I was off [?] by a sense of the importance of the work you wish me to undertake, that I delayed so long in making my reply to your communication. But I have at last resolved trusting to God's help to comply with your request ...

How thankful I will be if I am enabled to advert your noble missions and if in any shape or form I am permitted ⟨to promote the missions in?⟩ Feejee ...

122. *From Henry Owen*[1]   Foot of Leith Walk, Edinburgh,
                                                February 22, 1849
On Page 64, large Minutes is the following Question. "In what manner may a Chapel, or Preaching-house be settled?", from whence we are referred to a Foot note, stating "This form of Trust is now superseded by the 'Model Deed' which has been adopted by the Conference."

And eight lines from the foot of page 65 Large Minutes, are the following words — "Provided also that the same Preacher shall not be sent to the said Chapel for more than two years successively, without the consent of the Trustees, given in writing". When a Quarterly Meeting has invited a Minister to remain a third year on a Circuit this Clause appears to give the power of a *veto* to a Trustee Meeting over the Quarterly Meeting.

And this view appears to be strengthened by the sixth and last particular of an Addenda on the 48th page of the Large Minutes, where it is stated that "Nothing contained in these Rules shall be construed to violate the Rights of Trustees as expressed in their respective Trust Deeds."

And some of our Trust Deeds are framed according to the Clause above Quoted from Page 65, Large Minutes. Will you favour me with your opinion upon the following Queries. viz. First. Have our Trustees-Meeting, at the present time, a *Veto* over the Quarterly Meeting in those cases wherein their Trust Deeds are framed according to the Clause above quoted from Page 65 Large Minutes. Secondly — If so, is there not a discrepancy and contradiction between the above, and the *following Clause of the Model Deed,* and *the Judgment of the Vice Chancellor* in Dr Warren's Chancery suit upon that Deed?

Clause of the Model Deed in question. viz.
"In the exercise of their Official Rights and functions, the Trustees are subject to the General Rules, usage, and practise of the whole Body of the People Called Methodists throughout Great Britain, as the same General Rules appear in the Annual Minutes of the Conference from time to time published by them under the Authority of the Poll-Deed".

The Vice Chancellor's Judgment upon the above. viz.
"It is to be observed that the Deeds of Trust are not to be construed merely with regard to the words which may happen to be contained in the Deeds themselves; but must be construed and looked at as part and parcel of the whole Machinery by

130

which the Great Body of Wesleyan Methodists is kept together, and by which Methodism itself is carried on."

Thirdly — If there be such a discrepancy and contradiction between the above authorities, have we no clearly defined and settled law to meet this case, if we have where may that law be found?

I am writing a small Tract, Entitled
"The Wesleyan Polity not illiberal".

And I am anxious to have correct views of the Subject referred to in this letter. And to know whether the Trustees Meeting have, *in any case*, a Power to nullify the act of a Quarterly Meeting which have invited a Minister to remain a third year on a Circuit.

I regret being under the necessity of troubling you. But I know of no other person so likely to be able to give the information I am seeking and am anxious to secure. If, in any case, our Trustees have such a veto — A Veto at variance with both the Spirit and Letter of the Model Deed, I think it both unfortunate and unfair, both to our Ministers and to the great Body of our People ...

1. Henry Owen (left the Ministry 1861), Preacher, Edinburgh Circuit, 1847-49; probably settled at Leith to follow the Scottish fashion at this time.
2. Pierce (op.cit.) makes no mention of this apparent anomaly, which suggests that by 1873 the question had been resolved by making the power of the Quarterly Meeting absolute.

123. *From Thomas R. Jones*[1]   Newbury, July 16, 1850

... I was then most unaccountably (having travelled 12 years) put down to a 6 or 7 years (newly married) mans place in Scotland. I took the opportunity when in Glasgow with Mr Roger Moore's consent, to attend the University Lectures, but this raised opposition & I left at the end of the year for Dundee. There I had to struggle with debt & difficulty another year but managed to effect what no one before had ever attempted, to pay £250 Chapel Debt ...

1. Thomas R.Jones, Superintendent, Dundee Circuit, 1848-49; Preacher Newbury Circuit, 1849-50.

124. *From John McLean*[1]   Edinburgh, August 18, 1855[2]

You will not I am sure suppose from my letter yesterday, that I have turned Democrat since I came to Scotland, which it must be admitted is a region, perhaps, somewhat unusually charged with that spirit. I quite believe in the sentiment which your enemies charged you with, when I had the honour of living under your roof, and of which I think you have no reason to be ashamed, that Methodism is as opposed to democracy as it is to sin. By which I understood you to mean, that Methodism was unmistakeably and irreconcilably [sic] opposed to democracy as a system of government. But I also believe that you recognise the existence of a Christian people or flock as distinct from the Pastors; and that next to the glory of God all church arrangements should be made with a view to their benefit. Neither do I doubt that any powers which might with safety be put into the hands of the flock would by you be most freely and gladly consented to. In England, however, you are accustomed to regard the flock or people or congregation, as embodied or condensed (certainly *you* never thought that they were *represented*) in the Leaders and Quarterly Meetings &c. For the south of the Tweed this perhaps is the best; because in truth I fear you have given such powers to those meetings, that I greatly doubt, whether without the hazard of some fearful tumult you could apportion any of them, to the congregation. In Scotland it is different, because our entire ecclesiastical system may be considered to be yet in a state of solution; and also because in this country, the existence and rights, or as it would be more Wesleyan & scriptural to call them, the duties of the congregation are universally acknowledged. In the Free Church as well as in the Established Church this is undoubtedly the case. So also in the United, and other Presbyterian sections. You have no parallel to this state of things in England. Now I recommend the Veto Act in yesterday's letter with a view to this peculiar constitution of religious opinion and society on this side of the Tweed. I do not deny that I should without scruple place it myself upon much higher ground than that of *mere* expediency, though of course I am too established a Wesleyan to suppose that the scriptures make this or any similar detail of church arrangement, imperative, except where the prosperity of the work of God demands it. The reality of a *visible* Church, should I think be carefully kept up, along with the reality (not of an *invisible* Church, as our Calvinistic friends are too apt at once to run the thing to) — but of a *spiritual* and *converted* church such as I believe we have; visibly embodied in our own beloved and precious Methodist Societies.

Now such a regulated power of vetoing a minister, as I described in my last, might I think be safely and very advantageously committed to our congregations in Scotland. They are all supposed to be baptised. We admit their children to baptism. They are thus with their families, members of the visible community of Christ's people, even if they do not feel themselves worthy to be communicants. I am not sure whether the Free Church extends the veto law so far; but I am satisfied that it might be done with our system of Government with perfect safety and advantage. As for having lay Elders in this country, that I believe is absurd and unscriptural, and I am yet to be convinced that Mr Wesley ever gave the slightest sanction to it. That our Presbyterian friends emerging from Roman Catholic errors three hundred years since, should have fallen into this Protestant error, is no reason, why any section of the followers of John Wesley should adopt it. But a proper recognition of the Congregation, would have the effect I believe of making one class of our lay officers more decidedly scriptural, while it would render another class more exclusively secular and financial, agreeably as I cannot but believe with the state of things in the *primitive Church* and *certainly* in our primitive Methodism. Have you not noticed how the godly men of business of Mr Wesley's days, got superseded by the spiritual men, and how the secular spirit, accumulated upon our poor but pious leaders thereby, has been exploding in our Leaders and Quarterly Meetings whenever the external atmosphere has become favourable from that day to this?

In reference to Mr Samuel Jackson,[3] I named him as occurring to my thoughts of the moment, though I should be dreadfully afraid of a crotchet or of that timid or artful policy, which might practically have the effect of *establishing* a very imperfect state of things. With respect of the *necessity* of having an English Ex-president appointed to the general oversight of Scottish Methodism, perhaps I might have expressed my self with less qualification than I intended. The great thing is to have the person duly appointed. Scottish I think I ought honestly to say, I think at present he ought to be; but English in the sense in which every thorough Wesleyan ever must be English ...

1. John McLean, Supernumerary, Edinburgh Circuit 1855-66.
2. Part of this letter was published in *Early Victorian Methodism* p.417.
3. Samuel Jackson (d.1861 aet. 76), President of the Conference 1847. Governor at the Richmond Branch of the Theological Institution, 1847-58.

125. *From John Maclean* Royal Asylum, Morningside near
Edinburgh, September 30, 1856

You will have probably been informed that I have again experienced a relapse into one of my afflictive attacks and am again under medical care. The attack like all my former ones has passed away very soon, & except a degree of weakness which is now nearly gone, I am quite recovered to my usual tone of health. As none of my own relations survive, except such as are quite out of my chosen associations & as few even of my early Wesleyan friends are alive or in Scotland, I am made painfully to feel that I am a stranger in my own country. In a state of affliction, it is difficult to express the painful effect of this conviction on my mind ... I was going on in my work very pleasantly & with some signs of success, when this last attack laid me aside & I am now longing to be with my dear children & the little society at Dalkeith again ... I have myself a firm persuasion, that full employment in the ordinary duties of a Methodist Preacher is the thing most likely to promote my health both mind and body ...

126. *From John Maclean*[1] Dalkeith, April 1, 1857

In the pause between your preparations, and the great May meeting, let me amuse a leisure moment or two of your valuable time, by a little Scottish gossip. A new Wesleyan periodical has appeared here called the "Gleaner". Who the author is, I know not; but it is one of those things which had been left undone. It is ambitious, but fustian and juvenile in its style, made up of extracts which every Wesleyan of Scottish breed is familiar with, & conveying in an extract form some Memoir of a person styled the "Wallace-town reformer" (which I never read, but which has been for some years producing I suspect, a number of unsanctified professors in our societies) the hateful heresy of believing the testimony of a babe and is most [?] revivalist to the fact of pardon, instead of waiting for the testimony of the Holy Ghost. This is worse, especially in such a country as this, than the Sandemanian[2] assurance of the Morrisonians.[3] It is reported to have been originated at our last District Meeting, by some of our chief ministers; but this I refuse to believe and should be sorry to invite the proofs.

The refracted literary infection of this country, combining with the low standard of education and taste amongst our people, relieved by no elevating exceptions, as in former days, poisons ? the very element of growth, for mean authorship, tending to lower us in the estimation of even our mechanics, & making more cultivated men laugh at our bombast. What we want in the form of books is the diffusion of Mr Wesley's sermons. If any wealthy friend would take pity on our poverty & help us to scatter broadcast the admirable tract series from Berwick upon Tweed to Johnny Groats it would do real good.

The young preacher at Dunbar, an M.D.[4] is reported to have added 70 members to society in the first quarter after his arrival last Conference. This is either the most remarkable work of God that Scotland has known, or it is a great mistake. Time will show. Other denominations may count upon adherents, though they keep down the standard of experimental and practical godliness over the country. The only strength and safety of Methodism is a genuine awakenings issuing in scriptural conversions. There is a decidedly favourable tendency in some of the higher strata's of Scottish society towards Wesleyan Methodism, as learnt from the life & writings of Wesley, and from our great Missionary & educational proceedings. If this could be followed up by simple, modest, and earnest Wesleyan preaching and action I should anticipate much good. But how can this be reckoned upon in the absence of any permanent central focus of Scottish Wesleyan influence?

The strictly presbyterian part of the population are all preoccupied and pre-engaged, by the Scottish ideas & connexions; but there is a numerous, growing, and highly interesting portion of the community to whom our English ideas and connexions are a recommendation. Not the vulgar English revivalism of the large towns, of the last twenty years, against which I wish you would warn the young students; but the wise and holy & self-denying efforts of the old Wesleyans, & their successors. Rhetoric & all that sort of thing is very cheap here. What we want is the classical and apostolical style of preaching indicated in Mr Wesley's beautiful preface to his sermons, & of which all the eminent ministers of Methodism according to their various gifts have been such noble examples, since his day. Twenty of *your* good outlines, filled up with the affection and faith of a wise ministers heart, would set any Scottish town on fire. I would trust the Holy Spirit for doing his part.

English Methodism cannot afford to be set a light by Scotland. I pray you to ponder this. I remember saying when I lived in your house, and was privileged to observe your proceedings, that you did things, as if you had previously enquired what will be the effect of this on Methodism, a hundred years hence. It was this, far more than any personal kindness that won my understanding and heart & the conclusions of your discourses, which I used to hear by a hard run from Gravel Lane to Irwell Street, gave a depth and strength to my evangelical earnestness, to which under God I attribute almost all the real good, that my ministry has ever accomplished. O that you were young again, & would take a suitable appointment in Scotland. But you have a better prospect before you. May the Lord grant you a brightening old age, free from pain and trouble of any kind ...

Some of the brethren have been speaking of a circuit for me next year; but I wish to stay here another year, from the hope of seeing the work revive, as well as from a desire to take better security for the continuance of my health. There is nothing which goes so much against the grain with me as writing about my self or my affairs; but to you it seemed due to say this much.

To return from this long digression let me suggest the enquiry, what will be the influence of Scotland upon English Methodism in the course of the next thirty years, if you do not secure a thorough Conference Methodism on this side of the Tweed by means of some plan, that shall secure its permanent, and ubiquitous ascendancy over the preachers and people on this side of the border? Continue to make this a penal settlement for disordered or suspected missionaries. Send young unformed men, who are here as free to follow their crudest ideas, as if they were in the wilds of Africa, though with much greater risk of evil. Take them back just when they have got as much infected with the delusions of Scotland and Scottish courts, as spoiled Beaumont[5] for life & killed him, I dare say at last. Leave them to carry an importation with them of the bulliontist [?] and captivating modes of Scottish Erskineites[6] & others to make them great revivalists or popular preachers among our unsuspecting Yorkshire Methodists & in this soil rootage [?], I think I forsee consequences which ought to be provided against.

But I must not bother you further, as my little Helen whom you baptised has just warned me that the post hour is arrived ...

1. John Maclean, Supernumerary in charge at Dalkeith 1856-60.
2. Followers of Robert Sandeman (1718-71), Scottish sectary. Came under the influence of John Glas at Edinburgh University in 1734. Sailed to New England in 1764 and founded the first church of his connexion in Portsmouth, New Hampshire in May, 1765.
3. Followers of James Morrison (1816-93), founder of the Evangelical Union. Probationer with the Church of Scotland at Borbrach, Banffshire; eventually separated from the Kirk over his views on the Atonement. He and a number of

other ministers founded the Evangelical Union at a meeting in Kilmarnock (1843) and their churches became the nucleus of the Morrisonian sect.
4. John Stephenson, M.D. (1799-1861), Superintendent, Dunbar Circuit 1846-1858.
5. Joseph E. Beaumont, Superintendent, Edinburgh Circuit, 1833-1836.
6. Followers of the Rev John D. Erskine, D.D. (1721-1803), minister of Old Greyfriars, Edinburgh, 1767-1803; for many years a leader of the Evangelical Party in the General Assembly.

127. *From John Maclean*

Wesleyan Chapel House Dalkeith
December 17, 1857

... Will you be so kind as to direct that an Annual Missionary Report be sent without delay to Robert Scott Moncrieff Esq.,[1] – Dalkeith Park. It is worth your while. Although his name does not appear in your list of subscribers, he gave a sovereign to our collection last year and has just sent half a sovereign for the present year.

In continuation of my gossip, I beg to say that I think you ought to begin next year with appointing two General Superintendents for Scotland; Mr McOwan[2] to reside at Perth for the Northern District, & myself, if you can find no better, at Dalkeith for the South Western District. It will be a great advantage to Mr McOwan & to the work, that he should begin with a small Circuit, until he learns again fully to understand his countrymen. His appointment at Glasgow was a comparative failure, because he has become more of an Englishman than he was aware of, & the people who remember him as a shoemaker, have not the sense to appreciate his high qualities, so as to perceive the thorough sanctity of his demonstrative ministerial & pastoral fidelity. I assure you we Scottish people are very peculiar but we have some noble qualities which no man in the Conference I believe, understands so well as yourself.

The above arrangement will involve the division of the Scottish District, which ought never I think to have been made into one. At the same time the appointment of General Superintendents, who should interchange on the three year plan, or on some other well considered plan, and the older of whom should have a sort of superintendency over his junior colleague or colleagues will give to the Scottish work a unity of character and action which under existing circumstances two Districts might endanger.

As Drake[3] must be well acquainted with all the recent changes on our Scottish work, & is, I rather think (though I know scarcely any thing of him), gifted in *his way*, I would not myself object to his being Chairman of both Districts, if that was decided consistent with our Wesleyan antecedents & usages. But that a General Superintendency in perfect subjection to the English Conference you must have, unless you wish to throw us all away quoad our own beloved Methodism and make us practically the exclusive servants of the Free Church, or the Reformers, or the Ranters, or the New Connexion if they think it worth their while to try Scotland again, I am perfectly satisfied.[4] Can you believe it, I was yesterday canvassing Edinburgh for a Missionary Tea Meeting, & found a good deal of anxious feeling about getting an organ in Nicolson Square Chapel?[5] I had been aware that something was going on, in which I had not myself the least part, & was secretly pleased, I confess, if such an advance to the work of God could be secured, without as I was told the least difference of opinion or injury. But there are some signs of dissatisfaction beginning to appear, as any one acquainted with Scottish prejudice & history might have been prepared to expect – & what do you think of the advice of a leading Wesleyan Minister in Scotland under the circumstances? It is that the friends who are in favour of the organ, who are I dare say the strongest party, should break the rule of the Conference & then apply for a dispensation afterwards. The Lady who

135

told me this, is willing to furnish the organ at her own risk & was a member of my own Class many years since. I am sure I never taught her to act upon such unworthy advice; but it came from one of our Scottish Wesleyan Ministers, who had, she said, "a lang heid" — My reply to the Lady, who is very much attached to me, & will, I know, abide by my advice, was, "I am one of those whom they call *Tory* Methodists and *we* never *break* laws, or recommend others to *break* them". Yet this is the policy of a 'school', now becoming more formidable that I like to think of. If I were one of Cardinal Wiseman's[6] Priests, instead of an honest Conference Preacher, I would say "my curse, and the curse of St Patrick, upon all such divisive and anti-christian advice". But enough —

The plan which I recommend is eminently Wesleyan. It would have entirely recorded the ideas of Mr Wesley were he now alive. It has the further recommendation of being suited to the ideas so far, & also to the early practice of the Presbyterian establishment. I know that in England the feeling would be amongst a certain interesting class in favour of more stately & equally scriptural titles which Dr Coke[7] perhaps wisely consented to in America. But the case of Scotland should be viewed in connexion with the interests of the empire and the constitution. By the British Constitution the Queen is Head of the Presbyterian Church in Scotland & is therefore a Presbyterian as *certainly*, if not as *much*, as she is an Episcopalian. She has now a dwelling amongst us; and the argument becomes as it appears to me stronger in favour of adherence to Mr Welsey's deliberately chosen Terms or titles as to his principles as a clergyman of the Church of England, advising never to leave that church; & after all, as we used to say when I was a boy "Its *a ane* in the Greek." But I am willing to repeat what I said in my last "give us *the thing*"*that* I solemnly demand in the name of Christ and of John Wesley. But as for names call me anything you like, except a supernumerary, or superannuated, or a *lunatic* Wesleyan minister. To neither of these titles will I by the grace of God silently submit, any longer, without an *open* trial in Conference, or a decision to that effect by Her Majesty's Commissioners of Lunacy in Scotland, or some competent legal authority in England, who will I am sure deal equally justly with me ...

P.S. Is there any screw loose in Armstrong's[8] or John Scott's[9] department. We really must have proper protection against the Erastianism of the schoolmasters as well as against the anti-conference or at least the *un*conference confederacies formed of students at our institutions. I thank God of our *good* Wesleyan laymen we have nothing to fear; but if you knew what students and young men do in this country, you would perhaps be a little less afraid of polemics than in your excessive good nature & Evangelical Allianceism I fear you are in danger of becoming. If you *are* consenting to be put out to nurse in your old days, either by old women or young men *or young women* you really must forgive those whom you have implicated in the teachings of your prime, to take protection from the guns which may be fired at them from defences which it is impossible *they* should ever consider to be other than sacred.

1. Robert Scott Moncrieff (1793-1869), 2nd of Fossway, Kinrosshire, Advocate, Chamberlain to the 5th Duke of Buccleuch at Dalkeith 1828-69.
2. Peter McOwan, Superintendent, York Circuit, 1856-59; Chairman of the York District, 1856-59.
3. John Drake (1809-85), Superintendent, Aberdeen Circuit 1857-60; Chairman of the Edinburgh & Aberdeen District, 1858-62; spent 40 years of his ministry in Scotland.
4. There is again a suggestion of a move towards a separate Scottish Conference.
5. The organ was not finally introduced into Nicolson Square until 1864. See Hayes (1976a).

6. Thomas Coke (d.1814), Director of the Missions from 1786. See also Vickers, J. (1969) *Thomas Coke Apostle of Methodism* (Epworth Press).

8. John A. Armstrong (1830-93), Preacher, Macclesfield Circuit 1857-60.

9. John Scott (1792-1868), President of the Normal Training Institution, Westminster, 1851-69. President, 1844, 1852.

Index

141

143